You Had To Be There

ALSO BY ROBERT COLLINS

NON-FICTION

East to Cathay (1968)
A Great Way to Go (1969)
The Medes and the Persians (1972)
The Age of Innocence: 1870-1880 (1977)
A Voice From Afar (1977)
Butter Down the Well (1980)
One Thing For Tomorrow (with Joyce Brack, 1981)
The Holy War of Sally Ann (1984)
The Long and the Short and the Tall (1986)
The Kitchen Table Money Plan (with Barbara McNeill, 1992)
Who He?: Reflections on a Writing Life (1993)

JUVENILE FICTION

Legend of the Devil's Lode (1962)
Rory's Wildcat (1965)

You Had To Be There

*An Intimate Portrait of the Generation
that Survived the Depression, Won the War,
and Re-Invented Canada*

ROBERT COLLINS

Canadian Cataloguing in Publication Data

Collins, Robert, 1924-
    You had to be there : an intimate portrait of the generation that survived the depression, won the war, and re-invented Canada

ISBN 0-7710-2255-7

1. Aged – Canada.   2. Canada – Social conditions – 20th century.*
3. Generations – Canada.   4. Aged – Canada – Interviews.   I. Title.

HQ799.97.C3C64   1997   305.2´0971   C97-931187-X

The excerpted lines on page 188 are from Jenny Joseph's "Warning" from *Selected Poems*, published by Bloodaxe Books Ltd. Copyright © Jenny Joseph 1992. (U.S. distributors: Dufours Press.) Reprinted by permission.

The publishers acknowledge the support of the Canada Council for the Arts and the Ontario Arts Council for their publishing program.

Set in Bembo by M&S, Toronto
Printed and bound in Canada

McClelland & Stewart Inc.
The Canadian Publishers
481 University Avenue
Toronto, Ontario
M5G 2E9

1 2 3 4 5   01 00 99 98 97

For Fred Hamilton, Alex Nickason,
and all the other brave ones
who have left us.

"We shared an experience, an experience you can't explain. You had to be there."

Maurice Falloon
Foxwarren, Manitoba

CONTENTS

ACKNOWLEDGEMENTS

I'm deeply indebted to the 181 men and women (see pages 298-300) who generously opened their homes and their hearts to me and shared their memories and opinions. My only regret is that space does not permit all of their contributions.

Thanks also to Bob Levin, executive editor of *Maclean's* magazine who, in assigning me in 1995 to a commemorative article on World War Two, inadvertently set this book in motion.

Special thanks to Evelyn de Mille, Moira Farr, Margaret Fraser, Paul Grescoe, Karen Hanley, Debbie Hebb, Barbara McNeill, Dr. Peter Neary, and Jan Van Fleet for their support and valuable leads. I'm grateful to all of the following for providing helpful material: George Boyd, historian of the Bomber Command Association of Canada Inc., Linda Chiarvesio and Sheila LaCroix of the Addiction Research Foundation, Chris Douglas of General Motors, Philip Gordon of the Canadian Tobacco Manufacturers' Council, Karen Kiddey of Calgary's Suicide Information and Education Centre, Anne Mason Mirabelli of the Vanier Institute of the Family, Joanne Potvin of the Royal Canadian Mint, and Lila-Mae White and Jacqueline Arrindell of Mid-Toronto Community Services.

The excerpts from James B. Lamb's *Press Gang* and Jenny Joseph's *Selected Poems* are reprinted with permission. Earlier versions of Glen Hancock's mysterious wartime encounter with the stranger on a train appeared first in the Kentville *Advertiser*, March 21, 1986, and subsequently in *Reader's Digest* (Canada), May 1986. It is adapted here with Hancock's permission.

Excerpts from some of my own earlier writings on World War Two are also adapted here: "When Mother Was a War Worker," *Maclean's*, December 19, 1959; "When Canadian Women Went to War," *Toronto Star Weekly*, September 23, 1961; "The Angel of Belsen," *Reader's Digest* (Canada), November, 1990; "An Arsenal for Democracy" and "A Time for Reflection" from *Canada Remembers*, published by the St. Clair Group Inc. for the Canada Remembers Commemorative Committee, 1994.

When the waters were troubled, my daughters, as usual, were sailing right beside me. Lesley Anne transcribed roughly one million words of tape-recorded interviews. Catherine, professional editor and writer and my first reader, contributed many gems of wit and common sense. This book would have been impossible without their help, encouragement, and boomer-generation perspectives.

Finally, thanks to my editor, Alex Schultz, for his perceptive eye, his affection for words, and his understanding of the writer's fragile psyche.

INTRODUCTION
"PRIVATE SANCTUARIES"

In Ontario in the winter of 1995–96, the guaranteed formula for a raging, in-your-face kind of brouhaha was to utter the words "Mike Harris." This particular Sunday evening was no exception. As so often that winter and since, the argument went beyond differences in political ideology to expose the yawning chasm between generations.

We were at dinner in a small Italian restaurant: three men, four women – writers, an artist, an academic, a retired business executive, and a widow of three years who was still grappling with bereavement. The artist, a vivacious and charming baby boomer, was about forty, the youngest among us. Two others were in their late fifties; the rest of us would never see sixty again.

Somewhere between the calamari and the ravioli, the boomer spat out the premier's name like an obscenity. The widow, sixty-nine, momentarily abandoned thoughts of her dead husband and leaned over with fire in her eye.

"You don't like Harris?"

The boomer curled her pretty lip. "Surely that goes without saying!"

The Harris government was trampling on her fundamental beliefs and, worse, it had shot an arrow into the bosom of her dysfunctional family. Back in the free-spending days, the young woman's daughter by a first marriage had left home in a snit to live happily on welfare. Now Harris had chopped 21 per cent from Ontario's generous welfare payments and the teenager was suffering from acute pogey withdrawal.

So why didn't she go back to mother? we suggested.

"I can't manage her!" the boomer cried. "And *somebody* has to!"

That did it. "Not on *my* taxes!" snapped the widow. Others of us growled and muttered assent. How typical of a boomer! we thought. She expects the state to do everything, including babysit her spoiled brat.

It went downhill from there: the familiar litany of pros and cons that dominated newspapers, newscasts and private conversations for years as Harris tried to reduce Ontario's crushing deficit. The government measures were heavy-handed at times, wrong-headed in some of their priorities, but overall, in the view of many (not all) of our generation, necessary.

The boomer, like most of her age group, had grown up with government largesse. It was a way of life. Those of us over sixty-five remember leaner, more self-sufficient times. We kept saying, "If we don't do *something* about that debt, the country will crash!"

"But who's to say there *is* a debt?" demanded the young woman. What if it were all a numbers game, an evil plot devised by shadowy money interests? She'd absorbed the contrarian theories of author Linda McQuaig in *Shooting the Hippo*. The boomer wanted desperately to believe that the deficit was a myth; wanted the nastiness to go away; wanted the good times to roll again the way they always had.

At evening's end, no one's mind had changed, but a truth was reaffirmed: the views and perhaps the values of my generation are seriously out of sync with those of most younger Canadians today.

There are 3.6 million of us over age sixty-five, about 12 per cent of the Canadian population. We are the last link to a remarkable, almost mythic time. We are the survivors of the Great Depression and World War Two, architects of postwar Canada, parents of the celebrated boomers. We have lived through monumental change, unparalleled in any previous generation: from horse-and-buggy, Model-T Ford, and crank-handle telephone, to moon walks, space shuttles, and the Internet. We are better educated, more affluent, more vigorous, and longer-lived than any generation before us. We are more widely travelled and hungrier for study and self-improvement well into old age.

Yet in all of this we have clung to a certain innocence that no generation is likely to have again. Although many of us are equipped to the teeth with the tools and toys of contemporary society (computers, VCRs, fax machines, cellular phones) such wonders still mildly amaze us.

We are still "old-fashioned" in our outlooks. We are the last enthusiastic patriots; the last to go willingly (albeit fatalistically) to war for king (or queen) and country. We rarely flagellate ourselves over the Canadian "identity"; we think we know what it is. We are the last to accept authority with respect: authority of parents, teachers, police, governments, military officers. We are the last generation to have reached adulthood without television, credit cards, computers, push-button phones, or the Pill.

We are the last, as a group, to have entered our late teens with virginity intact. We are the last to believe widely in the sanctity of marriage, in the invulnerability of family, in mannerly children and courteous adults. We place high value on hard work, loyalty, and self-sufficiency.

You can easily spot us, even if the grey hair and wrinkles aren't a dead giveaway. We "dress up," meaning we are usually over-dressed by contemporary standards for most occasions. At parties, church, or the theatre, our men tend to wear suits or jackets and ties; our women favour dresses more often than pants. Our men still hold doors open for women, and our women still say "thank you."

We like music with lyrics we can understand. We hardly ever "right-size," "download," or "prioritize" anything. We cringe when young people exclaim, "That really resonates for me!" Most of us prefer to send letters on paper, rather than e-mail. We gaze bemused at the young lining up with bovine patience to get into movies or bars; we have detested lineups since the war.

We wonder how girls with rings in their lips and studs in their tongues can eat without slobbering. We don't understand how guys can blow their noses with rings in them. We wonder why pre-teens' hands never extend from the sleeves of their jackets. Do they have very long sleeves or very short arms?

In twenty years, give or take, we will all be gone. The world, for better or worse, will never see our like again. Generations are forever fading and turning to dust. Will our passing matter one iota to Canada? How and for what might we be remembered?

In considering a label for us, I toyed with Generation M, for "Mature." "Mature" is variously defined as ripe, adult, knowledgeable, experienced, developed. As a group we qualify on all counts (including over-ripe and ready for the dumpster, if you're feeling hostile). The idea was developed further in the May/June 1996 issue of the provocative U.S. magazine *Utne Reader*. It contained an excerpt from *The Sibling Society* by Robert Bly (he of *Iron John* fame) suggesting that people don't grow up any more. Bly claims that adolescence now stretches from about age fifteen to thirty-five. *Utne Reader* compared the faces of young adults of seventy to eighty years ago to those of today: the former *looked* mature; the latter look "preternaturally young."

Labelled or not, our generation matured in a hurry. Depression and war did that for us. We think we are the better for it. Certainly, we differ vastly from our children and grandchildren, much more than we differed from our elders.

And so we are bewildered, saddened, angered by the state of our country: the threat of its breakup; the lawlessness on its streets; the flagrant lack of discipline in its schools; the rash of personal bankruptcies and staggering level of household debt (reportedly near 88 per cent of personal disposable income); the general decline in human civility. What happened to the postwar Canada we launched with so many hopes and dreams fifty years ago?

And what is happening to us? Why the growing hostility toward us? There are even mutters of "intergenerational warfare," based on misconceptions such as the myth that we lucked into a life of ease and luxury.

Our generation made many mistakes. Some of them contributed to the attitudes of our boomer children. But this book will not dwell on blame or on trashing younger generations (well, hardly ever). Rather, I invite younger Canadians to re-examine and try to understand us – who and what we are and how we got this way – before they cast us adrift on ice floes off Baffin Island.

Why are we so careful – frugal, even – with money? Why did we march so willingly into war? Why did we lavish so much on our boomers? Kids, you had to be there.

This narrative includes interviews with 181 men and women of my generation across Canada. Some are well-to-do, some not. Some live in luxury homes, elegant townhouses, and condominiums with high-priced views of the Straits of Georgia, the Minas Basin, the St. Lawrence Seaway, Victoria's inner harbour. Others live in cramped one-room apartments, minuscule bungalows, and shabby old houses.

My subjects include Tories, Liberals, Reformers, and NDPers. Among them are former lawyers, teachers, farmers, postal workers, mechanics, journalists, politicians, clerks, nurses, professors, accountants, librarians, photographers, a pilot, a building contractor, a bookseller, a pharmacist, an actress and a cartoonist. They are trim and fat, white-haired, greying, or balding. Only one, as best I could perceive, has had what my daughter calls "the golden scalpel" (cosmetic surgery). The rest seem content with, or resigned to, the lumps, bumps, and wrinkles that time and fate have dealt them.

They include widows and widowers, divorcees and divorcés, homosexuals, and couples who have lived together so long – forty, fifty years – that they automatically echo each others' most innocuous words:

She: We came back and the front door was covered with grasshoppers.
He: There was a grasshopper plague.
She: There was a plague, a grasshopper plague.

I met a man who habitually refers to his spouse as "my wife" in her presence, and another who calls his wife "the missus." I encountered couples who bickered and contradicted each other, oblivious to the stranger in their midst. Some were relentlessly cantankerous, railing against today's youth. Others wagged their heads, glumly asserting that indeed the world is going to hell in a handbasket. But most that I met were people of intelligence, humour, and deep feelings. Naturally, so small a sample cannot pretend to represent all of our generation. The people who enthusiastically answered my newspaper advertisements and who willingly, even eagerly, agreed to be interviewed are by nature interested and involved. Many others sit in the shopping mall and stare into the middle distance, or hunch over the tube, thinking not much about anything except dinner. But there was enough consensus on some subjects to persuade me that much of what you read here reflects the views of the majority of our 3.6 million senior citizens.

These memories, says my friend Lach MacLean, a retired educator in Blenheim, Ontario, are "the private sanctuary of those who lived in those years." If you are one of us, you may find them heartening. If you are younger, you may find them enlightening.

We think our generation brought with it some values that should not be lost. We would like to be remembered for them.

I

DEPRESSION

"IT TEMPERED OUR SOULS"

A Sweet–Sad Time

From north to south
(from bad to worse)
Father Mother
. . . nursing
'depression' blues,
hitched up the horses
two wagon teams
hayracks loaded
and headed south . . .

Bade farewell
to fields of sterile grain,
to thunder-driven clouds . . .
Father fast-talking
minimizing fears; Mother's bosom
heaving, crying
opulent tears . . .

– from "The Exodus"
Patricia Ritz Andrews

She is seventy-nine, grey and bespectacled, but her voice is urgent and young as she relives in memory that defining event of her life, of nearly all our lives: the Depression.

"Oh, that time still haunts me!" Patricia Ritz Andrews sighs. "It will as long as I live."

It haunts us all. We can't and don't want to forget it. Its people and lessons deserve to be remembered. Andrews preserves them in verse. In her comfortable apartment in White Rock, British Columbia, looking out upon glistening Semiahmoo Bay and Mount Baker's peaks, she writes of withered grain fields, men beaten down by struggle and despair, bone-weary women, their faces flushed from hours bent over coal-burning cook-stoves, abandoned homesteads with walls burnished silver-grey by wind and age.

It was a sweet-sad time for most of us. For Andrews those years were, on the one hand, "probably the best of my life." And yet, "the sadness was deadly."

In 1932 she was barely into her teens on a farm near Leader in western Saskatchewan when the exodus began, when people realized that these were not just aberrant years but a catastrophe of immense proportions. Some packed everything and fled to northern Alberta's fertile Peace River land. The Ritz parents – "peasants . . . plebian, I guess you could call them" – originally from Rumania, took bad advice and moved the family to another farm in the arid southwest.

"It was the worst thing that could have happened. The farm went under. Absolutely went under. My parents placed me for a year with a family in Medicine Hat. They were kind but, oh, I was lonely! Already I knew loneliness at fourteen. I would weep at night and wouldn't know why."

She glances down her long hall. "Every time I sit on that toilet I think about my parents. I think, 'Here we are, Ted [her second husband] and I: two bathrooms, no kids.' We sit on that toilet as if this is our right! And I think of how my parents and my four brothers and one sister and I shared one outdoor privy."

Few of us would exchange our flush toilets for an outdoor one-holer, but the events of 1930 to 1939 are rubbed indelibly into our souls. Most of us are glad we endured it.

"Everyone should experience a depression and be made to

cope with it on his own," declares Glen Hancock, teacher and writer in Wolfville, Nova Scotia. "We were tested and we met the challenge."

"It gave us a set of values that we wouldn't have had otherwise," says retired farmer Maurice Falloon of Foxwarren, Manitoba. Bill Pratt of Tillsonburg, Ontario, former weekly newspaper editor, learned "that family means more than a bank account. I feel sorry for those who feel money is the only benchmark of success."

And lawyer Neil Davidson of Vernon, British Columbia, concludes: "It was pretty terrible, but I guess it tempered our souls from iron to steel."

They call it the "Great Depression" because it was worldwide, and there has been nothing like it since. Its origins, when recorded on paper, seem dry and prosaic, a pallid reflection of the real misery that ensued. The 1920s had been prosperous for most of Canada, with goods pouring out of our farms, forests, and factories at record rates. Credit was easy – too easy. Headlong overexpansion infected Canada, the United States, and others of our trading partners.

Investors grew wary. Stockholders began to sell. Selling turned to panic, culminating in the New York market crash of October 29, 1929. Investment, lending, and growth ground to a stop. World markets had more food and raw materials than they could handle while, ironically, people were starving.

No country suffered more than Canada, because so much of our economy, and one-third of our gross net income, depended on exports. By 1933, 30 per cent of the labour force was unemployed. The jobless rate never fell below 12 per cent until the Second World War. The birth rate sank from 13.1 per thousand population in 1930 to 9.7 in 1937.

One in five people depended on relief, the thirties' version of welfare. Tory Prime Minister R. B. Bennett became infamous –

and lost the 1935 election – for setting up relief work camps for young single men, where they would clear brush and do road work for twenty cents a day under military control. His intention, it seems, was to keep them from congregating in cities where they might cause trouble. It backfired. The camp workers unionized, and in June 1935 began an "On to Ottawa Trek" from Vancouver aboard freight trains. Two thousand of them paused in Regina while eight went ahead to Ottawa to negotiate. The talks failed. The workers staged what was meant to be their final protest in Regina, and the authorities sent in the RCMP and the local police. In the subsequent riot one policeman was killed, several people were injured, and 130 rioters were arrested.

By then the Co-operative Commonwealth Federation (CCF), forerunner of the NDP, had been founded in the West, demanding a wide range of government ownership and control of business. Saskatchewan in particular was ripe for social change. With crop failures and low wheat prices, it was hardest hit of all the provinces. Its income dropped by 90 per cent in two years. Two-thirds of the rural population went on relief.

Even when trade improved marginally in the mid-thirties, Prairie farmers were in a grievous state from the endless cycle of drought, dust storms, and infestations of grasshoppers, army worms, cutworms, wireworms, gophers.

In my own farming community, near Shamrock, in southwestern Saskatchewan, dust storms sometimes blackened the sun at midday. Our mothers served food under dishtowels to ward off the grit. At the one-room rural school our teacher routinely shovelled out sand that drifted under the door. Occasionally we were sent home early. My father met my brother and me to walk us back, fearing we'd be lost in the swirling topsoil.

The whole country seemed jinxed. In July 1936 one of the worst heatwaves in Canadian history blanketed much of the land. Winnipeg reached 106°F (41°C). In Toronto on July 9 the temperature reached 105°F, which, with the local humidity, made life in the inner city almost intolerable. Air conditioning for private homes was virtually unknown. Thousands slept fitfully in the crossfire of electric fans (the city sold out its stock of six thousand), sometimes blowing over melting blocks of ice. Other thousands fled overnight to parks, the waterfront, or the Canadian National Exhibition grounds with blankets and mattresses. When it was over, 542 Ontarians had died.

And the Depression went on for three more years.

DESPAIR

Hope Morritt, now of Point Edward, Ontario, lived in Edmonton during the thirties. How did her family survive the Depression?

We coped, but some didn't. When I was eight or nine I had a little friend named Mary. One time she had to go home for something, so I said I'd go with her. It was just a shack they lived in, two girls, a boy, father and mother; one big room and in the back it was bunks. There was a big long table with one loaf of bread, a big butcher knife beside it. I'll never forget the bread. It looked so stale.

The mother was sitting in a chair and she had her arms on the table. She never lifted her head.

Afterward I said to Mary, "Is your mom okay?"

"Yeah, she's fine."

"Is she asleep?"

"No."

"Did she know you were home?"

She said, "Oh, yeah."

I had a terrible feeling about it and told my mother. She told her priest and the church looked into it. In the end the two girls were moved to an orphanage in Edmonton, and the boy went with his father. But that woman was depressed. She went to a psychiatric hospital. That was somebody who would never make it.

I told that story to my son, and he said, "Why wouldn't she make it?" The baby boomers cannot understand that kind of hopelessness.

Glimpses of a Distant Past

Yet, if we step from the frenetic 1990s into the desperate 1930s, it seems at first glance a blissfully simple, safe, and quiet Canada. Our population hovers at 10.4 million, of whom 46 per cent are rural folk. The air is cleaner, the ambience serene. There is less crime and crime is less grisly. Hardly anyone locks a door. Some don't even own a latchkey.

In the country, sounds are muted – clip-clop of horses' hooves, creak and jingle of harness, rattle of wagon and buggy. The tractor's growl is not yet pervasive. City traffic is relatively placid – only about one million automobiles in the country in 1930 (and seventy thousand fewer by 1935). No muscle cars or deafening leaf-blowers, power lawnmowers, ghetto blasters, multi-speaker stereos, video arcades, jet aircraft. We will never come to understand the later generations' tolerance for noise, let alone, in the case of their music, their *craving* for it.

Here in the thirties, even city neighbourhoods have an oddly rural ambience. Some people keep chickens. Fresh washing flaps on backyard clotheslines: none of us has heard of clothes dryers. Refrigerators are rare: most city families have an icebox.

Here is a summer's-day ritual: the iceman clatters up to your door with a "Whoa, whoa!," burrows into his wagon, frees a crystalline block with his icepick (sending up showers of chips), seizes it with tongs, and lugs it indoors to fit under the icebox. Children skulking in the hedges — the iceman knows they are there and enjoys their subterfuge — dash out and salvage ice slivers to suck. Their mothers have already warned them: "Don't suck that stuff, it's dirty!" which merely enhances its charm.

In Montreal the rag man roams the lanes and alleys calling "*Des guénilles à vendre.*" In every city milk and bread come by horse cart. In one Hamilton neighbourhood you can place a twenty-five-cent bet with your bread man, a handsome, clean-cut fellow who doubles as bookie. Mothers assign their kids to scoop up horse manure from the streets to fertilize the garden. Any city household with even a scrap of earth has a garden to supplement the food budget.

Prices, like wages, are ridiculously low. A quart of milk costs ten cents. Bread is six cents a loaf. Eggs are five to ten cents a dozen, butter is twenty cents a pound, a whole chicken can be had for twenty-five cents, and a quality roast of beef sells for ten cents a pound. In Halifax, fishermen's wives from outlying villages go door to door selling quart milk bottles of delicious clam chowder for ten cents.

Time travellers from the nineties see a conspicuous difference in dress. Their own young people wear torn and faded jeans as a fashion statement. Thirties youth are ashamed of ragged clothing; it must be patched, and ideally blue denims are raspingly new and stiff. Nineties mall-goers or church-goers often dress *down* by choice. Their thirties counterparts dress *up* to go shopping, to the movies, and most especially to church.

Many women wear homemade frocks cut well below the knee. Underneath, many are locked into a "foundation garment" to restrain the body-not-so-beautiful: a full-fledged corset with whalebone stays, not the kind Madonna wears but the kind Queen Victoria wore (or should have worn). Even firm, trim young bodies may be encased in elastic girdles, hiding their curves and crevices from prying eyes.

Men, for dress-up, wear white shirts, neckties, and jackets or suits with wide lapels and pleated trousers hitched high above the waist with suspenders. Everyone wears a hat or cap (although there is no hole in the ozone layer and nobody's heard of the UV factor). Here in the thirties, looking one's best is a matter of pride.

That same brave front is evident in the music pouring from mantel radios and front-parlour pianos (in homes that can afford them). Songs that thumb their noses at hard times: "Happy Days Are Here Again," "I Found a Million Dollar Baby in a Five and Ten Cent Store," "I've Got My Love to Keep Me Warm," and "Wrap Your Troubles in Dreams," sung by the popular new crooner with the goofy name, Bing Crosby. His voice flows soft and smooth like cream over a bowl of Wheaties, Breakfast of Champions.

Are these people in denial, as their grandchildren would put it? No. It is a deliberate façade. They know all too well that life is perilous. Look into their faces, as in a snapshot of my own family in the year 1935. My father is grim and unsmiling, although he loves to laugh. My mother, too, is dark-eyed and serious.

Only my brother and I, urchins in overalls, are smiling. Our parents are bearing the brunt. We know these are hard times because the parents say so, but everyone is in the same boat. Like many children of the era, we don't particularly mind the poverty. Nor do we realize how this decade is marking us for life.

THE LITTLE RAILWAY GIRL

For Marilyn Chandler, home was a railway station. Her father, William, was a branch-line Canadian Pacific Railway agent in five successive Prairie towns. For seventeen years the Chandlers lived above waiting rooms and offices with chattering telegraphs, beside high wooden platforms and ribbons of steel track with thundering steam locomotives, whistles shrilling, coal smoke belching, brakes squealing.

The station was the hub of every small community and everything and everyone moved by train.

My entire childhood was spent in CPR strawberry-red station houses. People coming and going all the time, each town with its traditional characters: drunk, idiot, hero, villain. I helped my dad in the office. Sometimes I waited on customers. During the war I delivered telegrams, always with a sense of dread. I played acrobatics in the rafters over the freight shed, and my brothers taught me to drive a car on the platform.

In the fall there were crates of peaches, apples, and pears. My hands were just the right size to get through the slats and snitch some. In the spring there'd be shipments of baby chicks. Dad let me look for crippled ones to nurse. One, Biddy, grew into a magnificent white rooster who guarded our yard with such ferocity we had to send him to a farm.

The station agent was an important person. My dad was real friendly and outgoing. He just loved talking, much more than he should have, and then had to do all his work at night, much to Mother's distress. She'd be sitting alone upstairs.

Dad was a simple man. He didn't need money for pleasures. Mother had big ideas, ambition. She used to visit relatives in Winnipeg. They had more money. She envied them and would come home and bitch at Dad because we didn't have what they had.

Some of those living quarters when we took over were filthy hellholes, with vermin in the floorboards. Mother worked so hard to make us a clean, comfortable home. Then a big steam engine would come along and spew coal soot all over her fresh washing, rattle her pictures off the wall, and sometimes kill my pet cats.

Coming into new schools I kept a low profile. Kids are cruel. There was always the feeling that I was breaking up their little cliques. I just shyly made my way into new situations. That way I kept out of trouble.

It was lonely. But it was a real adventure.

Marilyn Chandler McFadden lives in London, Ontario, widowed and still sometimes lonely.

Pride and Misery

The Depression did not touch everyone.

"We weren't rich, we weren't poor," says John Dodds, now of Vancouver. He attended a Montreal private school and "didn't really know there was a depression at all." Neither did Arthur Bishop, also a private-school boy: "The Depression didn't mean a hell of a lot to us because we lived in a luxury penthouse in Montreal."

Others, although not wealthy, did not suffer because the family breadwinner, usually the father, had a job. In Fredericton, Fran Murray Peacock's father was a fox farmer. In Sudbury, Douglas Gardner's father was in the automotive business. Barbara Cumming's father was budget controller for the Toronto Transit Commission: "He worked all his life for the TTC and expected to, but he had a lifelong nightmare of losing his job."

In London, Bill Williamson's father, a sheet-metal worker with Canadian National Railways, "made twenty dollars a week, which kept a family of five." Any railway job – conductor, engineer, brakeman, section hand, station master – was golden, because the trains always ran. Doctors, dentists, veterinarians, barbers, while not necessarily rolling in cash, usually ate well because patients or customers often reimbursed them with butter, eggs, vegetables, a chicken, or a cut of beef. When a patient brought his doctor father a fresh chicken, remembers John Bigham of Burlington, Ontario, it meant the family was assured of good meals for a few days.

Beverly Holmes Watson's father was also a doctor. "He and Mother did the accounting at night, putting little red clips on the cards of patients who couldn't pay," she says from Buckhorne, Ontario. "Those red clips just about filled the book."

Everyone, even the four-fifths of the population that held some kind of job, cultivated a mixture of frugality and ingenuity. Farmer Leonard Shiels of Craven, Saskatchewan, lived on a ninety-cent weekly food budget, part of which he earned by selling bones scrounged from the prairie.

"We thought we were in heaven," Shiels says. He was, too, compared to earlier years when as a hired man he had worked one whole winter for no money, just board and his washing. The next winter he had had to pay for the washing.

In Montreal, Bernard Brouillet's father owned rental properties for one hundred tenants. His father wasn't wealthy – the tenants didn't always pay – but was comfortably off. Yet the son, a young man during the thirties, used to nurse one cigarette for most of a day: one puff, pass it to a friend for a puff, stub it out, take another drag an hour later.

And no caring person, whether directly touched by poverty or not, could ignore, or can ever forget, the pathetic little dramas being played out around them. In Kitchener, Helen Stumpf wondered why her friend's kitchen walls were papered with newspaper. "Later I realized it was out of desperation." Eric Golby recalls eating an apple at recess in his Toronto school: "Two or three kids followed me, waiting to grab the core when I threw it away."

Ruth Hewitt's father, a Regina veterinarian, once took her and brother Earl on a rural call. Each small Hewitt had an orange for a snack. One glance at the farmer's six children and Dr. Hewitt turned quietly to his own two: "Would you give your oranges to these kids?" They did. The smallest child stared at an orange and said, "What is it?"

Children today expect to have their own bedrooms or, at least, to share with no more than one sibling. In the thirties that was luxury. Jean Orpwood grew up in Toronto in a three-bedroom house with four brothers. One bedroom was rented out for some extra income. She and the brothers shared another: the boys on bunks, Jean on a single bed. When she grew older, she got the lodger's room. (It did not wreck her life; she ended her career as director of the North York Public Library.)

On the family farm near Trewdale, Saskatchewan, Mona Patterson, her parents, two sisters, and a brother lived in a twelve-by-twenty-four-foot shack. Mother and daughters slept in the only bed; father and son slept on a cot. Yet they were marginally better off than a neighbouring family of ten who slept on straw mattresses, all on a single wooden bench that ran the length of the house. One of those children went to school wearing a rubber boot on one foot and an overshoe on the other.

As now, kids were always growing out of shoes. Could this really matter when they cost only $1.44 a pair? It mattered if the parents were broke. Sunday School teacher Elisabeth Brown, of Stellarton, Nova Scotia, knew children who wouldn't attend church because they had no footwear. Only a teenager herself, she bought them shoes from her twenty-five-cent allowance, paying off the shoemaker at ten cents a week.

Many Depression children conserved shoe leather by going without. "I was a teenager before I quit going barefoot in the summer," says Michael Bartolf of Oxbow, Saskatchewan. "My feet were like leather. I could run through a patch of Canada thistle." In Melville, Saskatchewan, Jean Parker saved her only pair of shoes to wear just before reaching church or a community dance. Stan Hoffman walked three miles to school at Humboldt,

Saskatchewan, and hated it: in the winter his feet froze because he wore only socks inside rubber boots.

Extra clothes of any kind were a frill. Mona Patterson wore the same dress through one whole winter. When Olive McConville of Ponteix, Saskatchewan, left home to train as a teacher at the normal school, her sister donated a coat and another sister made three blouses (blue, pink, white) to go with Olive's only skirt.

Olive Farnden of Alameda, Saskatchewan, owned two school dresses (one in the wash, one to wear) and one for Sunday. Her five brothers each had two pairs of combination overalls. "When I was fourteen Mom was in hospital so I stayed home on Monday and did the wash. Bless my soul! Three of the boys got into a slough on the way home and messed up their clean Monday overalls. So I put them in bed while I washed and dried the overalls."

None of this was child neglect. Our parents made countless small sacrifices for us. One man told me that when food was scarce his mother habitually said, "I'm not hungry, you kids eat it."

The Ritzes of Saskatchewan were not the only family torn apart by poverty. For three years Ted Grant and his mother and sister lived with rural friends while the father hunted for work in Toronto. When Kay Heaney's parents lost their Sault Ste. Marie house, "we had to live with my grandmother. And I think it broke up my parents' marriage. They lived together but their spirit was broken."

The Ritzes weren't the only ones to abandon home either. In one family exodus, Jean Parker was smuggled in a boxcar, with a brother and a sister, the family furniture, and two cows. It was a five-day trip, from Edmonton to Judah, in Alberta's Peace River district, and her father couldn't afford their rail fare. Although the train crew was supposedly unaware of the stowaways, they gave Jean's father enough hot stew to feed a family, in exchange for milk from his cows.

Otto Beck's family also hid out in a boxcar from Salter, Saskatchewan, to Manitoba. The drought drove Otto out of Salter in 1937, only nine years after he had come from Poland to better his life. Their pitifully few household furnishings were loaded aboard. The cattle, pigs, eight horses, and a colt went into a cattle car. He turned an old wagon box upside down inside the boxcar and lined the floor with blankets. His wife and his two small sons and daughter crawled inside with a cache of canned pork and chicken, a five-gallon can of boiled milk, and two containers of water.

When the branch-line train pulled up, the train man called, "Otto Beck? You ready?" and hitched his boxcar on behind. Then he climbed in and plunked himself down on the overturned wagon box. Ernest Beck, eleven then, remembers, "There was only one inch of lumber between his behind and us."

"So where's your family?" the train man asked chattily.

"Oh, they left a week ago," Otto lied. The train lurched away at four p.m. on Friday and reached Winnipeg at two a.m. on Sunday. Otto retrieved his grubby little family and led them to the station for a wash. Then they took a streetcar to Selkirk, to find plenty of fishing, muskrat trapping, hay, and precious water. It seemed like paradise.

Men and women would do anything for work. It not only kept families alive, it was a measure of one's worth. When work was lost, self-esteem went with it.

"A lot of emphasis was placed upon the dignity of work," says Ruth Dillon Collins of Toronto. "My worst memory is of seeing men – no scarves, no hats, in the bitter cold of winter – lining up as far as you could see in front of a store advertising *one* job. That to me, more than anything, depicts the Depression."

In Winnipeg, Alan Cooper's father – an unemployed teacher – joined a line stretching around a block for a job with the local electrical utility. Most of the job-hunters were young and well-dressed. When Cooper, Sr., reached the head of the line he deducted ten years from his age. He got the job and held it for eighteen years.

When Mona Patterson needed new shoes her father told her, "Never mind, girlie, there's a carload of coal coming in and I'll get five dollars for unloading it. We'll get your shoes." "Unloading" meant emptying the whole boxcar by shovel and by hand. It was a hard day's labour, and he felt lucky and proud to get it.

In Victoria, after Peter Marchant's father lost his insurance-bond business in the crash of 1929, father and son went job-hunting together. "We'd go to schools and he'd say, 'Do you want anyone to mark your playgrounds or do any odd jobs?' Occasionally we got a little work." For money, of course, but also as a matter of pride.

From his condo overlooking Victoria's inner harbour, Doug Harvey thinks of *his* father, who manufactured wicker furniture until the Depression made wicker passé. At the time, their Toronto suburb was paying out-of-work men two dollars a day to sweep the streets.

"I remember so vividly seeing my father one day with this push broom in the gutter. I ran up yelling to him. He wouldn't answer, wouldn't even look at me. It took me years to understand."

Glen Hancock tells of a Wolfville neighbour who, one Depression winter, went to work early every morning, "lunch-pail under his arm, steps crunching in the snow. Until it was discovered that he didn't *have* a job. Where he went I don't know, but he felt a man had to be seen going and coming. Imagine! Today, of course, if you don't have a job you make your way as fast as you can to the welfare office."

Unemployment drove men to terrible extremes. Ted Grant's father went seven years without a job. On his search he often trudged over Toronto's Bloor Street viaduct high above a ravine. "Many times, Dad told me later, he felt like jumping off," Grant says. His father finally found odd jobs as an auto mechanic and truck driver.

In 1930 suicides of men ages thirty to thirty-five soared to 22.2 per hundred thousand (more than double the rate of only six years before). In the same year, 31.6 per hundred thousand men in the forty to forty-nine age group took their lives. Overall in the early thirties, suicide accounted for nearly 1 per cent of all deaths in Canada (in 1931 alone that would have amounted to a thousand deaths), a rate that would not be exceeded for another thirty years.

BY COVERED WAGON TO PARADISE VALLEY

In the summer of 1937 Herman and Irma Kleeberger, three sons, and two sets of twin daughters, finally gave up on Saskatchewan. Herman tightened the steel rims on his three-deck grain wagon (the wooden wheels had shrunk through years of drought) and covered it with canvas stretched over bowed ribs cut from Saskatoon bushes. He converted a horse-drawn hayrack into a canvas-covered mobile home and took his 1927 Chev off its blocks. Irma canned beef and salt pork for what would turn out to be forty-five days and six hundred miles on the road.

Earl, then age fourteen, laconically describes their incredible journey – wagon, hayrack, car – from Assiniboia, through Swift Current and Leader, across the Saskatchewan River by ferry, and into central Alberta.

By August 18 we were ready to leave. All the neighbours gathered to see us off. We had six or seven horses and nine head of cattle. Joe the canary travelled in the Chev in a cage. Bessy, our pet nanny goat, rode in a cage on the running board.

The front of the hayrack was a bedroom/kitchen with stove on one side and two double-bunk beds along the other. In back was a washing machine and livestock feed. A dozen chickens rode underneath. The grain wagon held household things and beds for the four girls.

Every day we started about eight-thirty and stopped about six. Mother and Dad drove ahead and located stops with feed and water for noon and overnight. We travelled sideroads mostly, to be easier on the horses' feet and to find grazing in the ditches. On steep hills the wheels had to be locked going down [to slow the wagons] and we doubled the teams going up the other side.

We stopped on Sundays to rest and do laundry. Mother would have chicken and dumplings ready at noon. She even baked bread. We'd put a quart jar of cream on a coil-spring bed and by noon we'd have butter from all the bouncing and shaking.

One night we kids were herding the horses and they got by us and headed back for home. It was a terrible dark night but we located them and wrangled them back to camp.

It must have been hard on our parents, but the rest of us had a pretty good time. We met so many nice people who gave us any vegetables and food they could spare and advice about feed conditions on the way. On October 2, we reached Paradise Valley, just west of Red Deer. My father and older sisters got jobs that first year. Then we got a farm near Sylvan Lake. Things improved after that.

Children worked as a matter of course. This is not to denigrate today's kids who hold part-time jobs, although Elisabeth Brown Golby says they are "treated like little prima donnas, pampered and protected from the stark realities of life." As a child she shovelled snow around house and stable, exercised two horses before school every morning, and mucked out the stalls. "When I brought the horses back, icicles hung from their nostrils and their breath was frozen all over my jacket." For this she earned twenty-five cents a week.

There *is* a difference between serving Big Macs or running a leaf-blower, and, as Glen Hancock did, harvesting salt hay from salt marshes. "I'd lift the heavy stuff up a slope, over the railway tracks, down the other side, across a footbridge and into our backyard where I'd stack it. My father sold it for fodder. I didn't get any money. It was just one of the things you did."

In Galt, Roy Francis was fifteen when his father died. Roy, youngest of five children, was broken-hearted. "I crept downstairs a couple of times that night – he was in a casket in the living room, they did that in those days – and sat by the door in the dark. I guess I thought it was keeping him company."

All the Francis kids were superior students. Roy accelerated through grade school and began high school at thirteen. He was also a budding tenor and studied classical singing for eight years. But after his father died, Roy Francis dropped out of school and music and went to work in a saw factory for fifteen cents an hour.

Boys then as now delivered newspapers, but the rewards were minute. Ron Laidlaw of St. Mary's, Ontario, delivered the Stratford *Beacon Herald* for, he recalls, three or four cents a week. The newspaper cost subscribers twelve cents a week, so Laidlaw waited two weeks to collect, hoping customers would let him keep the extra penny from a twenty-five-cent piece as a tip.

In Calgary, Stan Winfield inherited a paper route from his three older brothers. Among them, they kept the route for fifteen years, turning over most of the money to their parents.

Their father, a druggist, needed help; he'd been caught up in what seemed to be blatant anti-Semitism. In 1915 the Alberta Liquor Act had prohibited the sale of alcoholic beverages, but doctors and dentists were allowed to provide liquor for "medicinal purposes." Dispensing druggists had to keep proper records of such sales. In 1919 Winfield's father was fined for allegedly selling liquor without a bona fide prescription. (Most druggists were selling it in similar fashion. Some did not keep records; some actually sold liquor by the glass. Winfield, the province's only Jewish druggist, was the only one charged.) He lost his licence to dispense alcohol, a blow to his business. "From then on," the son remembers, "he was just a destroyed man."

The award for childhood entrepreneurism must go to the Finnbogason brothers of Winnipeg. When parents and five sons moved into Winnipeg from Lundar in 1932, nine-year-old Bill and his three older brothers went to work. On Saturdays, and weekdays after school, they delivered handbills, newspapers, and groceries. Most of their take went into the family pot.

"It wasn't because we were good kids," Bill insists. "It just seemed the natural thing to do. We knew our parents were having difficulty. Somehow they had instilled this unity of family into us. We did it with no questions asked."

Their *pièce de résistance* was butter. Every week for five years they imported fresh country butter by train and sold it to city customers. Each brother had a route, delivering by bicycle after school every Thursday and Friday, and all day Saturday, collecting on Monday, Tuesday, and Wednesday from clients who didn't pay on delivery day.

"It was a learning experience of inestimable value," says Finnbogason, who ultimately became Winnipeg's commissioner of works and operations. "I've never regretted it."

The Dole

"It seems to me that people on welfare now live better than the kings and queens of five hundred years ago," says Eddie Laporte of Moose Jaw. That's the perspective of one whose family of six lived on relief payments of eleven dollars a month in the thirties – about five cents per person per day.

There was no social safety net as we know it now. During the thirties nearly a billion dollars went into direct relief for the unemployed and destitute. Throughout the decade, successive federal governments contributed 35 to 40 per cent of the cost; provinces and municipalities the remainder. Since relief was administered by municipalities, the ground rules and amounts of assistance varied widely by region. A family of five in Calgary might get sixty dollars a month, but in Halifax only nineteen. In Toronto a family of five received a $6.93 weekly food allowance, while the same-size family in rural Quebec might receive $3.25. Newfoundlanders received six cents' worth of food a day for each family member.

Today, welfare for the needy is viewed as a right. The vast majority of those I polled remember the dole as mortifying, if not humiliating, and to be avoided at all costs. "My family would have come close to starving before asking for relief," says Norma West Linder of Sarnia. "It was a dirty word back then." In Oxbow, Saskatchewan, Hazel Armstrong Paton's parents "took a five dollars per month relief cheque one winter and felt terrible doing so. They spent all their savings first." Margaret Davidson Boyd of Kinistino, Saskatchewan, recalls other children eating "relief" apples at school: "They smelled *so* good, but we did without. My father would never accept charity."

Near Truro, Nova Scotia, Elizabeth Murray's father was over-seer of the poor for the neighbourhood. "There was a book of names he kept locked in his desk and it was never discussed. To this day I would find it difficult to look through that book."

Alan Cooper's father, the unemployed teacher, had prospered for a time in real estate, working with his brother. After the crash of 1929, he had to declare bankruptcy. The Coopers lost their modern house in Winnipeg and their Overlander car, and moved to suburban East Kildonan, with its mud roads, board sidewalks, water from a well and no telephone.

Cooper, Sr., had no income and no savings. When municipal assistance came through, he walked two and a half miles to a store, paid for what food he could, and charged the rest. Going to that distant store kept some of their neighbours from knowing he was on relief, his son says. "In 1935 he found work and paid off the old grocery bill by 1942."

The mere *suggestion* of being a welfare recipient was insulting to some. In Edmonton the school nurse sent Hope Morritt home with a note that said, "This child is too thin." Morritt's mother bristled. To her, it implied they were a welfare family. "Sorry, I can't fatten a racehorse," she wrote back curtly, and that ended it.

Arthur Witt, now of Brantford, and his two siblings actually insisted that their parents go off the dole. The Witts arrived in Alberta from Poland in 1930 but could only obtain relief after getting their citizenship papers in 1936. "Our parents then got it for two months. When we three children found out, we begged that they cut it off because of the stigma it gave us at school."

The stigma, for those who felt it, came partly from the ethos of our generation and partly because officialdom made it *seem* shameful. Proof of residence – ranging anywhere from six months to three years – was usually required. Ontario relief recipients had their driver's licences cancelled lest they use the pogey to operate cars. In some jurisdictions, relief families were refused telephones. Saskatchewan residents risked having relief cut off if they bought beer or liquor. In Quebec, recalls Beatrice Shaw of St-Laurent, "your welfare worker could visit and check up on you any time without notice." One day her parents were preparing to take a twenty-minute bus ride when they met their welfare worker at the bus stop. The woman scolded them for splurging on the ten-cent bus fares. They should walk, she said; there were better ways to spend their welfare money.

Applicants had to line up at the relief office and prove their need. Local bureaucrats could be patronizing or deliberately insulting. In Sault Ste. Marie the municipal government gave five-pound bags of flour or rolled oats to the needy. Fred Hamilton's father, who'd lost his job and had five children to feed, qualified.

He needed Fred's little wagon to haul the handout home. Young Fred was in the wagon, so his father pulled him along. The relief office was run by the mayor's young son, who berated the older Hamilton for living off other people. Why didn't he get himself a job?

"My father came out and he was crying," Fred told me shortly before his death in 1997. "He pulled me home in my wagon and he never, ever went back for relief. Never."

Instead, Hamilton, Sr., opened a nightclub. It was "a bootleg joint, but a pretty high-class one" and it prospered, because the community's leading citizens "all liked to drink now and again."

The lack of social assistance made life especially hard for single-parent families. In Moose Jaw, Hal Sisson's mother received a "widow's pension," forty dollars a month for herself and her four children. "The Liberal government of the time placed a lien against our home, intending at some future time to collect both principal and compound interest," says Sisson, now living in Victoria. "The lien was later cancelled, but it pissed me off to the extent that I became a lawyer, with the intention of harassing government as much as possible."

Douglas How's widowed mother in Dorchester, New Brunswick, also with four children, received "not one cent of government help. Absolutely nothing. My Uncle John, a stock-broker, sent her twenty dollars a month. One summer, when I was about twelve, she said, 'Uncle John hasn't sent his cheque for three months. I'm terrified it's stopped for good. If it has, we're in deep trouble.' A week later it came; he'd been in Europe. But five dollars a week made that much difference."

Although many of our generation feel that some of modern government's beneficence is excessive and has been abused, medicare is universally admired. In the 1930s, when everyone had to pay for medical care, our mothers treated our minor ailments. Once a reaper blade cut my father's finger to the bone. He drove into Shamrock, where the postmaster's wife patched him up. We went to doctors or to hospital only for major emergencies. Illness could ruin a family, as it almost did the Schienbeins of Neudorf, Saskatchewan.

A Simple Appendectomy

Herb Schienbein is a square-built man in his sixties with sandy grey-flecked hair, a powerful upper body, and an occasional wry smile that, all together, remind you of the movie actor Brian Dennehy. He became a successful realtor and building contractor, partly because of cruel lessons learned in the Depression.

In his home town of Regina, he tells me his story in intimate detail, mostly in dispassionate tones, now and again shaking his head or flashing his ironic grin at the memory of people and circumstances that shattered his family more than sixty years ago.

In 1936 his mother, Katherine, needed a simple appendectomy. There was no hospital in the village, so she went by train to Regina. There, says Schienbein, she lay in a hospital hallway for two and a half days until the municipality agreed to foot part of the bill for her surgery. (Her husband, Philip, could not afford to pay.) By then the appendix had burst and gangrene had set in. Although Katherine survived, she was plagued by medical problems for the rest of her life and had to undergo some fourteen other operations related to the original delayed appendectomy.

Two years later, creditors, including two doctors, took over Philip's farm to cover some of the medical bills. The family moved to Wolseley, forty-five miles away, taking along a single souvenir of the old home: one of the ornate wooden curtain rods that Philip's father had turned out on his lathe.

One day an RCMP corporal arrived at their gate with one of the doctors. They had come to claim the missing curtain rod. Herb's father was sharpening fenceposts.

"By then Dad was just beaten down by all that had happened. He struck out with a fencepost and wouldn't let them in the yard. I can still see my mother in tears with all this going on."

The Mountie and doctor left. (Years later the Mountie apologized to the Schienbeins; he said he had only been following orders that day.) Philip planted a new crop in 1938. Grasshoppers stripped it. The family moved again, by hayrack to Lemberg, thirty-five miles away, and rented a two-room house from a man going off to war.

Philip got a railway labourer's job at sixty-five cents an hour. When he was laid off in the winter he earned twelve dollars a month for servicing the local rink. Herb helped, often getting home at two a.m. after flooding the ice. Sometimes, in season, he and his father – after coming home from school and from work – stooked wheat sheaves or split wood by moonlight.

Herb also worked after school in grocery and drug stores for $1.25 a week, earning an extra thirty-five cents a week for carrying two pails of water a mile and a half daily. The madame of the local brothel paid him twenty-five cents for fetching beer from the hotel. Sometimes the hotel-owner tipped him another quarter. All of this taught him "what life was about. I don't think you can get that in university."

Young Schienbein took most of his earnings home to his parents, but for years he sent $1.50 a month to a Regina surgeon to reduce the remaining medical bill. In 1959, by then the manager of a Regina credit union, he scraped together a thousand dollars and settled the debt.

"That was the first time since 1936 that my dad was debt-free." His parents wept with relief. The names of all those doctors are still engraved in Herb Schienbein's memory.

"Guys just like me"

Frank Hamilton – a Saskatchewan farmboy who flew two wartime tours over Europe and subsequently became a member of parliament – "rode the rods" during the thirties.

The spring of '38, when I was seventeen, a neighbour lad and I decided to head for Alberta. We hitched a ride from Mazenod to Moose Jaw. I had a pack on my back and five bucks in my pocket.

Just west of Moose Jaw we settled into the brush and waited. A freight highballs by, not very fast, so we jumped up. My God, there must have been two dozen *other* guys in the bush! They *all* rose up and grabbed this freight.

My friend got into a boxcar. I ended up hanging on between a couple of cars. Away we went. Jesus! Rattle, clang, bang! The first stop, I was off like a shot and joined my buddy. Sleep? I don't think so. There'd be maybe ten or twelve other guys in the car. Some young, some old (to me), in their forties. And it was talk all night – would the CPR cops get us, and so on.

We had a can of beans and a loaf of bread. We damn near went crazy with thirst before we finally got there. Oh, were we dry! We rode her all night, and the next night got off at Lacombe. I got a job helping put in the crop. Then I went to work north of Edmonton, cutting willows about as big as my arm.

I came home that fall, same way. Once I rode up on the coal-tender. In the morning, getting near Edmonton, I got off and, oh God, I was just black! Found a little slough, washed up, and offered to work for the first family I came to. I got breakfast from them. I can't remember ever being turned down when I asked for food. I was always gung-ho to chop a bit of wood or hoe a row of potatoes. Any damn thing at all.

The next year, '39, we went again. We were in some little place halfway to Edmonton when a young Mountie marched a dozen of us out of town. "Keep going, boys," he said. The royal visit was on and he didn't want our bunch showing up.

One dramatic thing happened. Our freight stopped some place in Saskatchewan, and a guy came up with a team and wagon. He started chatting, and we were saying, "Alberta, lots of work there."

Suddenly this guy simply wrapped up the lines [reins], jumped off the wagon, and got in the boxcar. Was he some-body's hired man? He just left the team there and went west!

I learned a lot of respect for my fellow man in those years. Maybe I was lucky. I heard about the hobo jungles. Every city had one. But I never got involved in any of that stuff. The guys I associated with were all just like me. Yeah.

Riding the Rods

In the slang and in the songs of the day they were hoboes, tramps, bums. But in reality they were ordinary men, mostly young, down on their luck. They shuttled back and forth across the land, riding the rods. (Technically, the rods were any of the metal framework underneath a rail car, but most men rode in or on top of the cars.) They were looking for work or just keeping on the move, which was better than the deadening emptiness of staying in one godforsaken place.

They dodged the Mounties and the railway police, scrounged food from fields and gardens, and begged at back doors, often politely removing their caps. People shared whatever they had: a beef or bologna sandwich, fried potatoes or eggs, canned fruit, tea or coffee, a glass of milk.

The men usually ate in the woodshed, on the back steps, or at a backyard picnic table. If they seemed harmless some families took them into the kitchen, or better. In Kitchener, Barbara Schwartz insisted that hungry men be seated at her table *spread with clean linen*. In Virden, Manitoba, Sara Childerhose made them feel welcome and equal: she asked their names, shook their hands, found odd jobs for them, and told her son, "Get some warm water so Mr. [whatever his name was] can wash up when he comes in." Kay Townend's father, a United Church minister in London, Ontario, saw to their feeding, then phoned around to places that offered beds for a small fee – which he paid. Reverend Jack Griffith of Bowmanville likewise staked them to a meal whenever he could find a spare dollar. One man thanked him with a gift – a white swan painted on black silk.

Legend had it that friendly houses were somehow marked. Perhaps it was some inconspicuous but significant assembly of pebbles? An arrow pointing to a favoured house? It drove small boys to distraction. "God, how I searched and searched," remembers Jim Redditt of his boyhood home in Goderich, Ontario. "I looked on trees all around the place and couldn't find the mark." But the men came, and his widowed mother always found them a meal.

For all boys, these kings of the road brought a fillip of excitement into the circumscribed world of a Depression childhood.

In Melville, Saskatchewan, Max Macdonald spotted a gun in the hip pocket of a lad his parents had invited to dinner: "I was quite excited but didn't say anything. He sure as hell wasn't going to rob us, because there was nothing worth stealing. But it never occurred to my folks to turn those people away."

"The guys would sit on the back step with me and talk," recalls Bill Williamson of his home in London. "I heard great stories. None of them were real bums."

Many were like Walt McConville, who in 1934 was shuttling between Vancouver and his home in Ponteix, Saskatchewan. He and a friend grabbed a freight in Vancouver and joined a dozen others bedded down on the floor of an unused caboose. It had a stove, and whenever the train laboured up a grade the men took turns jumping out to scavenge coal along the tracks. At water stops they fanned out to forage for farm vegetables for their stew.

On another trip McConville lost his bag with his clothes and what little money he had. Desperate, he began knocking on doors in Calgary, offering to do anything for food. On his third try a family said, "Come and live with us until you find a job." They kept him ten days until he found farm work.

For many of our generation, social conscience was born at such moments. In Sault Ste. Marie, little Kay Heaney asked, "Why are you giving those men all our food?" as her mother passed out tea and peanut-butter sandwiches.

"Because maybe some day your brothers will need something like this," came her mother's reply.

On the Whitefish River Ojibwa Indian reserve, west of Sudbury, a man dropped off the train and knocked at Augustine McGregor's door. Young Lillian, one of ten children, slammed the door on the stranger.

"Who was that?" her father asked.

"I don't know. He hasn't got the same colour as us."

Augustine McGregor – son of a Scottish father and Ojibwa mother, wed to Victoria Pegoniasong (meaning "beam of light" in Ojibwa) – fetched the man back and fed him. Later Augustine, a staunch Catholic, told his daughter, "Those men are looking for work. They travel all over. They have no place to sleep. Don't ever slam the door like that." He added not unkindly, "You know, that could have been *Gitch'Manitou* [approximately "Great Spirit"] coming to the door."

In Sudbury, Douglas Gardner's generous-hearted mother, on coming upon a young man looking for a meal, would exclaim, "Poor boy, where are you from? Can we help?" The man, clutching his pride, nearly always offered to cut a lawn, rake leaves, split wood. "It was none of this, 'You gotta feed me,'" Gardner says.

He never forgot his mother's generosity and the men's dignity in the face of need. Gardner spent most of his adult life as a social worker.

"So Little Meant So Much"

Despite all the privation, it was not a time of unremitting misery. "I could not have grown up at a better time or in better circumstances," insists Glen Hancock. "We were more trusting. We were better Samaritans. We stopped occasionally along the way to gaze into the lilies."

Smelling the flowers, literally or metaphorically, was one of our versions of a good time. We expected so little that we were easily pleased, a trait that has stayed with us. And, as we say *ad nauseam*, we made do with whatever was at hand.

Much of this we learned from those creative geniuses, our mothers. They concocted nourishing meals from the unlikeliest ingredients. "Mother could whip up a meal out of flour and water," Oxbow's Michael Bartolf enthuses. "We ate a lot of dumplings, little wee tiny things. The first night we had them as soup. Then we drained off the liquid for the pigs, put the dumplings in a cool place for three, four days. Then Mother'd fry up a bunch with a little bit of fat and add tomato sauce. Boy, was that good!"

It seemed all mothers made rugs out of rags and created shirts, underwear, dishtowels and tablecloths from flour sacks, oatmeal bags, or sugar bags with the Robin Hood, Rogers, or Quaker Oats logo bleached out. Ruth Hewitt's mother in Regina made a snowsuit for her daughter out of her husband's castoff coat. Mothers everywhere kept our meagre wardrobes in repair, with patches atop the patches.

Every mother could perform legerdemain with bits of paper. They devised cheap colourful costumes – elves, brownies, fairies – from crêpe paper for our Christmas concerts. One year my mother produced for me a virtuoso Little Jack Frost outfit from white crêpe, cotton batting, and sparkles. She also made scrapbooks with pages of ironed cloth scraps.

In Plattsville, Ontario, Effie Stauffer made her children scrapbooks with pages of ironed wrapping paper, and filled them with neatly captioned coloured pictures cut from magazines or Christmas cards and stuck into place with flour-and-water paste. She and the kids would leaf through the books, making up stories. Mrs. Stauffer also dyed Easter eggs a golden brown from onionskins. A generation later, her daughter Helen passed on that legacy to her grade-school students.

Most of our entertainment was homemade – dances, concerts, card games (whist was a favourite), or the simple enjoyment of going calling. As a boy, Ken Campbell had his immediate family plus eight sets of aunts and uncles in rural Ontario, all within horse-and-buggy or Model T Ford range.

"Sunday afternoon was the time for visiting," remembers Campbell, now a United Church minister in Burlington. "People didn't seem to make arrangements ahead of time. They just went. We either visited relatives or stayed home and expected someone to drop in. There always seemed to be enough food in the house, no matter how many people came."

Nearly always it was that way: families having fun together at no expense. In Marion Elliott Pratt's household, a Sunday ritual was mother reading aloud to the children from the serials in the *Family Herald*. It was the same in my house, where books, newspapers, and magazines were almost as essential as food.

Every rural schoolhouse or small-town community hall could produce a dance at the drop of a hint. Mothers brought sandwiches, cookies, and cake. Couples contributed a nickel or a dime for the band, if they had it. The band – a fiddler or two and a woman hunched over a pedal organ or a battered upright – tuned up with a cacophony of chords. The "caller," chosen for his foghorn voice and lack of inhibition, limbered his tonsils to utter such rallying cries as "*Everybody waltz!*" or "*Ladies' choice!*" or, during square dances, "*Now swing yer partners, corners all.*" But first he sprinkled the dusty, splintered floor with peelings of paraffin wax. Small boys, his eager confederates, raced and slid on the wax until the floor had a modicum of sheen. Then the caller bellowed, "*Evvereebody two-step!*" And for a little while, couples (she in her one party frock and he in his best-and-only suit) whirled and sweated and laughed and forgot the hard times; while shy men skulked around the edges.

A picnic and all it entailed – sandwiches, devilled eggs, three-legged races, ants – brought high excitement. "Our whole family would go to the Toronto Islands or High Park," says Mary Racher Arnold. "There was always homemade lemonade – we couldn't afford ginger ale or stuff like that. Ice cream was a luxury. Once my uncle brought a brick, and my grandparents brought one, and my parents brought one. *Three* bricks! Boy, that was something!"

For Marianne Linge, a supreme thrill was travelling from Capreol to the annual Canadian National Exhibition in Toronto – for the rides, of course, but particularly for the milk. *Milk?*

"We didn't have a refrigerator or icebox at home. We had a hole in the ground where we kept things cool, but the milk was always warm. I used to spend half of my money at the Ex on cold milk."

In rural Canada there was a weekly rite, unvarying, obligatory: going to town on Saturday night. "Everybody went, everybody," says Ted Turner of Regina. "If you wanted to see anybody, you'd find them in the village on Saturday night." Turner generally asked his father for a nickel to spend: "Then you had a hell of a decision. Were you going to buy an ice-cream cone or a chocolate bar or some licorice?"

Lillian Flint of Sylvan Lake, Alberta, treasures those memories: "Amazing what you could buy for a penny, and what patience the elderly storekeeper had as we kids debated over the goodies: licorice pipes, wax false teeth, little bags of sugar crystals that you sucked up through a straw. And what a joy to have a whole nickel! No question where it went: on an all-day sucker, sort of fish-shaped and coated in chocolate. If you were lucky, inside its wrapper was a slip of paper meaning you got a *free* one. Total bliss!"

Unlike the super-organized kids of today, whose extracurricular schedules of sports, music, dance, and general betterment would stagger the CEO of General Motors, we had time to play. Fun was rarely something we bought or paid to see.

THE DAY THEY DIPPED WENDELL

As a boy in Toronto, Doug Harvey plodded unwillingly each Sunday to church, until he discovered the drama of baptism. Harvey recalls the day they baptized . . . oh, let's call him Wendell, to protect the innocent. It was Depression-era entertainment.

My mother never went to church. My old man never went *near* a church. So my uncles would drag me and my cousin Jimmy to Baptist Sunday School. We were about ten. The minister was Reverend B. A. Loney. Naturally, we called him Baloney.

I detested church, but I liked this great big baptismal tank sunk down at the front. In a Baptist baptism, the minister would dip them down three times, backwards. Jimmy and I used to get to church early to get seats in the front row, because a lot of them didn't realize they were gonna get immersed backwards. When the water ran up their nose, they thought they were drowning, and they'd throw spray about three rows back.

There was a kid there, Wendell. Wendell never washed. He didn't like water. None of us scrubbed too much, but Wendell's famous trick in the winter, when his nose was running, was to take his cap off and blow his nose in it and put it back on.

Jimmy brought me the news: "Wendell's getting baptized this Sunday. Are you going?"

"*Am I going!?*"

We were there a half-hour early, in the front row, the organ playing. Wendell had a gown or something over his clothes. The minister had hip waders on, and he led Wendell down into this tank. We're up on the edge of our seats, waiting.

Whoosh! Down he went under and the water ran up his nose. Well, Jesus! Wendell came up like a torpedo! Knocked the minister down and water flew back over everybody.

Baloney was just fierce! There were no words, just a fierce struggle. He grabbed Wendell again and forced him back under. By God, Wendell, up he comes again, knocks down the minister, and gets on top of him. Baloney's waders are filled with water, so he's anchored. Water's flying all over. And there's Wendell crawling up the steps like a wet rat.

The minister never did dip him three times. And laugh! Even

the old staid congregation, the women with their hats and the men with their red faces wanting to burst out with laughter. Yeah, that was the only thing that kept Jimmy and me in there.

We made a pact on the way home that we would *never, ever* be baptized.

Glen Hancock and friends of Wolfville, Nova Scotia, lacking a football, used somebody's cap stuffed with grass. In Oxbow, Michael Bartolf and his brother never had storebought toys; they manufactured them from the junk pile. Stan Logan, a former Winnipegger now living in California, fashioned guns from clothespins and rubber bands cut from old inner tubes. Sometimes he and his friends walked the wooden sidewalks, eyes down, searching for lost coins to be fished out between the cracks. Sometimes a kid, overcome by avarice, crawled under the sidewalk, got stuck, and had to be pried out by a father with a crowbar.

My frequent companion was the mythical Pedro Gonzales, Mexican gunslinger. I rode beside him on an imaginary horse, loping in three-quarter time and muttering *cloppata, cloppata* sound effects. My brother and I played hockey on a rink made with buckets of water lugged from the well. Each of us was a complete team. In seconds I transmuted from Syl Apps, centre, to right winger Gordie Drillon to defenceman Bucko McDonald to Turk Broda in goal, depending on my position on ice and the speed of my mouth (I also broadcast the play-by-play).

Little girls, as is their nature, came up with purely charming diversions. Fran Peacock of Ridgeville, Ontario, cherishes a memory from her home town of Fredericton: "In the spring my best friend from grade eight and I would take an iron frying pan — so heavy one of us had to tie it to her shoulders — and bacon and eggs and hike at six a.m. up a high hill overlooking the valley. Then we'd cook breakfast and talk until it was time to go to school."

Perhaps we were less accomplished and less fact-packed than today's kids. They – with their fingers flickering over computer keyboards – undoubtedly have greater hand-eye coordination. But there's not much for the imagination in video games. We had childhoods of invention and dreams.

Naturally, and despite our vaunted self-sufficiency, we longed for things we couldn't have. If in the end we got them, the delayed gratification – delayed sometimes for years – was part of the plea- sure. Masochistic though it may sound to today's young, the waiting made every simple gift or small reward all the sweeter.

I saved my trifling earnings for four years until at fourteen I could afford a bicycle. And I nurtured it until I went away to war. In Winnipeg, Bill Finnbogason "would have killed" for a blue leather windbreaker with grey piping on the pockets. Finally his parents were able to buy it.

Mona Patterson had an affluent neighbour who squeezed oranges and threw away the rinds dripping with juicy pulp. "I would have just loved to have those rinds. I told mother once and she said, 'Don't you *ever* ask for them!'" Pride forbade it. But at Christmas Mona always found one orange in her stocking (which tasted extra good) and, usually, one present. "One year it was a fountain pen. Once I got practical woollen mitts. That was Christmas. So little meant so much."

Little, indeed. For a weekly treat, Olive Farnden's mother cut up one chocolate bar between nine children. Lach MacLean of Blenheim, Ontario, was "truly thrilled" to get a hockey stick or a book for Christmas. To Norma Ritchie Williamson, raised on a farm near London, a present wasn't necessarily a present in con- ventional terms. "I still remember getting a dressing gown that the whole family chipped in to buy. That was really something."

Yet even the smallest trinket might be withheld if our manners didn't measure up. In Ponteix, Saskatchewan, Olive McConville's mother had a big black purse. "Dad called it the Bank of Montreal. She always had a treat in there for a special occasion. Just before my birthday one year, I knew she had a present for me so I snooped. There was a nice little comb in a case with a mirror. But because I'd snooped I didn't get it; one of the others did. I learned my lesson."

Is it any wonder that even sixty-odd years later we have no patience with the younger generation's lust for instant gratification, or bidding wars over Tickle Me Elmo dolls?

All right, there were *some* pre-packaged pleasures, and we rose to them like gophers to a grain field, if we could find and afford them. Take movies. Toronto, like other cities, had five-cent Saturday matinees. Lucky kids like Doug Harvey lived for them.

"Our ambition was to see Tarzan," Harvey says. "The Saturday matinee was chaos city. Nobody sat down. They screamed and yelled and jumped on the stage and belted each other and threw hats."

Suddenly, a hush. Tarzan came riding along on his elephant. "When he leaped on the lion and stabbed him, every kid just roared. On the way home we'd say, 'Now if Tarzan had only . . .' We could have done it better." Harvey doesn't remember Jane, but he was pre-pubescent at the time.

In my corner of Saskatchewan, movies were shown in Gravelbourg, sixteen miles away. It was a trip that required more planning than a space-shuttle launch. Problem one: we could not afford licence plates for the 1929 Chev, so dodging the Mounties was vital strategy. Problem two: dry weather was essential, because rain would turn the dirt road into gumbo pudding. Problem three: four admissions cost a prohibitive sixty cents. But once there, the singing sweethearts, Jeanette MacDonald and Nelson Eddy, could transport us far from dust storms and grasshoppers for an afternoon. How sweet her voice! How rock-solid his jaw! How pure their love!

A radio – now so commonplace, so cheap that every child can own one – was a luxury item. A Rogers six-tube Dual Wave radio cost $79.95 from Simpsons. The innards of all radios were filled with vacuum tubes that burnt out regularly (transistors were unknown). Where there was no electricity – which meant much of rural Canada – radios required wet batteries that had to be recharged. Few families, mine included, could afford one until Depression's end.

But then, ah, the wonder of it all. Radio taxed the imagination, and we had imagination in spades. We could hear Jack Benny's impeccable timing but had to imagine his masterful double-takes that kept the studio audience roaring. We guffawed when guest W. C. Fields threatened to feed Edgar Bergen's dummy, Charlie McCarthy, to the woodpeckers, but we had to visualize W. C.'s bulbous red nose and Charlie's goggle-eyed insouciance. It was part of the fun. (And yes, boomers, Bergen was the father of your very own Murphy Brown, telephone huckster, Candice.)

There were radio soaps. On the farm we tried to arrange lunch hour ("dinner," we called it) around "Pepper Young's Family," maybe, or "Big Sister," or "Oxydol's Own Ma Perkins." Ma, corny as Kansas but wise as Solomon, was our favourite. The old harridan was actually a liberated woman; she ran a lumber-yard with the help of an amiable simpleton called Shuffle. (His name came out "Sheffle" in Ma's nasal drawl.)

Ma Perkins spent most of her days meddling in people's lives, which was a lot more fun than selling two-by-fours. But compared to the steamy goings-on in today's soaps, ours were as squeaky clean as an Oxydol wash. You never caught Big Sister *in flagrante delicto* with Pepper Young, or Ma Perkins doing it with "Sheffle." Mind you, Ma was not called Ma for nothing, but

Shuffle, no rocket scientist (he couldn't even work a chainsaw), probably thought babies came from the tooth fairy.

Even *I* knew that they came from the stork.

When Babies Came from Belly Buttons

All right, I knew that babies didn't arrive in a sling, toted by a big white bird; I had watched cows and cats give birth. But beyond that, I, like my contemporaries, especially in rural Canada, was a sexual ignoramus. Our boundaries extended no more than five or ten miles in any direction. I was fourteen before I rode a train and eighteen before I kissed a girl (the train ride was better).

"If there was sex, it must have passed me by," says Ron Laidlaw, who lived in sizeable St. Mary's, Ontario. In cosmopolitan Wolfville, Nova Scotia, Glen Hancock thought "it was exciting just to hold a girl's hand."

Robert "Chick" Childerhose's earliest date in Virden, Manitoba, had all of our generation's awkward innocence. He was in grade ten when his local air cadets staged a ball. The girl sitting behind him in school tapped him on the shoulder.

"Who are you taking to the ball?"

"Nobody."

"Take me."

"Okay."

They had a good time. It was a bitter night when he walked her home, wearing his greatcoat and wedge cap and feeling "very military. At her front door I wanted to kiss her, but didn't have the nerve. Suddenly she grabbed me and kissed me so hard I was twanging like a tuning fork. I don't remember getting home . . ."

Our naiveté was totally predictable, given our environment. We had no TV shows with squirming heavy-breathing couples, no X-rated movies, no *Penthouse* magazine, no topless or bottomless bars. Nearly all of our sex education came by osmosis – from dirty jokes at recess, from crude sticklike drawings on school toilet walls (wherein the characters depicted didn't seem to be having much fun), and from those teases in the lingerie section of Eaton's catalogue (men with discreet bulges in their all-wool combination underwear; women coyly holding up the edge of their armoured corsets but revealing nothing, nothing, nothing). Rarely did we learn one iota from our parents.

"GO ASK YOUR SISTER"

Gladys Graham Byrnes, a cheery widow in her early seventies, now living in Creemore, Ontario, faced puberty in the thirties with the customary handicap: a parent who refused to talk about IT.

When I started menstruation, I didn't know what was happening to me. I didn't have a clue. After about two days, I said to my mother, "I think there's something wrong with me."

She said, "Go ask your sister. She'll take care of you."

So my sister Marie, four years older, was the one who told me all about that. And she also said, "You'll hear a lot of dirty jokes, but sex is a beautiful thing when you're in love." I've always thought back on how wise she was.

Then I started going out in cars. One day I was up in my mother's room and heard her downstairs saying, "She's going out in a car."

"She's WHAT?!" my father said.

"She's going out in a car. With a boy. I think you'd better talk to her."

He said "Anne, *you'd* better talk to her."

She came upstairs and along the hall. She knew I was in there, using her rouge. And she said, "Did you hear that?"

"Yes, I did."

"I guess you could tell me more than I could tell you."

I said, "Yeah!" Actually, I had a lot to learn, but that's exactly what I said. Really, it was so ridiculous. They didn't know how to tell us.

Irene Irons Grant and Elizabeth Rudge Tucci were exceptions: both had enlightened mothers. Grant's mother had been so ignorant as a child that she thought once a kiss had made her pregnant, and spent several uneasy weeks before the mirror, waiting for her belly to bulge. She vowed no daughter of hers would suffer the same. Likewise, Mrs. Rudge told young Elizabeth the facts. When her daughter was in Grade Eight, a classmate told her that babies came from a lady's belly button. Elizabeth promptly set her straight.

But most mothers, and all fathers, were hopeless. When John Dodds joined the navy his father said awkwardly, "Well, remember there are girls." That was the extent of Dodds's sex education.

Typically, Patricia Ritz Andrews married at nineteen knowing nothing about sex. "I'd never been with a man in my life. In those days we were all virgins, men or women. We never talked about abortion or babies born out of wedlock or anything. Why didn't my mother talk to me?"

Because she was a typical thirties mother.

Consider Bernice Quinto, good Catholic girl, who as a teenager was "heavily into the Catholic Youth Organization. Every Friday and Saturday we met as a group. After Sunday Mass we'd all go to a delicatessen across the street and have hot dogs and French fries and talk about getting together that night. I was seventeen or eighteen, and that's what dating was for me."

When she was fifteen, a worldly wise neighbour (just into Toronto from Bulgaria) told Bernice and her friend June how babies were born.

"Do you *believe* her?" June demanded as soon as they were alone, eyes huge.

"Maybe that's how they have babies in Bulgaria, but they sure don't have them like that here," Bernice said with authority. "Mom told me she went down to this hospital and there was a big table where all the babies were laid out. And I was lucky because Mom chose me."

And so we limped into adulthood.

A Touch of Magic

By 1939 most of Canada was numb from ten bad years. Would the hard times never end? Were the rumours from Europe to be taken seriously? Was the world mad enough to go to war again? Was there no light or grace left on earth?

Then the word came racing down the nation's party lines: the King and Queen were coming to visit! We were (excluding some Quebecers) passionately loyal subjects. We were still the Dominion of Canada. Eighty-nine per cent of the population was Anglo-Saxon. We stood stiff as pokers to sing the national anthem, which was "God Save the King." Once, during the subsequent war years, when our home finally had a radio, my father – caught off guard at bedtime by the anthem sign-off, but a patriot to the core – sprang to attention in his Penman's dropseat underwear, and stood firm until the last note.

We admired this particular king, who had reluctantly accepted the throne: decent, dutiful George VI with his painful speech impediment. His dark-eyed smiling Elizabeth, with all the social ease that was so difficult for him, was his perfect foil and consort. We had clucked our disapproval when his playboy brother, Edward VIII, abdicated to marry his fancy-woman American divorcee. And we had chuckled appreciatively at the British commoners' parody on the Christmas carol in winter, 1936:

Hark, the herald angels sing!
Missus Simpson's snitched our king!

Long afterward, it was said that old men in high places had contrived the royal visit of '39 to help bring Canada onside in the imminent war. Few of my guileless generation entertained such thoughts. If we had, we would never have associated the royal couple with such duplicity. We were simply delighted that they had bestowed this honour upon us. No reigning monarch had ever before set foot on Canadian soil. Over in London, the *Toronto Star* correspondent penned this purple prose: "Men's imaginations are touched by the thought that from this little green ancient island set in warring Europe's stormy seas two people go forth to a vast dominion across the seas . . ."

Across the vast dominion, small towns went into orgies of tree-planting, city-hall scrubbing, and Boy Scout/Girl Guide rehearsing. The *Empress of Australia* sailed for Canada on May 6. From his vessel in the English Channel, young Peter Marchant, late of Victoria, in England to escape the Depression and now enlisted in the Royal Navy, watched as the entire Home Fleet turned out to see them off: "Battleships as far as you could see, a wonderful sight. It was the last real peacetime review. After the war those things were gone."

When they landed at Quebec City in view of the historic Plains of Abraham, Canada's press fell slavering in adulation: "THUNDERING CHEERS ECHO ALONG CLIFFS," rang one headline. The King, with most of his fifty uniforms packed for the tour, the Queen, with innumerable gowns, hats, and fox-fur wraps, boarded their special blue-and-silver twelve-car train and headed west. "MONTREALERS CRAM THE STREETS," "A MILLION TORON-TONIANS CHEER THEM," the papers gushed.

Reporters lost their wits and their cherished cynicism: "His Majesty has a real man's voice, warm and cordial. . . . His tanned skin, clear eyes and strong handgrip tell a story of health and clean living." As for Elizabeth: "The camera misses her inner light . . . quite like someone out of a fairy tale . . . you expect her to dissolve in thin air at any moment . . ."

The *Toronto Star* rose to new heights of drivel when the Queen "looked directly at this reporter. . . . Receiving a nod of encouragement he controlled his shaking knees and arms as best he could and walked slowly toward the end of the coach. . . . No words were exchanged but the Queen continued to smile and the reporter took pictures."

Virtually every Depression alumnus I have encountered remembers the visit with startling clarity, the way those of a later generation remember where he or she was on the day John Kennedy was shot. Each recalls taking train, bus, streetcar, or rickety automobile to the nearest parade route, just downtown or fifty miles away. Maybe the couple passed them in an open car. Maybe they waved from the observation platform of the slow-moving train. Maybe they were tiny distant figures seen from a high window or the back of a crowd. (My mother, peering over heads in the temporary chaos of Moose Jaw, saw only the Queen's hat, but pronounced it good.)

But everyone remembers. One man reports with satisfaction – after nearly sixty years – that he "made eye contact" with the

Queen. (He wouldn't have used that nineties idiom then; he would have said, "She looked me right in the eye!")

In Fredericton Fran Murray and five girlfriends wangled Red Cross armbands through an influential father. That put them into the front ranks, with a view that most of us would have killed for. All over the country, children, such as Herb Gallifent in Hamilton and Elizabeth Rudge and Doug Harvey in Toronto, planted pennies on the railway tracks just before the royal train passed. Many of the old one-cent pieces, almost as big as today's two-dollar coin, were still in circulation at the time, and the flattened penny became a prized souvenir.

After the visit, some women devised flowered hats like the Queen's. "Aunt Myrtle came to visit us in St. Thomas," Gene Rowe Tingley says. "She weighed about 350 pounds, and she was wearing a replica of the Queen's hat. She looked so silly." It was simply further testimony to our adoration.

When war came, less than four months later, our hearts went out to Britain and her royal family. They had brought a touch of magic to our lives. Now we were ready to give those lives for king and country.

II

WAR

THE ONLY THING TO DO

You Had To Be There

The youngest of us was only thirteen when World War Two ended. Yet for most – whether we served in that war or worked, waited, and worried at home – it was a pivotal moment in our lives.

Our patriotism and the rhetoric of those times may seem archaic to younger Canadians now. But everyone who lived through the war remembers the grim reality of an enemy that threatened the entire Western World, and remembers the total commitment of a Canada that never wanted to fight but, when faced with it, was determined to win.

Forty-two thousand of our uniformed men and women died; nearly fifty-five thousand were wounded. The rest of us, the luckier ones, emerged at the end of the war intact but irrevocably changed. We had taken a short cut to adulthood. We hurried to make up for lost time and – although few of us would express it in these terms – to keep the faith with those who had died. This feeling of time lost and debts owing drove the work ethic that we brought from the Depression and carried into the fifties.

What follows here is not about battles, nor even much about heroism. Nearly everyone who came under fire was a kind of hero. Rather, this is about children of the Depression in uniform: what the war meant and did to them. And about the millions of civilians without whom the war could not have been won. About some of the inexplicable wartime events – luck? fate? providence? – that spared certain lives. And how all of this helped mould us into the kind of people we are.

That distant war must be incomprehensible to many young people today. A story has it that recently a student at Toronto's York University, after hearing a lecture on World War Two, asked his professor, "So, who won?" Well, it *was* more than fifty years ago. Does anyone care except us?

Some do. Historian Michael Bliss, born in 1941, says, "the debt we owe to the people who fought is incalculable." And in 1995, *Globe and Mail* TV columnist John Haslett Cuff, reviewing Robert Nielsen's film *No Price Too High*, about the wartime generation, wrote:

Even I, the rebellious and chronically cynical and disenchanted spawn of "the Endless Party of the Sixties," felt a love and pride of country I don't ever remember experiencing before . . . because [the film] resonates with the articulate, often impassioned voices of seemingly "ordinary" – but in fact extraordinary – human beings. . . . [Nielsen thinks the war] marked this generation of Canadians as exceptionally adventurous and resourceful, affecting the destiny of Canada itself for years to come. Their achievements are simply too significant not to be more fully acknowledged.

Accolades from writers younger than ourselves surprise us, but we think they have it right. Whether or not we were "extraordinary," we think our war mattered. None of the revisionist history, composed by people who were not there, will change that feeling.

We know now that our leaders, both political and military, sometimes screwed up, that training and equipment were sometimes wanting, that censorship, in World War Two as in every war, glossed over the harsh facts of errors and defeats. We know that German and Japanese civilians were slaughtered, but so were Dutch, Belgian, French, Polish, Scandinavian, and British civilians, and millions of Jews of many nationalities.

We know that thousands of Canadians died wastefully, and we grieve for them, far more than the second-guessers can (check the snowy heads at any Remembrance Day ceremony). They were friends, brothers, husbands, sons, daughters. But those who fought, and the rest who served in uniform or in war plants at home, have a right to be proud. That time, that experience, has set us apart ever since.

We were not militant people. We grew up with veterans of the first "Great War," and their horrific experiences soured any taste we might have had for battle. Yet 1,136,999 of us, men and women – 10 per cent of the population – joined up, because it was the right, necessary, and *only* thing to do.

"Did we ask about pension plans when we were handed over to the loving care of a drill sarge?" asks Max Macdonald of Regina. "Did we ask about death benefits when we agreed to serve anywhere in the world for as long as we were needed? An appallingly one-sided contract!" Of course no such questions crossed his or anyone else's mind. So Macdonald, a railwayman's son from Melville, Saskatchewan, went to sea for four years, because "it seemed like the thing to do."

But (we hear some youthful voices asking) *why did you sign that "appallingly one-sided contract"? Why didn't you question your politicians and your generals? Why did you march off so willingly like sheep? We wouldn't have fallen for that warmongering crap!*

Kids, you had to be there.

"Occasionally, someone writes that we could have made a deal with Hitler if Churchill hadn't been so bloody-minded," says Jim Lamb of Baddeck, Nova Scotia, who served six years in the navy. "If we had, a lot of guys would be alive today. But everyone forgets that, little by little, old Adolf had been pushing his way through Europe. The people wouldn't have stood for making a deal. It was, 'Okay, let's have at this bastard.'"

Or, they have never been properly taught the history of World War Two and Canada's part in it, as the eminent historian J. L. Granatstein has repeatedly warned. So they do not know the mood of the time, nor that many of us went to war because we loved Canada. Not many said it aloud, then, and not many will say it now. A few, like Willard Holliday of Victoria, candidly admit: "I felt that I should do something for my country." He joined the navy. So did Jean Marie Danard, oldest of four children in a Kirkland Lake, Ontario, family. It was a matter of duty. Her younger and only brother was slated for university. She told herself, *Someone* from our family has to go!

Glen Hancock of Wolfville joined the RCAF in part because "it was clear that the old flag needed to be supported." But he also went because all his friends were going. "I couldn't wait to get into it. And I assumed that I'd be on the winning side."

That was part of it – a romantic crusade and a welcome escape from Depression drudgery. "We were coming from nothing – no money, couldn't go anywhere, never saw anything," Doug Harvey reflects. "And we read about the Battle of Britain – guys shooting down Huns – and said, 'God, let me out of here!'" Harvey, the kid who'd enjoyed Sunday baptisms, became an RCAF bomber pilot.

Calgarian Stan Winfield, who'd peddled newspapers to help his parents, also "wanted the adventure. But I knew terrible things were happening over there. And I'm Jewish, and I really wanted to be part of it all." He went into RCAF ground crew.

Merle Tingley of Montreal joined the army to learn a trade. Bill Williamson of London signed up because "I was absolutely crazy about flying. Nothing else. No patriotism." Larry Holmes, from Smooth Rock Falls, Ontario, joined the navy just days after war was declared; he didn't want to be a small-town banker all his life.

Hal Sisson, then of Moose Jaw, makes light of it (after knowing him fifty years, I still can't tell when he is pulling my leg). "The time came, if you didn't do something," he says, "the army was gonna [draft you]. I thought, How drunk am I gonna have to be when they yell 'Fix bayonets!'?" He joined the RCAF.

So did Sara Thomson from Depression-battered Belleisle Creek, New Brunswick. She had left home to work for thirteen dollars a month as a household servant, from seven a.m. until eight p.m. daily. "I was looked upon as an outcast, not a real human being," she says. Often she couldn't afford a three-cent stamp to send a letter home. At twenty she had owned nothing but hand-me-down clothes for nine years. "It was bone-crushing," she remembers. "There was no way out." But now there was.

In 1943 she joined the Women's Division (WD) and, as she later wrote in *To Spread Their Wings*, a self-published memoir: "My life changed forever. . . . I have never known a more satisfying moment than the one in which I put on my complete uniform. . . . For the next three years I would never have to worry about what to wear. . . . I felt a new and better life had opened up for me and I would never go back to the way things were before."

The three Francis brothers from Galt joined up within weeks of one another. Older brothers Ben and Bert joined the Highland Light Infantry of Canada right after the fall of France in 1940. Their regimental numbers were A37234 and A37235. Little brother Roy – short but stocky, and something of an athlete – was hot on their heels, number A37284. Ben and Bert were upset with him; it left their mother and two sisters alone at home with no man. But his mother said stoically, "If he thinks it's right, he should."

For Arthur William Bishop there was a unique dimension to the war; his "Old Man" was William Avery Bishop, the most famous Canadian warrior in living memory. Air ace Billy Bishop, VC, was credited with downing seventy-two German aircraft in World War One. By the end of World War Two Billy Bishop was an RCAF Air Marshal. They didn't come much higher. The son was known in his early years as Billy Jr., implying great expectations.

There was more. Young Bishop's uncle was Hank Burden, soon to be group captain in charge of a squadron overseas. A cousin, Group Captain Johnnie Fauquier, would become known as the greatest Canadian bomber pilot in World War Two, one of the legendary Pathfinders and "dambusters." In effect, the kid was born into a military royal family. If he joined up, which seemed inevitable, would he ever be treated as an ordinary mortal?

He enlisted. During training he was rated as an "average" or "average plus" flier, but he graduated as fighter pilot, a role every red-blooded boy coveted in those years. By summer 1942, Pilot Officer Bishop was on his way to England.

He was small of stature, like many fighter pilots – a dashing figure in battle dress and white silk scarf. He was considered a prodigious drinker, in a time and place when boozing was an art form. Maybe it was a way of proving something. His main concern, in those days, was keeping the "Old Man" off his back.

One day Air Marshal Harold "Gus" Edwards, chief-of-staff overseas, called Bishop in from his operational Spitfire squadron.

"Are you behaving yourself?" Edwards said jocularly.

"What do you mean by that, *sir?*" Bishop said tartly.

"Just asking," the Air Marshal said.

"You mean the Old Man wants to know if I'm drinking too much," Bishop said. Ordinary mortals did not address air marshalls in this manner, but Bishop, by his own account, "didn't give a shit." "Tell him to stay out of my hair, *sir*. I'm on Ops."

Bishop, Jr., went on to fly a full tour out of England and, after D-Day, on the Continent. He was shot down once, but landed safely behind Allied lines. On another occasion, he was air-testing his Spitfire over England when flames broke out.

"You're on fire, you're on fire," yelled a voice in his headset.

"Don't you think I fucking well know it?" Bishop shouted back. He was too low to bail out. He crashed into trees and woke up in a field, where a farmer offered him a drink of brandy. Years later he mused, "I never got scratched the whole fucking war."

Maybe not, but Arthur Bishop had finally stepped out of the "Old Man's" long shadow.

WHEN THE PADRE CAME ABOARD

Jim Lamb of Baddeck, Nova Scotia, served six years with the navy, ending as a corvette commander. This poignant memory still brings tears to his eyes.

In the early days we were losing the war at sea. Every crossing had the potential [for death]. It was a harrowing business. I remember one time we had a new crew and we'd made a double crossing. We got in. Everyone was a bit shattered. And this guy, Ivan Edwards, came aboard.

I'd seen him play football for Queen's and later with Hamilton; he was a helluva football player. He was a chaplain. I was the first lieutenant. He said, "I wonder if I could have a word with the boys?" These buggers always used to come down about noon so that they could scrounge a drink and stay for lunch. I didn't like them because they interfered with the ship's work. I had to get work out of these guys.

But anyway we got them together. And I can't remember everything he said, but I remember he brought tears to my eyes – even now, when I think of it. He said, essentially, "You're going through a very hard time. You don't understand it." And he said, "Christ loves you. He's not leaving you alone." . . .

He really shook everybody. These were all eighteen-, nineteen-year-old kids. And his point was: *This is part of the great system of living. I don't know why you have to suffer this and why those fellows have been drowned out there. But it's part of something, and you're with somebody. And you're not alone.*

It made a great impression.

For most of us, the war was, in part, a time of discovery – of faraway places, of self, and of people unlike ourselves.

"All of a sudden there was a world out there that didn't go to private school and didn't go to the big Presbyterian Scottish church," says John Dodds, the Montrealer who, unscarred by the Depression, had joined the navy to get away. "I saw the other side, which I never would have seen."

"Not the least of the benefits of the war was the mixing that would never have happened otherwise," agrees Jim Lamb. "It was a great part of the forming of the nation."

It was also, for many, an exhilarating time. The uniform flattered all but the most grotesquely misshapen men. The sailor's bell-bottoms and middies hugged the bum and midriff respectively. Army and air-force battledress tunics narrowed the waist and made shoulders look brawnier than they were. With shoes gleaming, brass glistening, wedge cap at jaunty angle, permitting a cockscomb pompadour glistening with Brylcreem to plume out on one side, we were irresistible, we thought. Or would be, when our acne cleared up.

Conversely, the military uniform – especially tunics with patch pockets – were not kind to the shorter female figure. The average CWAC (Canadian Women's Army Corps) recruit, it was recorded, stood five-foot-two, weighed 132 pounds, and wore a size-16 uniform. But tall slim women, especially in the navy Wrens uniform, were knockouts.

And one of women's many contributions to the military was their civilizing effect on men. An army adjutant general announced in 1942 that "the presence of women has raised the tone of the mess." What he meant was, men were coming brushed and combed to meals, cursing less, eating with forks instead of knives, and sitting at, rather than crouching over, their plates.

Much of the servicemen's spare time was devoted to *cherchez la femme*. On route marches, the NCOs – if seized by a rare benevolent whim – bellowed "Eyes Right!" as we passed a bevy of pretty girls. We smiled. They smiled with pleasure or blushed in confusion. It was not considered bad to be a sex object. Young women presented their chests in their pointiest brassieres and tightest sweaters; the sweater girl was a wartime icon. On the street, bold men routinely whistled at girls (the wolf whistle, it was called), and bold girls were unabashed.

We travelled in pairs or packs. Our favourite word was "swell." We chewed gum incessantly. We discovered booze and cigarettes. I began smoking after falling in love with an Irish girl who smoked. The ritual of plucking two slim white cylinders from my tunic pocket (cigarettes courtesy of the good folk of Shamrock, Saskatchewan), gently cupping her hand in mine to light up (or, if I was feeling particularly Humphrey Bogart-like, lighting both and passing one from my fevered mouth to her ruby-red lips), it was all so . . . *swell*.

There were new friends with every posting. New places that we had never, in our wildest Depression dreams, hoped to see: the opposite ends of Canada, Times Square, Nelson's Column, the Champs-Élysées. We gained front-row seats at history's unfolding, as in the case of Erol Hill, RCAF airframe mechanic from remote northern Ontario, who, in occupied Germany, witnessed the war-crimes trials of Nazis Goering, Goebbels, and Hess.

It was a time of once-forbidden sex with consenting strangers, whispering "But I might be killed tomorrow" and half-believing it. A time of young men swirling young women through the intricate weaving patterns of the jitterbug, skirts planing out like saucers with a tantalizing flash of thigh. Of music forever linked to that war, wistful ballads of love and parting: "I'll Be Seeing You" and "White Cliffs of Dover" and "When the Lights Go On Again." A thousand pianists with a single accomplishment – a nimble left hand that could coax out the rippling, rumbling eight-to-the-bar of boogie-woogie. And the World War Two anthem, Glenn Miller's "In the Mood," soaring in a thousand drill halls, Legion halls, Knights of Columbus halls, *palais de dance*. After fifty years, "In the Mood" still quickens my pulse in a flood of memories.

Normal life was on hold for the duration. No Sunday dinner with parents, brothers, and sisters. No spouse in bed beside you at night (or, at least, not your own spouse). No watching your baby's first steps. No career plans. Everything was postponed for "some day." You could plan and hope for the future but never know.

For some, the future never came.

The Short Bright Life of Gérard Vallières

Many Quebecers were passionately opposed to fighting "England's war." Fifty-nine per cent of them told Gallup poll-sters in 1942 that Canada wouldn't be at war if she were not tied to Britain. When national registration was enacted, Montreal mayor Camillien Houde advised his people to defy it. He was promptly interned for four years, but much Quebec sentiment stayed with him.

Yet many other French Canadians served valiantly. Helen Margison remembers seeing young soldiers changing out of uni-forms and into civilian clothes in the bus depot in Montreal before going home on leave to families who presumably didn't know their sons had joined up. Two days or a week later, they were donning their uniforms and returning to war.

Gérard Vallières was one who served. His life and death, even after fifty years, bring a smile and a tear to such friends as Bernard Brouillet of St-Laurent. Vallières grew up in the 1930s. He was a typical "son of the crisis," Brouillet's term for Depression-era people. They met when both were attending small colleges affiliated with Université de Montréal.

They and their friends drank, joked, played pranks, talked endlessly of politics. Vallières stood out among them, in part because he was six-foot-two, powerfully built, with strong hand-some features, in part because nothing seemed to get him down.

Gérard Vallières had style. As a youth he thumbed his nose at the Depression by wearing a jaunty Borsalino hat with the big brim, favoured by certain film stars. Classical music was his passion, and Enrico Caruso was his idol. Often Brouillet's phone rang late at night, a familiar voice would murmur "CFCF" or "CKAC," and, sure enough, Brouillet would find a Caruso aria was on the radio.

Even adults couldn't resist the exuberant Gérard. "My parents loved him," Brouillet remembers. "I brought him along one time to our place in the Laurentians. He helped paint a cottage my father was building, all the time singing at the top of his voice."

After college Vallières got a job selling men's clothing in Eaton's. One day a woman customer asked why they sold suits with two pair of pants (a practice common in the thirties).

"Because if your husband becomes too fat or too thin, depending on you, madame," said Gérard politely, "he will always have a spare." He was fired for impudence.

He found another job that entailed driving a car. Naturally he drove, as he lived, with gusto. He crashed, and the car was a write-off.

In February 1941, Vallières told his friends, "I'm going to the war." Not many months later he phoned Bernard. "I'm going away. I'm not supposed to tell you when, but are you free tonight?"

Bernard rounded up six of the old friends, and they met at the Mount Royal Hotel, Gérard immaculate in the uniform of a lieutenant in Le Régiment de Maisonneuve. They ordered Scotch all round, and Gérard loosened his tie. They ordered another; his jacket came off. After the third, he boomed, "By the left, quick march!" and off they paraded to Peel Street. Driving home, they paused several times to let Gérard throw up.

Finally, after much stumbling about, they dropped him on Brouillet's living-room floor. In the morning he was sleeping peacefully. When Bernard returned from work that night to a lingering odour of whisky, he found a note on the couch: "Many, many thanks for everything."

Brouillet never saw his friend again. "We wrote to him, sent him cigarettes. He answered. It took us a while to find out he was sending the same darn letter to all of us."

In England, Vallières wrote home of the "extraordinary cleverness" of English drivers who drove on the wrong side of the road, as was his own habit. He sent a postcard to Bernard at his friend's tiny home town of St-Esprit (knowing every local resident would hear about it): it was a picture of 10 Downing Street, with "A Bordello Street in London" printed boldly on the back.

Vallières went from England on loan to the British army in Africa, rejoined his regiment, became a company commander, and went to France. Six weeks after D-Day, the dispatch came: Major Gérard Vallières had been killed in action on July 22, 1944, in Normandy, near Saint-André-sur-Orne.

Later Bernard learned the details. Vallières' company had been pinned down by a sniper. A man volunteered to go after him, but Vallières said, "No, no, you guys are all married and I'm not." He crawled out and was killed. He was twenty-six.

Vallières' name, with others, is engraved on the war memorial at the entrance to Eaton's in Montreal and in the memories of his friends.

"I often ask myself what he would have been," Bernard Brouillet says, "if he had lived."

Fervour and Fear

It was never just a military war. In Halifax, young David MacDonald, son of the dean of Dalhousie law school, witnessed it from his doorstep. Soldiers marched past his home on Oxford Street, en route to the docks and overseas. He stood on Citadel Hill, watching ships limp back into harbour, battered by enemy fire.

When blackouts came, the family doused every light in the house and repaired to a basement room, fitted with food, blankets, first-aid kit, and a bucket of sand. (Many major cities had black-outs and air-raid wardens, in the event that Nazi submarines – which *did* penetrate the St. Lawrence – would shell the likes of Toronto the Good or Ottawa the Dull.) In the summers, the teenage MacDonald worked in shipyards.

The war ended before he was old enough to join up, but he remembers his feelings with stark honesty: "I was nervous, as I suppose a lot of guys were. I wasn't eager to go to war and put my life in danger, but I would have done it. Since then I've wondered whether I would have been brave enough, or able to control my terror well enough."

But the millions who didn't get into the armed forces fought their own war in a thousand earnest ways. They bought bonds, gave blood, collected scrap. Consider the case of Gordon Smart, southern Saskatchewan teenager in the summer of '42. As head of the Bateman/Shamrock chapter of the Victory Boosters Tobacco League, he cycled miles around his neighbourhood, coaxing broken harrows, discarded ploughshares, and defunct cultivators from local farmers for scrap at $7.50 a ton. I was his helper; at the time we were both too young to enlist. We gut-wrenched four tons of the stuff into a truck and to a government depot, where it sold for $15 a ton. The $30 profit sent a tidy batch of nicotine to our fighting men, who (as I later discovered overseas) frequently swapped their free smokes for souvenirs or sex.

Canadians also sent milk to Britain, took British refugee children into their homes, and knitted and sewed deep into the lonely nights. In Alberta, Jean Parker Holt "made more men's pyjamas for the Red Cross than I like to remember." Every Sunday, Winnipeg schoolgirl Pat Wilson listened to "The Shadow" on radio (with its trademark opening lines: "Who knows what evil lurks in the hearts of men? The Shadow knows!" followed by a maniacal laugh) and "knitted scarves that went on forever." In Nova Scotia Elisabeth Brown churned out socks "the way they built the Liberty ships. I could turn out a pair in three or four days."

The home folks planted Victory gardens and laboured on farms. Margaret Davidson of Kinistino, Saskatchewan, helped shovel harvested grain for her father at age twelve because most hired men were at war. Women worked in troop canteens and wrote letters to maintain troop morale. From Oxbow, Saskatchewan, Hazel Armstrong corresponded with six service-men simultaneously. In the end she married airman Keith Paton, who was never on her list.

Patricia Hamilton, in the city of that name, was a patriot to the core. She cried and cheered watching war movies, knitted scores of ditty bags (for servicemen's odds and ends), tucked letters into them, and once included "her" photo (actually her pretty older sister). A lovestruck soldier wrote back that he wanted to meet her. Fourteen-year-old Patricia hastily replied, "Sorry, just got married!"

And they worried and prayed for their sons, daughters, broth-ers, sisters, fathers, and husbands in the war zones. "My brother Gordie was overseas from 1943, an RCAF bomb aimer," says Lillian Dunn Flint of Sylvan Lake, Alberta. "We lived with *National Geographic* maps on the dining-room wall so we could follow the news." In St. Thomas, Gene Rowe's father stood in long lineups outside stores, sometimes knowing only that the line was for *something* in short supply, maybe a treat to send to his Spitfire-pilot son. The boy died overseas.

Every visit, every letter or phone call was precious. One Christmas Bernice Quinto's brother rode the train from Halifax to Toronto and back on a three-day pass. He reached home at six a.m. Christmas Day, dined with the family at eleven-thirty, and caught his train back at three-thirty that afternoon.

Another time he phoned from some night spot in the United States.

"Listen, Dad!" he yelled over the music in the background. "It's the Harry James Orchestra!"

"*Talk* to us, son!" his father shouted back. "I can hear Harry James on the radio any time."

THE LAUGH-A-LOT CLUB

Even amid wartime prosperity, untrained Depression-era teenagers such as Mona Patterson of Trewdale, Saskatchewan, had to take mundane jobs. A sense of humour often lightened the drudgery.

I had a dream when I was a child: I always hoped to be a schoolteacher. It never happened. They couldn't afford to send me to high school. So I worked for a schoolteacher, taking care of her kids and doing janitor work. And on New Year's Day, 1941, I went to Moose Jaw.

I did housework. Worked at one place just a few months. I got three dollars a week, was up about five o'clock in the morning and really worked hard all day. I was supposed to get a half-day off on Thursday, but often I didn't get out until about four o'clock. She came up with all sorts of things for me to do at noon on Thursday – bake cookies, scrub the floor, do this, do that – before I got out.

Then I went to a big home and was the maid for two sisters. I got twenty dollars a month – quite a raise – but often had to get up during the night to help one of the women, who had multiple sclerosis.

I ate in the kitchen. But they were kind to me. A lot of employers were not nice to the girls. I always had the full Thursday afternoon and every other Sunday afternoon off.

We had a group – all housekeeping girls and maids, about twenty of us. We called ourselves the Laugh-A-Lot Club 'cause we had to laugh about something. We used to meet at Zion Church, and later at the Y. Oftentimes we'd get a sing-song going. Sometimes a Miss Busby used to speak to us on growing up and whatnot. Of course we felt we were grown up.

We'd each put in ten cents and take turns making supper. We would buy day-old buns, and sometimes it would just be pork and beans and buns and apples. Or sometimes girls would make pancakes. It was amazing what you could do for ten cents.

Mona Patterson later managed a grocery store in Assiniboia, where she met farmboy Eddie Laporte. They now live in Moose Jaw, have been married fifty-one years, and still laugh a lot.

For twelve-year-old Gildas Molgat from Ste. Rose du Lac, Manitoba, the war began early. On September 2, 1939, he, his father, and two brothers boarded the liner *Athenia* in Liverpool after a visit to his grandmother in France. The next morning war was declared. That night they were torpedoed. Gil lost his shirt and shoes, but his father got all of them into the same lifeboat. They were rescued the next day, taken to Ireland, and eventually got home intact.

For most others at home, the war became real in 1940 with national registration to mobilize our human and material resources. Everyone carried an identification card to be produced on an instant's notice if demanded. It seemed to be a step towards conscription, which Quebec, in particular, passionately opposed. In late 1944, with reinforcements urgently needed at the front, several thousand conscripts were ordered overseas. The issue very nearly split the country. Many conscripts turned into good and brave soldiers but always bore the nickname "Zombies."

Anything less than total commitment to the war was considered near-treason. There were constant reminders of enemy spies. Mail from overseas was censored; posters showed scary scenarios of Allied trains and troopships sabotaged because of "Careless Talk." A propaganda piece described "How to Spot a Jap" and not confuse him with Chinese, who were good guys.

Anyone remotely suspected of being an enemy alien was liable to harassment or worse. Many loyal Canadians were shamefully treated. Bernice Quinto's Italian-born father owned a barbershop in Toronto's King Edward Hotel. When war broke out, customers told him they wouldn't come back until it was over. Bernice's older sister couldn't get a job until she changed her name to Quinn.

In Oxbow, Saskatchewan, the RCMP ordered Michael Bartolf's German father to dismantle his radio shortwave. The local storekeeper advised the Bartolfs to go out on the street if they wished to speak German. Young Michael joined the cadets; some of his mates called him "Hitler Youth" and gave him the Nazi salute.

Conscientious objectors and pacifists were deemed similarly disloyal. In Leamington, Ontario, United Church minister Reverend Jack Griffith's anti-war views made him so unpopular that by 1941 he felt compelled to move to another parish. A young man in my rural neighbourhood refused to go to war on grounds of religious conviction, and was jailed. Alex Nickason of Guelph, like many with pacifist roots (Mennonite in his case), served as a non-combatant. Nickason joined the field ambulance corps on the day war was declared, later moved to a tank welding unit, went to France six days after D-Day, and remained close to the front lines to war's end.

Even now it is surprising to meet people who opposed the war. In England, schoolboy Stanley Westall, now of Mallorytown, Ontario, was "bitterly angry" at his parents for not doing something to avert it. Toronto high-school student Beverly Holmes first thought it "a kind of a romantic lark." Then the names read out at school assembly changed from boys enlisted to boys killed. "It began to dawn on us," she says, "that these kids were going away to kill other kids." She vowed no child of hers would ever go to war.

The most flagrant injustice was the ousting of more than twenty thousand Japanese Canadians – immigrants and Canadian-born children alike – from the Pacific coast after the bombing of Pearl Harbor. Given the patriotic fervour of that time, and fear of an attack on Canada's west coast, few Canadians objected. After all, Japan was the enemy, and a brutal one. Only those close to the scene knew that these Canadians, loyal as the rest of us, were being treated as aliens.

"One day we came to school and they were all gone," remembers Barbara Cumming Gory, then in Vancouver's Kitsilano district. "Our social studies teacher was very irate, and told us what an absolutely outrageous thing this was. But nobody did anything about it."

Not Wanted in His Country

Around midday on December 7, 1941, Frank Moritsugu and six teenage *Nisei* friends – Canadian-born sons and daughters of Japanese immigrants – were hanging out at Dorothy Mizutani's home. It was their Sunday after-church ritual in Kitsilano; they would gather in the parlour behind Mizutani's dry-cleaning shop for tea and biscuits, the latest knock-knock jokes, and the newest musical hits on the radio.

They were kidding around, flirting – Frank had a crush on pretty Dorothy – oblivious at first to the words interrupting the big-band music through bursts of static on the radio. Somebody turned up the volume, and then the news hit them: Japanese planes had bombed Pearl Harbor.

They looked at one another, stunned, frightened, mostly silent. Oh God, we're in trouble now! Frank thought. They poured out of Dorothy's place and ran home. Frank cut through an alley to his backyard and met a caucasian friend.

"Hi, Les," he said automatically.

"Hi, Frank," Les said. "Boy, the Japs have gone and done it now, haven't they!"

"Yeah, I guess they have," Frank muttered. "Excuse me."

His four brothers and three sisters were waiting. "*Niisan* [big brother] has come," cried one of the younger boys. Frank joined his father, Masaharu, and his mother, Shizuko, in the kitchen. They stood by the radio, wondering what the news would mean for them. It seemed to augur bad times. Just how bad, the Moritsugus couldn't imagine.

Masaharu Moritsugu emigrated to Canada in 1915. By 1921 he had enough money to return to Japan and find a bride through a marriage broker. He and Shizuko, a teacher, married on Christmas Day. The next year they settled in Port Alice, in the distant reaches of Vancouver Island. Frank Akira Moritsugu was born there. When he was four, the family moved to Vancouver.

Frank grew up fluent in English and Japanese. Shizuko had studied English in Japan, and she and Masaharu were avid readers of Japanese magazines and an English-language daily. Masaharu liked the sports pages, especially baseball, and he enjoyed a popular comic strip of the day, "Bringing Up Father" (featuring henpecked Jiggs and his domineering wife, Maggie). Other Japanese-Canadian parents were less proficient in English; conversely, many of their children spoke little Japanese. The Moritsugus had feet in both worlds.

Frank and his siblings attended kindergarten in English. At ten he joined a local judo club and at the same time was a Wolf

Cub in an Anglican church troop. "I learned about Baden-Powell, the Empire, and all that."

He also, for a while, attended an extracurricular Japanese school, where *Nisei* kids could keep up on their parents' language and culture. He learned Japanese pop songs from his parents' 78-rpm records and North American hits from the radio.

"That's the sort of strange mixture we were," he remembers.

In high school he was a star: honorary prefect, member of the student council, editor of the award-winning school paper. He and two others received hundred-dollar scholarships to study journalism at Drake University in the United States. But, of course, he dared not dream of becoming anything so grand as journalist, doctor, or engineer. Japanese Canadians still weren't allowed to vote.

Bright kids like Frank had few options. The choice for a boy was to find a job in Japan (in prewar times), or, as in his case, go to work with his father. Frank was small, five-foot-two, but strong and fit. After high school he joined Masaharu at landscape gardening.

He already knew about discrimination. Of the 23,500 Japanese Canadians in 1941, 95 per cent were in British Columbia. They were variously accused of trying to overrun the province with their growing numbers, of monopolizing the coastal fishing industry, of endangering white living standards by accepting low pay. When war broke out, they were not allowed to enlist and were issued special identity cards, marking them as second-class citizens.

Still, Frank thought, they *were* Canadian citizens. Surely the federal government wouldn't let them down.

He was nineteen when Pearl Harbor was bombed. A week later – landscape work being slack in December – he got a job on *The New Canadian*, the only English-language newspaper for the

Japanese community, and the only one the RCMP didn't shut down. He learned the rudiments of journalism, but his future looked bleak. In rapid order, the Japanese schools were closed, all Japanese Canadians were ordered indoors after dark, and their cars and radios were confiscated.

As Japanese troops overran Hong Kong and took Singapore, there was hysteria at home. In Vancouver, Japanese-owned shops were vandalized. Angry letters to the press demanded expulsion of the "Japs," as did Vancouver's city council.

In mid-February Frank quit his job to take over the gardening business; his father was being shipped to a work camp in the province's interior. It was still daylight when his father caught the train, so Frank could see him off without breaking curfew. Masaharu Moritsugu was a proud man. He had been boss in a pulp mill, had run his own business, had been a leader in the community. A gregarious fellow, he had often chatted with his customers about the New York Yankees.

Now, standing on the platform with suitcase and kitbag, he looked small and beaten. "I had never seen him so defeated in all my life. He looked as though somebody had just knocked him down. *This was my father!* I felt so terrible."

Three days later, another announcement: all males of Japanese descent, citizens or not, were to be shipped out. (No Italians or Germans were ousted.) Frank Moritsugu's country had failed him.

The young men had a choice of going to logging camps in northern Ontario or doing road work in interior British Columbia. He and brother Ken opted for B.C. so they would be closer to home. He was sixteen months in Yard Creek camp, right beside the main CPR line. His father was interned in a camp beside the CNR line.

"If we were potential fifth-columnist saboteurs – eighty to a hundred men, ages eighteen to forty-five, and the only guards were three or four Home Guard guys with Lee Enfield rifles, we could have overpowered those poor buggers and blown a bridge," Moritsugu says of the absurdity. "If we were so dangerous, why did they put us beside two transcontinental railways?"

Frank and two others ended up as kitchen flunkies, peeling vegetables. The food was ordinary but plentiful (stew with rice was a staple). They worked early and late but had time off between shifts. Mostly, it was boring, "a strange going-nowhere situation." There was no barbed wire, but no one tried to escape. "Where in hell would we go?"

Frank wrote at least two letters a day and usually got a daily censored letter back. For a while he wrote to two girls (one of them Dorothy Mizutani, whose family had moved to Toronto), telling each that he loved her deeply. Then the two girls compared notes. "I had to start over from scratch."

To help pass the time, some men played mah-jong. Moritsugu started out at whist and got into serious poker. They ordered battery radios from Eaton's or Simpsons mail-order catalogue, received them with surprising ease, and were able to stay abreast of the hit parade and CBC's popular daily variety show, "The Happy Gang."

The following winter they skated on local sloughs with skates ordered from the Eaton's catalogue. They were paid about thirty-five dollars a month; Frank and Ken each sent twenty dollars to their families. They bought salmon at twenty-five cents apiece from a neighbouring Finnish community, and for a while attended its dances until the local men took exception ("The little blonde Finnish girls thought us city guys were pretty cute.")

In time, Frank and Ken were allowed to visit their parents and younger brothers and sisters, now all together in a camp at Tashme, crammed into one tiny shack amongst hundreds in the makeshift settlement. "Dad and Mom looked shockingly older," says Frank.

Finally the older Moritsugus were transferred to St. Thomas, Ontario, to perform farm work on the estate of former provincial premier Mitchell Hepburn. Frank joined them in March 1944. Japanese Canadians were still not allowed to enlist.

At last, in early 1945, with increasing numbers of Japanese prisoners-of-war being taken in Asia, the British army needed language experts. Frank joined up, and, in spite of everything Canada had done to him, was proud of his uniform. "I was able to walk around with 'Canada' flashes on my shoulders and go overseas and be treated like a Canadian."

In July he landed in India, but to his chagrin, he was earmarked to teach Japanese to fellow *Nisei* who lacked his fluency. Then he joined a British intelligence unit slated to go to Japan ahead of the occupation forces, but that was cancelled.

He went home to his family a sergeant in the spring of 1946. Soon after, an RCMP constable knocked on the door with the wartime registration card that Frank had turned in on enlistment.

"Your photograph looks pretty weatherbeaten," the Mountie said. "Better get new ones taken. And send us two copies for our files."

Moritsugu flung it back at him. "You fuckin' asshole, get the hell out of here!" he raged. Frank's mother was shocked at his barracks language, but the Mountie didn't come back.

Yet for several years after, even those Japanese Canadians who had served in the forces had to carry registration cards, and report to the RCMP if they travelled more than fifty miles from home.

Home Front

Most Canadians were oblivious to, or unconcerned about, the plight of the British Columbia Japanese. For those on the home front there was one concern: Canada, how can I stand on guard for thee? One way was to buy Victory Bonds, War Savings certificates and stamps (sixteen twenty-five-cent stamps made a four-dollar certificate, which in seven and a half years was worth five dollars). From January 1940 until war's end, Canadians poured an incredible $8.8 billion into the effort. We tucked bonds or certificates into Christmas stockings. A Nova Scotia woman saved pennies for two years to buy a hundred-dollar bond. An Edmonton-area trapper turned five fox-skins into a bond. A thirteen-year-old Vancouver lad worked Saturdays in a factory and ran a weekday paper route to buy war-savings stamps.

Companies laced their advertising with instant patriotism. "Take up your pen for Victory," cried Parker, showing a happy penman writing out a bond application. "I'm patriotic!" burbled a magazine-ad model, rolling her pincurls in Kleenex tissue instead of curlers, thus saving metal and rubber for guns and tires. "I'm doing a man's job but I'm still a woman on the surface," murmured a make-believe war worker, scrubbing down with Palmolive soap. Bell said its telephones were working for victory; RCA said its radios were. Kodak was snapping soldiers' pictures; Coke was keeping them refreshed.

We were warned not to make waste. The Department of National War Services prodded housewives to save fat and bones to make glycerine and glue for weapons and planes. Glass, rubber, old saucepans and toothpaste tubes (for the aluminum) – we recycled them all, fifty years before the blue box. We scavenged whatever the government told us to scavenge. Marion Elliott of Tillsonburg, Ontario, collected infinite quantities of milkweed pods, supposedly to make stuffing for kapok jackets. Whether they did, or how much of our other accumulated junk actually found its way into the tools of war, we'll never know. But it made the home folks feel part of the effort.

Some omnipotent authority or other was forever nagging us to "Do your part," and we did. National Revenue assured its captive audience that "income tax is fair to all" and was helping preserve "your very existence." In 1938 Ottawa had collected $42 million in income taxes; by 1943 it was $815 million. The hard-nosed Wartime Prices and Trade Board scared housewives silly with its directive: "You need not hoard – you must not hoard – YOU MUST OBEY THE LAW."

Material for domestic clothing was scarce; no more cuffs on men's trousers, no more roomy bloomers for women, and no elastic waistbands. One day on the streets of St. Thomas, Gene Rowe felt buttons popping and her ridiculous non-elastic drawers sagging to half-mast.

Silk went for parachutes, so most stockings were of unflatter-ing cotton lisle. Young women stood in bathtubs and painted their legs with ersatz-stocking colouring, finishing off with a line down the back for a seam. It fooled most men, but no other woman.

When rationing came in 1942 – sugar, coffee, tea, butter, meat – it brought annoyance more than pain. Eleven million ration-book holders embraced it, happy to make their small sacrifices. "On the way home from school, we always went in to see if the store had any veal kidneys, which weren't rationed," says Lillian Flint. "Mother could do wonders with them."

Restaurants had meatless Tuesdays and Fridays and urged cus-tomers to "Use less sugar and stir like hell. We don't mind the noise." Liquor was hard to find; Gooderham & Worts assured consumers that its alcohol was "fighting the icy hand of death" as de-icing fluid on military aircraft.

Gasoline was rationed ("A gallon a day keeps Hitler away"). By mid-war, non-essential motorists were limited to 120 gallons a year, enough for about two thousand miles. With tires and spare parts also scarce or non-existent, many drivers put the family heap on blocks for the duration and turned to car pools and public transit. When transit sagged under the strain, offices and war plants began staggering their working hours.

Amid this flurry of earnest effort, cheaters and black-marketeers enjoyed the war. Unscrupulous landlords squirmed around the rent-control regulations and stiffed gullible working girls with exorbitant rents for squalid rooms. There was a black market in automobiles, tires, and gasoline, in meat, butter, coal, and liquor. Even second-hand tables and sofas were sold at rip-off prices to war workers or servicemen and their wives, desperate for furnishings in makeshift city quarters.

"For citizens who were asked to make relatively few sacrifices," wrote Jeff Keshen in *The Good Fight: Canadians and World War II*, "the amount of cheating in wartime Canada was certainly noteworthy."

Indeed, the sacrifices deemed necessary in Canada were trifling compared to the real privation overseas. Many of its survivors are now Canadian citizens. "At school, when you'd finished a page on your exercise paper, you'd turn it upside down and write in between the lines, to save paper," says Sheila Hanson, now of Mallorytown, Ontario. When the Hansons emigrated to Canada after the war, husband Malcolm ordered his first Canadian steak: "It was a confrontation with gluttony!"

Rose Baines was a Yorkshire schoolgirl during the war. Now Rose Dyson, a retired actress in Toronto, her abiding memory is the perennial blackout darkness: "Absolute pitch dark. We carried torches. On moonless nights you couldn't see a thing. The traffic was all muted lighting. The trains, the buses, everything stopped early. I felt as if my youth was going by."

Food, clothing, fuel, and home appliances were severely rationed. Even neutral southern Ireland felt the pinch. "Although we were never actually hungry, I remember my mother drying out tea leaves and using them over and over again," says Elsie Sheane Towson, then of County Wicklow. "Fuel was just the pits. Before the war you would see graffiti: 'Burn everything British except their coal.' Boy, we could have eaten those words during the war, because our only fuel was wet soggy peat. We were very cold and very miserable. We had expedients like the hay box, a wooden box packed very tightly with hay. For stew or porridge, you'd cook the meal as far as you could, then burrow the pot in the hay and close the lid and it would slow cook, believe it or not. We were put to the pin of our collar, as the saying went."

The Irish got no sympathy from Britain, where civilians were dying. Olive Millward of Birmingham was eighteen when her best friend was killed by a bomb. Today, Olive Millward Williams of Etobicoke, Ontario, can still hear the dead girl's mother in the hushed funeral – sobbing, sobbing, sobbing.

In south London, Mary Byrne Parfitt, like millions of others, lived through the Blitz. Her family bedded down nightly in their concrete air-raid shelter. "At first it was exciting, going to bed in bunks in a hole in the ground," she says. "It became scary. The worst were the V2 rockets. There were no air-raid warnings. You couldn't prepare. We'd be sitting in school and there would be an explosion." And they wondered if their parents or neighbours had been hit or if the next one would hit them.

"People ask me, 'How did you sleep through those raids?'" says Lily Currie of Regina, then a London teenager. "You *had* to sleep, so you became immune to it."

There was worse. In Normandy during months of onslaught from land and sky, Odile Bidan and her parents took shelter in a trench, called the "pit."

"We were petrified with fright," she recalls in Vancouver. "For several years after that, I developed a kind of crouching position from all that time in the pit. There was fear in me that I carried for a long time. Not of bombing. I transferred that fear into all kinds of things: fear of water, fear of this, fear of that. . . . I don't really want to go into it."

Luck, Chance, and the Unexplained

Over and over on the war's front lines, Canadians discovered the fragile balance between life and death. One night over Norway, navigator Flight Lieutenant Rae MacLeod's Halifax bomber took a shell through the mid-upper gunner's turret. The gunner wasn't scratched. "Luck all over the place," MacLeod says.

Lean, soft-spoken Ron Jeeves from Wolseley, Saskatchewan, was with the Canadian Corps in Italy when a single shell fell among five men. Jeeves, after recovering from three shrapnel wounds, was the only one to return to the regiment. "One out of five to get back," he muses. "Was it luck or something else?"

Alex Nickason transferred out of the 11th Royal Canadian Field Ambulance into the Royal Canadian Electrical Engineers, just days before his old outfit went into the carnage of Dieppe. Good luck? "I call it a guardian angel," he told me fifty-four years later.

"IT SEEMED THAT SOMEBODY TOUCHED ME"

Fred Hamilton of Sydenham, a big man with craggy features, red hair gone to grey, had — until you got to know him — a presence that did not invite confidences. Shortly before his death in 1997, I asked if the unexplained had figured in his military life. Hamilton hesitated, then:

I don't like to talk about it particularly, because it's probably just more imagination than anything else. But the very first patrol that I took out, we were moving up a small country road, and the Germans mortared the road we were coming up.

So I was lying in the ditch there. And you just can't believe the feelings of fear that flood through you when all this stuff is going *bang*, *bang* all around you, and you don't know what's happening, and you're almost deafened by the noise and the flashing lights.

Then it just seemed to me that somebody touched me on the shoulder and said, "Don't be afraid. It's all right." And that was it. I calmed down. I might have been up and running, which would have been a bad thing to do.

Bill Williamson's bomber crew had already survived some hairy raids before the final trip on their tour of operations. (A "tour" was, with occasional exceptions, designated as thirty operational flights.)

The night before that thirtieth trip in August 1943, Williamson and his seven crewmates were walking back from the pub to their 427 Squadron base in Yorkshire. A black cat ambled out in front of them.

On impulse, Williamson yelled, "Let's outrun it!" He and the bomb aimer did. The others, amused and unconcerned, let the cat cross their path.

The next night their Halifax was near Osnabrück, headed for Berlin, when cannon-fire from a JU88 night fighter set their starboard wing on fire. They veered and jettisoned their bombs. Another blast shot off a wing and destroyed the intercom. The Halifax went into a spin.

Just before the bomber hit the ground, Williamson freed the escape hatch and baled out. Although there was barely time for his chute to open, he landed safely in some woods. He heard the downed aircraft explode. He buried his chute, tore off his sergeant's stripes, observer's wing, and "Canada" shoulder patches, studied his escape map, and walked west towards Holland.

He was on the loose for seven days, walking at night, mostly in rain in low, wet country. One evening around dusk, fed up with the drizzle, he started out early and found himself at the edge of a German village. It seemed quiet, so he decided to walk through it; to a casual onlooker his unmarked battledress could pass for a German uniform.

A small girl appeared from nowhere, reached up, and grabbed the lanky Canadian's hand. She began chattering in German. Williamson understood nothing but muttered "*Ja, ja!*" at intervals. Finally he waved goodbye and slipped away.

At the heavily guarded Dutch border he jumped a train, but a train man spotted him in an open coal car. His luck had run out; he spent the rest of the war in prison camp.

But it wasn't until some time after his capture that Williamson learned just how fortunate he had, in fact, been. Only he and the bomb aimer had survived the crash; the other six – whose paths the black cat had crossed – were killed.

Williamson today thinks it only an interesting coincidence, yet acknowledges that "every one of us [survivors of the war] is here by sheer luck and a miracle."

In October 1944, Glen Hancock was on an English train headed for York, where he would catch a bus to rejoin 408 Squadron at Linton-on-Ouse. Just that morning he had been discharged from military hospital in London. His bomber had been shot up over the Ruhr and forced down in Allied territory. Wireless air gunner Hancock had taken flak in the shoulder and leg.

Oddly, given wartime crowding, only one other person shared Hancock's train compartment: a huge man in striped trousers and black jacket – rather like an undertaker – with black bowler hat, umbrella, and black leather case. Hancock took an instant dislike to the man. He seemed to be a typical "limey," superiority oozing from every pore.

They rode for miles without speaking. Then the man, producing lunch from his case, said, "Will you have an apple?" Hancock refused – although he hadn't eaten since morning – but in spite of himself was soon caught up in a fascinating philosophical conversation.

The man proffered his card, which proclaimed him to be A. E. Helliman. Hancock never found out who A. E. Helliman was or what he did, but guessed it had something to do with boosting military morale. By the time they reached York, where the older man changed for Harrogate, they were friends.

On parting, they shook hands, and Helliman moved away. Then he turned back: "Would you mind if I prayed for you?"

Soon after – on October 14, 1944 – 408 Squadron flew in one of the war's biggest raids: *two* one-thousand-bomber raids in a single day on Duisburg, a heavily defended Ruhr port and industrial city. On the second trip, around midnight, Hancock's Halifax was twice attacked by enemy fighters, then pinned in the blue beams of German searchlights. Hancock, monitoring radio traffic from Bomber Command, heard flak rattling against the bomber's belly. The air was thick with the smell of burnt cordite. The crew, numbed by noise and fear, did their jobs by instinct.

Then Hancock remembered A. E. Helliman's parting words, and suddenly felt "a strange, twilight-zone calm."

The next day he dug out the stranger's card and sent him a note, asking simply: had Helliman prayed for him? Back came a reply: yes, he *had* prayed. He also volunteered the time: precisely during those worst moments over Duisburg.

Later, heading home after finishing his tour, Hancock wrote to Helliman again. He could not find the latter's card, nor his letter, but had kept the address in his diary. There was no reply. And back home in Nova Scotia Hancock discovered the *address* had now inexplicably vanished. The incident began to obsess him. He had written to his father about the incident; his father could remember no such communication.

Hancock wrote to the Harrogate chief of police, who replied that he knew of no A. E. Helliman anywhere in the city. Years later he met a Harrogate man visiting Canada who agreed to search for the mysterious Helliman when he returned home. Again the same answer came back: there had never been such a person there. Hancock visited Harrogate himself. There was not even an A. E. Helliman in the cemetery.

Who or what was he? Hancock doesn't know. "But I know he existed," he says. "And I believe in the power of prayer."

Rosie the Riveter

In 1939, 575,000 Canadian women were employed outside the home, mostly in clerical jobs. By 1944, 935,000 worked in offices and factories, and several hundred thousand others laboured on farms. It was the birth of women's liberation.

Fully half of these women were doing what once was deemed men's work, and doing it well: assembling radio tubes, operating small machines, paint-spraying, spot welding, punch-press work, filling fuses – and driving rivets, of course. "Rosie the Riveter," a pop song of the day, became synonymous with women in war work. Every woman in coveralls was a Rosie.

Not until 1942, with the growing shortage in manpower, did the men who ran our country twig to this other perfectly capable source of labour. Then in a rush came compulsory registration of all women ages twenty to twenty-four, an order-in-council that led to the establishment of day nurseries and the Women's Voluntary Service, which organized housewives for everything from donating blood to hoeing Victory gardens. By the end of 1942, the emergency war-training program had graduated about twenty thousand women in a score of technical trades. A Gallup poll showed that most Canadians favoured paying women the same wages as men. It didn't happen, but the women came close; a female aircraft-production worker, for example, averaged seventy-nine cents an hour, compared to a man's eighty-two.

Every city had Miss War Worker contests (before sexism was given a name), with contestants packed into curve-fitting coveralls. Movie houses ran morning films for women coming from or going to shift work. There was an Anti-Noise Week. Window posters cautioned: "Please – A WAR WORKER IS SLEEPING." A hit song of the day went, "Milkman, Keep Those Bottles Quiet."

Many were like eighteen-year-old Agnes Brunning, from a farm family of eleven near Prince Albert. In the summer of '43, the word went out that Defence Industries Limited (DIL) near Toronto wanted women on its assembly line. Terrific wages: fifty to eighty cents an hour. Agnes hopped the eastbound train, sitting up two nights on the day coach, nervous and elated. She had never been more than a hundred miles from home.

At Toronto she joined a female influx from east and west, all bound for a burgeoning defence "city" twenty-five miles east (in postwar, the town of Ajax). Many of the nine thousand employees, mostly women, lived in one of twenty-one residences, each with a house mother riding shotgun.

Agnes started work the next day, learning on the job. DIL filled artillery, anti-aircraft, and mortar shells with explosives. Its coverall-clad workers handled gunpowder, percussion caps, detonators, and cordite (a smokeless propellant with nitroglycerine as the main ingredient) – a potentially lethal mix.

Each shift had to pass security, giving up wedding and engagement rings, earrings, chains, anything metallic that could strike a spark, and, of course, cigarettes, matches, and lighters. (One addict caught sneaking a smoke was jailed for three months.) Workers kept their fingernails clipped short, for fear of trapping granules of explosive, and wore shoes without nails or metal eyelets. They were allowed one touch of femininity: a sprig of curls dangling from the front of their bandannas. Agnes's brunette curls turned coppery red from chemicals in the cordite.

Eight hours a day she tucked detonators into bundles of cordite. To break the tedium, they sang pop tunes as they worked: "Paper Doll," "Mairzy Doats and Dozy Doats," and "Don't Get Around Much Any More." After work there were dances, movies in the rec hall, and parties galore.

Agnes, a non-drinker and not much of a party girl, was homesick. She wrote home every week and saved her money. She could earn as much as a hundred dollars a month – a dizzying sum – and spent every spare penny on her family.

"I vowed my mother would never wear patched-up stockings again," she says fifty years later.

Her loneliness ended when she met Jim Robinson, who hauled cordite into the plant. They married ten months later, and eventually found a little wartime house in Ajax. Widowed now, she lives there still.

Women also drove streetcars, pumped gas, trimmed meat in packing plants, bottled beer in breweries, and moved log booms at pulp mills. Hamilton's Steel Company of Canada had them cleaning railway tracks and loading freight cars. In Toronto they oiled engines and fired up boilers for the CNR. Canadian National Telegraphs hired 150 uniformed "messengerettes" to deliver telegrams in the major cities, a job previously done by boys now gone to war. Schoolgirls called "farmerettes" pitched hay on summer holidays.

Jean Young of Flin Flon, Manitoba (mother of Canadian writer Scott Young and grandmother of Neil Young) became a timekeeper for the Hudson Bay Mining and Smelting Company at age forty-seven – "green to the ways of the industrial world, shy and afraid," she would tell me years later. She boosted her

Above: The truly "Dirty Thirties": wind lifted clouds of parched prairie soil, blackening the skies at mid-day, while farm families huddled indoors, their crops and hopes blown away. (Glenbow Archives, NA-2496-1)

Right: When a dust storm ended, fields were stripped of topsoil, roads were layered with sand, and miniature sand dunes grew along the barbed-wire fence rows. (Saskatchewan Archives Board, R-A4823)

No money for gas or repairs, so autos (*sans* engine) were converted into horse- or ox-drawn "Bennett buggies," named after Canada's luckless prime minister of the early thirties. (Glenbow Archives, NA-2434-1)

Above: Their worldly goods in one tiny trailer, despair in their eyes and slumped shoulders, this family is fleeing the dried-out prairie for some place, *any* place, offering rain and a little hope. (Glenbow Archives, ND-3-6742)

Left: No more words necessary – the sign says it all. Canada's Depression jobless rate never fell below 12 per cent until World War II. (Toronto Star)

Right: They were called hoboes, tramps, bums, but most were just ordinary men down on their luck, criss-crossing Canada, seeking work and a change from being stuck in one desolate Depression-era place. (Glenbow Archives, NC-6-12955[c])

Below: Thirties' transients "rode the rods" (boxcars) across the land, dodging Mounties and railway police, who, at best, would kick them off or, at worst, club them or jail them. (Glenbow Archives, NC-6-12955[b])

The haves and the have-nots: the unemployed line up in Vancouver for food handouts. "Relief," the thirties' version of welfare, was negligible by today's standards, yet most people were ashamed to accept it. (Vancouver Public Library, 12748)

In a march like this, originating in Vancouver, young men headed for Ottawa in 1935, protesting federal government work camps. At Regina, police moved in. In the subsequent riot, one man was killed, several injured, and 130 arrested. (Vancouver Public Library, 8811)

The CCF party (forerunner of the NDP), born in Saskatchewan in the thirties, answered the cry for social change. Twenty-five years later under charismatic premier Tommy Douglas (centre) it would bring medicare to Canada. (Saskatchewan Archives Board, R–B2895)

Top left: The 1939 Royal Visit (here, in Regina) brought a touch of grace and grandeur to a Canada crushed by the Depression. Worshipping crowds everywhere welcomed George VI and Elizabeth (today's Queen Mother). (Saskatchewan Archives Board, R–B172)

Bottom left: In wartime Britain's sociable pubs, young Canadians discovered civilized drinking. At the Wilton Arms, privates Bill Montague, James Smith, and John Partington (l. to r.) share a congenial pint with the locals. (National Archives of Canada, PA–147116)

Whether she made Bren guns, shells, or ships, every female in overalls and bandanna was a "Rosie" (from the pop song "Rosie the Riveter"). More than a million like Veronica Foster did vital war work as well or better than the men. (National Archives of Canada, PA–119766)

After Japan entered the war (and in June 1942, a submarine lobbed a few shells harmlessly onto Vancouver Island), British Columbia panicked. Here, school children prepare for a gas-attack drill. (Vancouver Public Library, 44965)

When Japan overran Hong Kong and took Singapore, hysteria peaked in North America. More than 20,000 Japanese Canadians – many of them Canadian-born – were ousted from coastal B.C., for fear they might aid the enemy. (National Archives of Canada, C-46350)

An RCMP constable checks the documents of Japanese-Canadian evacuees at Slocan City, B.C. Whole families were shipped to interior work camps – an infamous episode in Canadian history. (National Archives of Canada, C-47387)

Wartime rationing (here, in Montreal in 1941) was trifling compared to the privation in Britain and Europe. But for home-front Canadians it was also symbolic: one way of helping beat Hitler. (Montreal Gazette, National Archives of Canada, PA-108300)

A sedate form of the wartime jitterbug. Most young Canadians at home or abroad favoured a more exuberant swirling, skirt-spinning, girl-hoisting version, to the irresistible beat of the big bands. (Canapress Photo Service)

The Allied invasion of Europe and ultimate victory began on D-Day, June 6, 1944. Here, four days later, an armada continues the massive flow of troops and war material to the French coast. (National Archives of Canada, PA-116339)

On VE-Day (Victory in Europe), May 8, 1945, a mob – mainly naval personnel – ran amok in downtown Halifax, looting liquor stores that officialdom had foolishly closed. (National Archives of Canada, C-79564)

spirits each morning with a dab of cologne, drawing wisecracks – "You smell like a bloody drug store" – from male co-workers. But on her last day they stood her on a big machine, gave her a watch engraved "To Jean from the Boys," and threw a party.

"As far as I could see were the dear dirty faces," she remembered. "It was a part of my life I shall never forget."

When the war ended, many women gave up their jobs, often regretfully, to returning servicemen. But they had blazed the way for the working women of today. And the home-front warriors would never forget that time of tears and wry humour, self-discovery and rare achievement. A time when, ironically, Canadians were united as never before or since.

The Making of Men

What became of Fred Hamilton, Glen Hancock, and Bill Williamson after their rendezvous with the (possibly) supernatural? What of others from our little cast of Depression alumni? How did they fare, and how did the war mark their lives?

Many men went into battle with a sense of immortality. Doug Harvey was one: "Oh sure, the other guy'll get shot down, but I'm invincible. Probably, that was a form of self-protection."

But for the foot soldier, where death was just over the next ridge, as close as the next mortar burst, the feeling of invulnerability faded fast. In the European campaign, Sergeant Fred Hamilton's twenty-four-man scout platoon went through ninety-six men to stay up to strength. The anxiety became exhausting.

"You thought, 'I can't keep being so lucky. My turn has to come, and soon,'" Hamilton told me in 1996, months before his death. "You were constantly tense inside, waiting, knowing that something had to happen to you, because the odds seemed to be that way."

In August 1944, Hamilton's scouts were assigned to check out enemy strength in the forest leading to the Seine river-crossing at the town of Pont de L'Arche. The results would govern the brigade attack the next day.

Hamilton and his men brought back detailed information on road craters, minefields, road blocks, and the state of the bridge. For this, France's General de Gaulle awarded him the Croix de Guerre with bronze star. The speed and accuracy of his reconnaissance, said the citation, "had a decided effect upon the final success of the crossing. . . . Sgt. Hamilton led his men with skill and daring. The leadership and complete disregard for personal safety exhibited by this non-commissioned officer has at all times been an inspiration to all ranks of the battalion."

By the end Hamilton had lost most of his close friends. It made him wary of new friendships for most of his life. He never wanted to get too close to people again.

When Bill Williamson was released from prison camp, he had a spur-of-the-moment chance to hitch a quick ride home on an American B-17, on one condition: he would have to leave all his luggage behind. He dumped everything on the tarmac, including a precious prison-camp diary and his good-luck scarf, and turned his back on the war.

Had he changed? "I was a naive little twit when I joined up. I didn't swear, I didn't tell dirty jokes. I was a little sissy. A real goody-goody. The kind of guy that I couldn't stand by the time I got out."

Glen Hancock completed thirty trips over Europe (earlier he'd flown twenty-nine over the Atlantic with a reconnaissance squadron hunting submarines). He had married during the war and now found himself on his own with a family. It was a responsibility he'd never anticipated. Temporary solution: he went into the peacetime air force.

It was a bad war for the Francis brothers from Galt. The Highland Light Infantry landed at Normandy with the second wave on D–Day. Three weeks later Roy was knocked out with shrapnel in his left hip. Bert had already been hospitalized with burns resulting from a shell–burst. Ben, a sergeant major, won the Military Medal for holding his company together in vicious hand-to-hand combat at Buron against the 12th SS Division, notorious for murdering prisoners.

Bert – who'd been a Sunday-school teacher and YMCA instructor back home – died in an English hospital. In August 1944, Roy returned to his regiment and Ben at Boulogne. They fought together at Cap Gris-Nez, where the Highland Light Infantry captured the Channel guns that had bombarded England's coast for years. Then, in the Scheldt estuary, a shell killed Ben Francis – he whom a school inspector once called "the most brilliant child I've seen" – a mere hundred yards away from his brother.

From then on, Roy Francis "lived and fought in a constant daze, consumed with rage and hate. I led more patrols at the front. I had dozens of close calls." They fought at Nijmegen and closed in on the Rhine. Then in late 1944, Francis's colonel and padre ordered him home. He was the last son left in his family and he was taking too many risks.

"I didn't want to go," he remembers. "I still had paying-back to do. And felt I couldn't face my mother."

For years after, he slept fitfully, with constant nightmares. Before the war he had been quiet, studious, and "a little bit religious." After, he was cynical, inclined not to trust anyone, and an agnostic. He graduated from university and was a newspaper man all his life. "I don't believe anyone fully recovers from wartime battle experiences," Francis says. "The problems are too searing for that."

Lieutenant Charles Smith, tank commander, was captured when Rommel's forces overran the British Eighth Army at Tobruk after four weeks of heavy fighting. Just before the

Germans surrounded him, Smith tried to escape by sea but his homemade raft sank.

"The POW experience, strangely, was almost rewarding," he says in Vancouver. "You had to dig inside yourself, into your own resources, to keep your head. You never knew when the bloody war would end."

In 1944 Allied bombs hit Smith's camp, killing one POW and wounding others. "Since then," he says, "every day for me has been a bonus."

As a prairie farmboy, John Archer got to town so rarely, he jokes, he "didn't know whether it was in the store or the church where I should take off my hat." Courtesy of the war, he got to North Africa and Italy as an artillery captain. After landing on a mine for the second time, he was sent home in 1944 with "a mouthful of shrapnel and bits in my back. But the thing that got me down more than anything was to go through the Hitler Line as we did and come out with only fourteen of forty-three men. I had to sit down and write, 'Dear Mrs. So-and-so, I have to tell you that your son died bravely. He was such a good companion. . . .'"

Archer came back resolved that it must never happen again. "It's all right to pray," he says in Regina. "But the Lord expects us to do something ourselves." As a broadcaster, historian, and former president of the University of Regina, he lends his weight to Canada's peacekeeping efforts.

Doug Harvey flew a full tour, including eleven trips over Berlin ("They gave me a watch for it; one of the clowns that dropped the most bombs on Berlin.") In March 1944 he was part of the immense armada that bombed Nuremberg and lost ninety-seven aircraft in one night, Bomber Command's costliest attack of World War Two. And somewhere in the throng that same awful night, Frank Hamilton – who once had been no higher off the ground than a CPR boxcar – was piloting *his* bomber.

Hamilton won the Distinguished Flying Cross (DFC) on that occasion for nursing his crippled aircraft, with starboard engine shot out and on fire, back to England through fighter attacks. Earlier he had won the Distinguished Flying Medal for picking his way home through the Alps, again with a missing engine, unable to fly higher than six thousand feet, not enough to clear the peaks.

Both Hamilton and Harvey (who also brought home a DFC) acquired the poise, and knack for sizing up men, that comes with command. It served Harvey well in civilian life. "I saw a lot of fear, and it didn't put me down. So I said to myself after the war, 'Nobody's gonna bother me.'"

As public-relations manager for Massey-Ferguson in Toronto, Harvey watched other men around the boardroom. "Suppose somebody had goofed up. The president would run his finger around trying to find out who. Now these guys were older than I was, but they'd get a little green, because if the finger stopped at them, there went the perks: the golf-club membership, the car, and all the rest of it. And they would sweat. And lie. The shoulders were hunched.

"All we ever looked for in the air force was the guy with the big shoulders. He'd turn and say, 'Yeah, it's my fault. So what? What are you gonna make of it?' *That* was leadership."

In his six years in the navy, ending up as corvette commander, Jim Lamb survived the worst that the Atlantic war could offer. "I ended up doing something I was good at," he says, "and it was very fulfilling. When the war ended, in some ways I wished I was dead. It just seemed that all my friends and the whole life I'd lived had gone."

Not long after discharge, he looked out from a train over Hamilton harbour to see *Camrose*, the corvette he had commanded in the final year of war, awaiting the scrap heap in a ship-breaking yard. Lamb jumped off the train and made his way to the bridge of the abandoned corvette. He would later write these moving words in his memoir *Press Gang*:

Here I had lived and had my being in a world of adventure and danger and strain – a world, moreover, in which I had a real part to play. Once this ship, with her power and her armament, her instruments and her trained and disciplined crew, had been my responsibility. I had taken her, sometimes alone, sometimes in company, across the great oceans; in her we had fought together against the forces of the elements and a ruthless enemy. On this little wooden platform I had experienced both the anxiety and the exultation of command; here, on this flimsy perch, had been shaped what sort of man I now was.

Like Jim Lamb, Max Macdonald lived through the war at sea. He sailed in Atlantic convoys, into the Normandy beachhead on D-Day, and worked the English Channel from then until the end of the war. From Regina, retired publisher Macdonald – tall, balding, piercing gaze under black brows – remembers.

"I'm not saying the war wasn't justified. They would have been silly to let Hitler run over the whole bloody world. But to think that a group of people will decide that their version of the world is worth killing a lot of people over – I have a very difficult time with it. I guess it began when we fished some bodies out of the Channel, and all we got were pieces of meat. I was revolted by that."

A SAILOR'S VIEW OF D-DAY

On June 6, 1944, Petty Officer Max Macdonald of Melville, Saskatchewan, was a coder serving aboard the corvette Kitchener.

On June 5 we closed up to action stations at midnight and started across. When daylight came and the dawn broke, I looked out and felt quite comfortable. It looked like the entire English Channel was filled with ships. Some of them had drogue balloons to foul up any aircraft attack. It looked like you could *walk* across.

We were with an American task force – a British corvette and ourselves, and the rest were all American ships. It was Omaha beach. Some big British battleships were firing on the coast to clear the way.

They say now that it was the most treacherous of duties for ships – not excluding the North Atlantic run, which was also kind of a bad deal – because there was shore fire. There were aircraft. There were mines, and there were submarines, all lurking around to do you in.

Reading about it now, it seems a lot more dramatic than it seemed at the time. We were just doing our job.

About a month after D–Day, with the Nazis driven inland, Macdonald's corvette got shore leave in Cherbourg. He saw a French family pushing a cart loaded with all their worldly possessions through the shambles with no place to go: "These poor folks wandering along, just dragging one foot after another with everything they owned in a damn raggedy old cart."

Macdonald went into the war with "a vague notion that it was a great heroic thing to do. But it really was demeaning in a sense."

Macdonald, Fred and Frank Hamilton, Doug Harvey, and the rest were still in their early to mid-twenties when it ended, yet they had already seen and done more than young men of later generations would see or do in a lifetime. In civilian life, Lamb noticed, as did most other veterans, "I was the junior fellow, but, God, I felt older than any of them. I was twenty-five years old and felt fifty. They all seemed like children to me."

The Angel of Belsen

Around war's end we became acutely aware of the Nazi death camps. Just before VE-Day (Victory in Europe), Glen Hancock crewed on a bomber carrying international observers to Bergen-Belsen. The smouldering furnaces and charred human remains haunted him for years after. A couple of weeks earlier, Flying Officer Ron Laidlaw, RCAF photographer – former paperboy from St. Mary's, Ontario – drove his Jeep into Belsen. It had just been liberated. Laidlaw was there by accident, lost from his unit when he heard about the camp. His shock was profound.

"The smell. The smell was just atrocious. British soldiers were ordering German guards to bury some of the bodies in big pits. They were really rough on those Germans, making them go right down into the pits. It was like mush. It was truly awful."

Laidlaw shot photos with his last roll of film. He never tried to sell them. They are his private record of one of human history's most inhuman acts. Back home he "was angry for a long time. I didn't get along too well with some of the people at work."

A month later, Sergeant Stan Winfield went to Germany with 84 Group disarmament staff. Assignment: gather and catalogue *matériel* to make sure the Germans wouldn't rearm. It was a fruitless exercise; Germany was shattered. Then Winfield found a cause – Belsen – and an unlikely hero in his boss, Squadron Leader Ted Aplin, a man with a burning social conscience.

Torontonian Aplin had volunteered in 1942, although as an "old man" of thirty-three with three children, he could have stayed home. Soon after they settled in at Celle, Aplin visited nearby Belsen. He returned shaken and outraged. That night he wrote to a friend back home: "I have just seen Belsen and am ashamed. Ashamed that Gentiles all over the world have not risen in one vast crusade to erase forever this evil mark on their record."

The dead were buried in mass graves, but the barbed-wire fences, guard towers, incinerators, and piles of burned and broken shoes, clothing, bones, and identification tags remained. The sickly smell of death still hung over the place.

About fifteen thousand survivors were housed in a former German barracks. They were mostly Jewish women and children, with spindly arms and legs and distended stomachs. Dysentery was rampant. Many were dying of tuberculosis or typhus. They received basic food and clothing, but were allowed no contact with the outside world while the occupying powers figured out what to do with them.

Aplin sought out Winfield. "Come back with me," he urged. Traditionally, officers and "other ranks" were not bosom buddies, but a bond was forming between them. They went into the camp wearing gauze masks.

"It's an admission I don't like to make," Winfield confesses, "but I felt a sense of revulsion. I just didn't want to look any longer."

Aplin saw it as an opportunity.

"We're going to recruit every man in camp," he said. "We'll get them to write home for food and clothing, and you and I will get it out to those people." Winfield caught fire. Maybe his duty in Germany had meaning after all.

They rounded up volunteers on the base. Each was allotted a code number that people back home could mark on return parcels. Clothes, shoes, chocolate, canned food, playing cards, toothbrushes, toothpaste, shaving cream, lipstick, combs, poured into Celle in coded bundles. A friendly postal clerk routed them to Aplin and Winfield. Once a week they trucked them to Belsen, travelling at dusk so as not to attract attention, for this was highly unofficial.

One Sunday they took some Belsen children on a picnic, with sandwiches, doughnuts, chocolate bars, gallons of powdered milk laced with chocolate to disguise its flat taste, and musical instruments. The children, scrubbed and brushed, their threadbare clothes washed, were beside themselves with excitement. Most did not know what "picnic" meant.

Aplin set out to find families of Belsen inmates around the world, helped relocate fifty Jewish orphans to London, helped a camp inmate with a shattered leg get successful surgery (she later emigrated to Toronto). But Aplin's flagrant use of RCAF vehicles for non-military purposes and his tendency to bend rules were getting him into hot water with RCAF brass. "I have not been getting along very well with the top officers," he wrote his wife. "Discussions have been bitter and recriminatory and I have no doubt they will try hard to make things tough for me."

Many of his superiors belonged to the peacetime permanent air force. Aplin, Winfield, and most other airmen were wartime volunteers, and there was no love between them. Aplin believed some of the permanent force were there to cash in on easy postwar duty and the rampant black market. Tension increased. Aplin feared he might be demoted or shipped out. So did Winfield; it was easier to sack a sergeant than a flight lieutenant.

Then Aplin went home on compassionate leave (his wife was ailing) and the brass heaved sighs of relief. In Canada, the media and Jewish community nicknamed Ted the "Angel of Belsen." He died in 1973, but Winfield has never forgotten him.

"I wonder if, without him, I would have been as acutely aware of the horror of what the Germans did," he muses. "Certainly that was the most important thing that happened to me during the war."

Victory

Finally it was over. Most of us remember where we were on VE-Day, May 8, 1945, or on VJ-Day, August 15, marking the defeat of Japan.

In Brantford, Private Frank Moritsugu – soon to be bound for India – watched the victory parade, proudly wearing his month-old army uniform.

In Halifax, officialdom unwisely closed the liquor stores. A mob, mainly naval personnel, went berserk, rampaging through the downtown, laying waste to stores and stealing 6,987 cases of beer, 1,225 cases of wine, and more than 5,000 cases of assorted liquor. Citadel Hill, young David MacDonald observed, was "pulsating" with fornicating couples: "Just one big quivering cathouse!"

"Her tears on my hand"

On May 8, 1945 – VE Day – Wren Ruby Evans, a navy motor-transport driver originally from Moose Jaw, was in Victoria. Ruby Evans Lamb now lives with her husband in Baddeck, Nova Scotia.

When the news of the Halifax riot reached the west coast, we were all confined to barracks – I suppose to ward off possibility of trouble in Victoria. We were leaning out the windows, watching the crowds go crazy below.

All of a sudden my wrist was wet. I looked up and the Wren leaning over my shoulder was weeping. I didn't know her very well, but I knew she'd lost her husband early in the war. In the air force, I think.

Afterward she told me, "I never cried when he was lost. I don't think I really believed it. I just got into the service 'cause we were still going to fight this war, the two of us. And now they say the war is over. That's the end of him. I'm alone in this world."

And she was weeping. It hit her with a great bang that he'd

really gone and she was alone. As long as she was involved in the war she had something to cling to, a bit of him.

She wasn't a close friend. But I always remember her tears on my hand.

That same day I was on leave in London, the best place on earth to be. With an escort of English aunts and uncles, I bused into the city centre, into the canyons of crowds uttering a single animal-like roar of pure joy.

I would gladly have waited all day to see Winston Churchill and the royal family come out on the balcony at Buckingham Palace to accept the people's homage (as eventually they did). But Kitty, my ranking aunt, was grievously afflicted with age and varicose veins. I dutifully joined the family retreat to suburban Plumstead, where Aunt Kitty, in a miraculous recovery, led us all in mugs of ale and a spirited song *and* dance rendition of "Knees Up, Mother Brown."

In Toronto on VE-Day, Bernice Quinto was riding the Bathurst streetcar with her parents. Suddenly there was an explosion of noise. Crowds materialized from nowhere. Uniforms thronged the streets. Her mother touched her father's shoulder: "Billy, what's happening?"

"I don't know."

Then the streetcar stopped, and soldiers were playfully trying to pull passengers out the windows. The conductor stood up and shouted "*The war is over, the war is over!*" And everyone in the car was screaming, or crying.

Some looked back on the war with a certain nostalgia. John Dodds, navy signals officer, sailed the Triangle Run – Halifax/ St. John's/New York – handing over or picking up convoys from other escorts at predetermined points in the Atlantic. The convoys were harassed by submarines and battered by some of the foulest weather known to seamen, but Dodds, self-styled fatalist, recalls no particular fear. He remembers the war as his "greatest experience." A photo of his corvette hangs on his apartment wall in Vancouver. "It was a team effort, the finest. Boy, that was as close to real family as you'll ever get."

Sara Thomson, the WD photographer for whom RCAF service in Canada meant more happiness and security than she'd ever known, was stunned to be discharged. "It was one of the worst moments I have ever had. Your whole life changed. Your home gone, your meals in the mess hall, your friends, the whole ambience of your life, from the sounds you hear as you drift off to sleep . . . to the clothes you wear."

Others came out frustrated because, through luck of the draw, they hadn't done what they'd hoped. Lach Maclean, for one, had trained to be a pilot. There was a pilot surplus, however, so he'd become an air gunner. Then he was turned into a human guinea pig. MacLean spent three months, two or three times a week, in an aircraft simulator, clad in the newly invented anti-gravity flying suit. As scientists outside cranked up the G (gravity) forces, MacLean and his fellow guinea pigs, bristling with wires and sensors, lapsed through phases of unconsciousness into blackout.

It was important research, developing what would become the forerunner of the spacesuit: "They wanted to see at what point you could recover enough consciousness to regain control of some sort." It did nothing for MacLean's career or his health. In later life he needed operations on both legs, and thinks the problem might be related to those severe experimental pressures on his lower limbs.

In August 1945, the atom bombs fell on Hiroshima and Nagasaki. Now the war was *really* over. Most of us were elated.

"I was ecstatic," admits Neil Davidson, then an RCAF air-traffic controller. "No question in my mind that it hastened the end of the war. And prevented a lot of loss of our lives, and probably Japanese lives, too."

Two days after the Japanese surrender, I, a callow twenty-year-old, wrote home from England:

> Well, it's over! ... It all happened in such rapid fire fashion that I don't know what to make of it. . . . The atom bomb may be inhuman but I guess we wouldn't feel guilty after what the Japs have done. . . . I also see by the paper that the British Empire is not accepting any responsibility for using the bomb. I think that is darn foolish. We've got it now, for better or worse, and we'll never be able to hide it. We can just hope to God there won't be another war in our time . . .

I was still posing as Sir Galahad, pure of heart and language ("darn foolish"), for my mother's benefit. And like nearly everyone else, I had no inkling of nuclear warfare's true horror. Soon after, when Gallup asked Canadians, "Do you think the Allies should or should not have used the atomic bomb against Japan?" 77 per cent approved.

Dearly Beloved – I

Wives, mothers, fathers, kids had been looking forward to the homecoming for *so* long. Now they and the returning servicemen and -women tried to pick up the threads of lives that had radically changed over six years. It was not easy.

Here were young men – back with Mom and Dad from grim places and rough companions – inadvertently blurting out at dinner, "Pass the fuckin' butter." Here were women and men who had found new love away or at home. Here were brides from abroad settling into our insular communities. Fifty-three per cent of Canadian women told the Gallup poll they disapproved of British war brides. They believed the Brits had "stolen" the flower of our young manhood.

Returning on a troop train in 1946 – men peeling off at every city and town – we watched a fellow airman step down at a certain Ontario station. His sexual exploits in occupied Germany had been legendary. Now, as we nudged and winked from the coach windows, he walked into the arms of (we assumed) his wife or fiancée – an exquisite creature in yellow frock and matching hat. As the train chuffed away, we wondered, with our new-found worldliness, how that one would work out.

Some of us had found love and lost it. The Irish girl I adored was, it turned out, weighing her options. In the end she opted for a Yank sergeant who also loved her. She went to the States, watched her uniformed idol turn into a hard-scrabble farmer with bib overalls and a drinking problem, bore him six children, and divorced.

Sometimes she wonders what might have been. Sometimes I do. Never do I hear the strains of "Sentimental Journey" without seeing her as I first glimpsed her – seventeen, slim and rounded in a green sweater, alone and hopeful on the fringe of a Belfast dance floor.

Let us visit a few who found and kept their love . . .

Jim Redditt – he who searched in vain for hoboes' marks outside his boyhood home – finds the love of his life early in the war: beautiful Jean Cole of Stratford. During lunch hours he whistles the most romantic tune he knows – Brahms's Lullaby – under her office window at Kresge's. She comes to the window and smiles down. They marry while he is with the navy in Halifax and begin housekeeping in a tiny, frigid backwoods cabin.

May 9, 1945, VE-Day-plus-1: Ron Laidlaw, memories of Belsen still swirling in his head, meets seventeen-year-old Vibeke Probst in a delirious crowd in Copenhagen. It is all highly circumspect: her father, mother, sister, and brother are in tow.

He nicknames her "Vips," as in Very Important Person. Eighteen weeks later they marry in Denmark's oldest church. Vibeke is in white, radiant as a picture-postcard bride. The civilian males in the wedding party wear formal dress. Laidlaw is in uniform, his fair hair freshly cut high above his ears.

Ron gets Vips aboard a freighter bound for North America just before Christmas 1945, by crossing the skipper's palm with cigarettes. Fresh from sophisticated Europe, she is shocked when her new in-laws in bluenose Ontario serve a "dry" Christmas dinner. "Beautiful dinner, lots of turkey, cakes, cookies – and a glass of cranberry juice! Then New Year's Eve – they toasted the new year in ginger ale!" Vips creates a few shockwaves herself by not wearing a bra.

Britisher Charles Smith, out of prison camp and at loose ends, returns to Germany to work on *Soldier*, an occupation-army magazine. Its translator and girl-of-all-work is Hilde Weber, a stunning brunette whose father died in a Nazi prison camp. Hilde herself narrowly missed prison for mouthing off at the Nazis. Smith, devilishly handsome with a jet-black forelock falling in his eyes, proposes the next day. Hilde makes him wait three whole days before saying yes.

From his base in Norfolk, Flying Officer Roy Bien of Coastal Command – an older grade-school friend of mine, whose dashing appearance in air-force blue cinched my own decision to join the RCAF – goes cycling to the town of Fakenham. He stops for dinner, takes in the dance, and is smitten at the sight of petite Doris Wright. Bien develops legs of steel cycling the eighteen-mile round trip from base to Fakenham two or three times a week. They wed in June 1945.

Elisabeth Brown, the dark-eyed, quick-tongued beauty from

Stellarton who bought shoes for poor children, has a wartime job in a Halifax bank. One night her roommates at the YWCA need an extra for a blind date. (Where would any of us be without the much-maligned blind date?) She goes reluctantly. They dine aboard a merchant ship. The slim, dapper radio officer, Eric Golby, offers to show her his wireless room. "You keep your hands to yourself," she warns.

Golby is a perfect gentleman. At evening's end he even *carries* her over a mess of oil and molasses on the wharf. They marry in 1946, she in a dress made of parachute silk, and honeymoon at a relative's place with no electricity, no water, and no plumbing. But so what? They are Depression-era kids, and in love.

In Regina, Ruth Hewitt, the veterinarian's daughter, keeps hearing about brother Earl's army friend Ron Jeeves, the wounded hero from Italy. Jeeves has a look at Ruth's photo and likes what he sees. One day in 1946, Ruth's mother puts a chicken in the oven, because guess-who's coming to dinner. The bell rings. Ruth answers the door with, "Well, you must be Ron."

"And you must be Ruth."

From such prosaic beginnings, love is born. They marry three years later, when Ron is settled on his farm.

September 1946: Joe Arnold ties the knot with Mary Racher, his wartime sweetheart since her seventeenth birthday party, when he came as a "spare" man and ate most of the chocolate cake. Now they sweep out of a Baptist church in Toronto, Mary with her luminous smile; Joe, wide-eyed, beaming, great shock of black hair, looking younger than twenty-five, and certainly not old enough to have flown a tour over Europe as bomb aimer, put out a fire in a burning Lancaster over Germany, and won the DFC. Only Mary, wise beyond her years, knows that in the winter just past, happy-go-lucky Joe has been close to tears, remembering friends who didn't get back.

On a foul December day three months after the Arnolds' wedding, Sergeant Fred Hamilton, still in uniform pending discharge, is freezing his toes off at the ferry dock in Sault Ste. Marie, waiting for (what else?) a blind date. He's ready to pack it in when she arrives. Kay Heaney, the erstwhile little girl who asked why her mother gave their food to transients, has grown up very nicely.

She is late because she's had too many boring blind dates and expects more of the same. Surprise! On their second night out, Kay, firing straight from the hip, says, "Well, are you gonna kiss me or are you just gonna stand here and freeze to death?"

And the rest is marital history.

Coming Home

Some came home with wanderlust still in their veins. Merle Tingley, who'd hoped to find a trade, became an army newspaper cartoonist. Upon discharge he went job-hunting across Canada on a motorbike. When his money ran out, he slept in a barn, where his companion, a cow, chewed the handle grips off his bike. Finally he landed a lifetime job as cartoonist with the *London Free Press*.

Willard Holliday, the unabashed patriot, spent the war on supply ships along the east coast. After a postwar year with an advertising agency, he quit and cycled across Canada ("I wanted to see my country at close range") on a single-speed bike. The hills were brutal. In Banff a mother bear with cubs gave him the evil eye. After that a lifetime in the civil service was tame.

The Canadian government did right by us after discharge. We received a cash gratuity based on length and location of service plus a chance to buy property (as did Tingley and Laidlaw), furnishings (as did Roy and Doris Bien), or get an education. Neil

Davidson, having earned a law degree before joining up, used his credits to buy a law library.

Nearly fifty-four thousand of us went to university. For those like me, whose parents never dared hope their children would get higher education, it was heaven-sent. The federal government paid the institutions $150 per veteran to cover administrative costs. We received free tuition plus monthly stipends during the school year (sixty dollars for single students, ninety dollars for married).

Latterly, the occasional querulous twenty-something has cited our free postwar education as yet another example of our alleged joy ride through life. That, as Max Macdonald says, is absurd: "We earned it!" He studied journalism at the University of Western Ontario, as did Fred Hamilton and Roy Francis. Lach MacLean took economics and political science at Western. Jean Marie Danard did the same at the University of Toronto. Arnold Steppler, one of my close air-force friends, studied pharmacy at the University of British Columbia.

Peter Marchant, after watching George VI and Elizabeth sail for their historic visit to Canada in 1939, served in the British navy to war's end as navigator on convoys and on minesweepers. Bombs and shrapnel fell around him. Ships blew up around him. The stress and strain of constant sea warfare preyed upon him, but he never had to swim for it.

He came out at twenty-six, a lieutenant commander, returned to Canada, drove a bread wagon in Ontario, then discovered that his British service qualified him for a Department of Veteran's Affairs credit. He got an undergraduate degree in geography from McGill and was well on the way to an M.A. when he landed "the perfect job" in exploration and construction work with the British Newfoundland Corporation.

John Archer and John Dodds had both started university before the war. Archer went back for an honours B.A. in history and ultimately a Ph.D. and a Bachelor of Library Science. Dodds got a law degree but ended up in the investment business. Sara Thomson studied art at the Saint John, New Brunswick, Vocational School; Bill Williamson attended the Ontario College of Art. Bill Finnbogason took engineering in Manitoba. Erol Hill completed a carpentry course.

Frank Moritsugu for a while worked in Winnipeg for *The Japanese Canadian*. Then he sold an article to *Saturday Night* magazine and its editor, the illustrious B. K. Sandwell, encouraged him to go into journalism with "a good liberal arts" education. With DVA credits he got an honours degree in political science and economics from the University of Toronto.

Canadian campuses coped remarkably well with the torrent of veterans. In 1944 our universities had only 35,132 students; in 1948 they enrolled 79,346. The University of Toronto, which took more vets than any other (University of British Columbia and McGill came second and third), set up a satellite campus for science and engineering students at Ajax in the former explosives plant where Agnes Brunning had worked. The University of Saskatchewan's "No. 4 Campus" was a former RCAF Service Flying Training Station on the edge of Saskatoon – fire hall, cafeteria, H-huts, and all – housing hundreds of the university's 8,705 veterans. The University of British Columbia moved 112 wartime huts onto campus.

When applications began pouring into the University of Western Ontario, registrar Helen Allison made up a policy on the spot. Four groups would be considered: veterans with good academic credentials; high-school students with good credentials; veterans with borderline credentials; and high-school students who just barely made it.

"If any have to be left out, it's the last group," she told the president. "We should take the rest without argument."

They hauled in temporary buildings, crammed dozens of extra chairs into classrooms, used every square inch of space.

"We held evening classes, Saturday classes, and I even held a Sunday make-up class, which was illegal in Ontario," says Dr. Ed Pleva, later head of Western's geography department. "I once taught twenty-two lectures a week, and that didn't include labs."

We students existed on the cheap, but that was second nature to us. We lived in basements, single rooms, or dormitories with double-decker bunks. Fred and Kay Hamilton found an "apart-ment" among the air ducts in a house basement, with a laundry room for a kitchen and one (shared) bathroom upstairs.

We dressed neatly for class, the way our parents and drill sergeants had taught us. Women wore skirts; men wore jackets, ties, short haircuts, and usually white shirts. "It took twenty minutes to iron one of those damn things," recalls Mary Arnold. "God, I just hated them!" She hated them more the day Joe threw them in the coin laundry with a pair of wine-coloured socks. When they came out pink, Mary made him bleach them in the bathtub.

We were uncommon students, no smarter than the younger ones but infinitely more motivated. We drank the mandatory gallons of beer but, having learned how to hold it, got to class the next morning. We were eager to learn and did not accept pronouncements from the lectern as gospel. We challenged and argued with our learned professors (alarming some and delight-ing others).

"Veterans were really wonderful to teach, especially in psy-chology, because they were mature and had ideas," recalls Dr. Mary Wright who went on to chair Western's psychology department from 1960 to 1970. "They'd experienced life. They didn't just sit and absorb things."

"The veterans had been and seen," John Archer says. Their life experiences were unlike anything the classrooms had witnessed. Once a history professor asked Archer to define nationalism. "Sir," said the student, back from battle with shrapnel in his face, "I'm not sure you can define it. But anyone who stood with the

Polish Corps, and listened to them playing their national anthem, will understand why they would leave one country and march all around the world just for the sake of that song and what it means to them."

The professor nodded approvingly. "You and I must have a good long talk."

Stan Winfield, who studied law at the University of British Columbia, enjoyed the learning experience but disliked the place. With Belsen still on his mind, he "was offended by the lack of discipline, the lack of interest, the lack of appreciation of young people who had not encountered any problems, any deprivation throughout that entire war. I wanted to tell them about my experience and how lucky everybody was and what a great country this is. But they were completely disinterested."

"In the fifties, teaching became dull as dishwater," adds Mary Wright. "It was back to nineteen-year-olds who seemed not that enthused about being at university. The veterans certainly were."

That was because we wanted to get on with it: get out in the world, get homes and families and nice normal jobs with no guard duty. We wanted to make up for lost time.

We were prime material for the 1950s.

III

BURSTING INTO THE FIFTIES

"A New Buoyant Canada"

I n this magical year of 1950, God's in His Heaven (well, surely He *is* a he?) and all's right with the world. As we peer into the second half of the century, we feel truly blessed. Did ever a people have it so good?

We lucky ones, having come through the war, are afloat on what one historian will call "a rapidly mounting wave of prosperity." Everywhere, the country is ready to build and grow: the St. Lawrence Seaway, the Trans-Canada Highway, the Toronto subway; an ocean of oil in Alberta, aluminum at Kitimat, uranium in northern Saskatchewan, nickel at Thompson, Manitoba, iron ore in the Ungava.

A first-class letter travels for four cents and a Gallup poll says three-quarters of us actually *like* our postal service. And why not, with delivery twice each weekday and once on Saturday?

Innocent times, these. Extramarital sex is not yet rampant; the Pill is years away, and we are still wrestling with condoms and prewar prurience. Political correctness means voting Liberal or Tory.

Even our crime is relatively benign. A good old-fashioned bank robbery is big news. The best-known serial killer is Jack the Ripper. "Swarming" is for bees, and "house invasions" are for termites.

A newspaper costs five cents a copy and our intelligentsia are reading "Pogo," a sophisticated satirical comic strip starring a mild-mannered Everyman kind of possum – that's right, *possum* – in Georgia's Okefenokee swamp, where many of the critters look like U.S. political figures.

On our own political scene, the federal Liberals are in power – so what's new? – but there's a fresh (well, make that *new*) face at the top. The eternal pragmatist and fence-sitter, William Lyon Mackenzie King, prime minister longer than most of us can remember, has finally stepped down. Hail, Louis St. Laurent, sixty-eight, courtly "Uncle Louis," as the press calls him, fluently bilingual and non-threatening to Anglos, the way we like our French Canadians. He'll be remembered as a shrewd administrator of a talented cabinet. No disrespect to Uncle Louis, but it doesn't take a genius to run Canada in this climate.

The real-estate market has gone bananas. New houses are popping up like crab grass, and *on* crab grass. Everywhere, the stores brim with riches. A new "fresh frozen" coffee is allegedly more flavourful than the stuff Mother used to make (which, come to think of it, tasted like a train man's boot). The *Financial Post* tells us, "a whole meal (including French-fried potatoes) can now be assembled quite readily with frosted goods."

Our new immigrants gape in wonder at the pyramids of fresh fruit and slabs of meat in the markets. Roast beef at ninety-five cents a pound is twice what we paid in 1945, but with prudent budgeting (at which most of us excel) we manage. Our average weekly wage is $45.08, and *Maclean's* magazine says a family of four can spend $18 a week on food, $7.50 on rent, $5.75 on clothing,

$2.25 on fuel, and so on down to $1.50 for transportation — and still have $2.00 left over for savings.

There are hints of marvels to come. Advertisements for a Dictaphone show an office girl — all stenographers are called "girls" — exclaiming, "Look! I've just grown another pair of hands!" (No more shorthand note-taking, you see.) More astonishing: a great clunky machine called "computer," the size of a locomotive, is about to radically change the way we live — although none of us can imagine how much. Nor can we really credit the outlandish suggestion that men will someday travel into outer space. It's exciting enough just to be within range of the world's longest undefended border and pick up "Howdy Doody" or "Kukla, Fran and Ollie" on American television. Two years from now the CBC will bring us our own TV.

Just two sour notes in this symphony of joy: that Russian bastard Joe Stalin (our former comrade-in-arms) is rattling his H-bomb, and war is looming in Korea. Surely not again, just as we've settled down and begun to get our lives in order?

Well, whatever comes, we will survive, as we have survived before. Let us get on with this fabulous year. Soon every Canadian over sixty-five will get forty dollars a month pension, regardless of need; 80 per cent of the populace will applaud this when queried by Gallup. Before the fifties end, we'll have automation, the Hula Hoop, rock 'n' roll, Sputnik beeping from outer space, and a new affliction called "stress."

Decades hence, a prairie historian named John Archer (at this moment rounding off his university career on his veteran's credits) will say, "Some of us made the world over in the fifties." Hula Hoops and "You're nothin' but a hound dog" are not exactly what he or we had in mind. But, as you shall see, sometimes we got it right.

On the verge of the new decade, Canadian Press reporter Douglas How – the Dorchester widow's son, back from the war – trailed Prime Minister St. Laurent from Victoria to St. John's. Uncle Louis was taking the nation's pulse to see if he should call an election. (He did.)

"The country was just *glowing*," How remembers. "One day, somewhere in Alberta, it hit me: 'By God, we have left the Depression behind.' It was a new buoyant Canada."

We had entered the war as a producer of grain and ore, and came out a manufacturer and trader. A nation of only 11.5 million people had become the world's fourth-largest supplier of wartime munitions and machines *and* had given $3.4 billion worth of aid to its allies.

On the domestic scene, the most dramatic change was in the number of owner-occupied dwellings. By 1951, 65 per cent of Canadian families were living in their own homes, a gain in ten years of 49 per cent. The suburbs were the places to be. In the ten years leading to 1951, the population in cities proper remained nearly static, but that of suburban Toronto, for example, had grown by 86 per cent. Overall, fourteen metropolitan areas from Halifax to Vancouver had added five million people – about as many as Canada's *total* population fifty years before.

In part, this growth of the suburbs was linked to our new mobility. In 1941, 37 per cent of Canadian families had cars. By 1951 it was 43 per cent; by 1953, 52 per cent. We drove 1,913,355 passenger vehicles in 1950; by 1960 we'd more than doubled our automobile population to 4,104,415.

The thing called the motel (not hotel, not motor court, not cabin) mushroomed along our roadsides. A *Financial Post* writer called them "just a twentieth century version of the stage coach inn." The writer was Peter C. Newman, who rose from these modest beginnings to become the mega-selling author of later decades.

By 1953, Canada had three thousand motels, and the industry was setting new standards. Red neon was banned in their road side signs lest it confuse motorists. (Whether they might mistake it for a stop light or house of ill repute, the article did not say.) Ontario motels were not allowed to proclaim "modern conveniences" unless equipped with telephone, electric lights, water-flushed indoor toilet, and hot and cold running water. We had come from coal-oil lamps and outdoor privies but were now above all that.

Deep thinkers were predicting in *Maclean's* that by the year 2000 half of Canada's people would live in a rural atmosphere with "room to breathe and see the sun." That didn't mean a farm (the rural population was dropping rapidly). It meant something like Don Mills, a "model" community going up on what were then the fringes of northeastern Toronto. Its builders were backed by E. P. Taylor, the rich industrialist. It occupied 3,300 acres along the Don River, and was expected to have four elementary schools, a shopping centre, sewage-disposal plant, parks, factories, and fifty-three different styles of home for every income level. Prices ranged from eleven thousand to seventeen thousand dollars.

Shopping malls were beginning to spread their tentacles across the land. In 1950 West Vancouver claimed Canada's first shopping mall, the $1.5 million Park Royal. In 1954 Hamilton announced the first Canadian mall with "air conditioned indoor streets." Its seventy-odd stores, sprawling over seventy acres, cost eighteen million dollars and assailed shoppers' ears with canned music.

Today, some of us who were newlyweds then are the elderly persons whose hearts or lungs can't stand the bite of a Canadian winter. So, in indoor malls like Hamilton's, we take our daily walks – five or ten laps around, then into a Diana Sweet's or a Tim Hortons to hoover down enough fattening pastry and coffee with cream to destroy the fleeting moment of good health.

SO HOW DID YOU LIKE TORONTO, MRS. GOLBY?

In the 1950s our cities became magnets for young small-town and rural folk, eagerly seeking their fortunes after the war. The jobs were there but the ambience was not necessarily better.

After Eric Golby got out of the wartime merchant navy and married no-nonsense Elisabeth Brown of Halifax and Stellarton, they moved to his home town of Toronto. And how did Elisabeth like the people in this smug self-important Centre of the Universe after sociable Nova Scotia?

They had no sense of humour. Nobody said good morning to you in church. The only time they'd talk to you is when they wanted to borrow something. I'd get so fed up with that.

I was one of these people who always spoke out about things. I was invited to go to an auxiliary, these missionary auxiliary things where they go down to Africa and try to Christianize all those poor innocent natives.

So after it was all over – talk about a catty bunch of old women! There's something about a cup of tea that brings out the gossip. On the way out, the minister, a very sweet gentle Anglican minister, said, "Mrs. Golby, what did you think of the meeting?" I said, "All I can say is those natives down in Africa could teach you people a thing or two." I said, "Leave them alone. They're fine without it." So that didn't go over too well.

One New Year's party, the men were all on one side talking about all the beer they could drink and the stock market. The women were over here talking about their various pregnancies and their grandchildren who had diarrhoea. Who wants to talk about that stuff when you're at a party?

Elisabeth and Eric Golby moved to an acreage near Tottenham, Ontario, with a kennel full of Kerry blue terriers, who are a lot more fun than Torontonians.

Dearly Beloved – II

For those not married immediately after the war, wedded bliss now became urgent. Everyone was doing it. Up to the mid-fifties, around 250,000 of us married each year. Being solid, responsible, and wed was part of our life plan. We didn't live together without benefit of clergy. We tied the knot.

A man unwed in his thirties was considered a loser or, maybe, a "queer" (our graceless term for gays). A woman unmarried by her mid-twenties was the despair of her mother, aunts, and girlfriends. When Merle Tingley, *London Free Press* cartoonist, proposed to Gene Rowe, the bright, acerbic advertising salesperson from the *St. Thomas Times Journal*, she didn't really want to marry. She was having too good a time at her job. Her mother was "terribly upset." *Didn't want to get married?* She was twenty-seven! What kind of daughter was she? How could Mrs. Rowe face her friends? Fortunately, Gene didn't let the side down.

We married with ridiculously little money by modern standards. Ed and Beatrice Shaw of Montreal, after honeymooning for three days in Toronto's Walker House Hotel, had ten dollars left in the bank and "never gave it a second thought." When I married Ruth Dillon of Toronto in 1952, I had five hundred dollars. It seemed a magnificent sum. We drove to Banff in my oil-burning 1949 Studebaker and one night slept in it. Coming home, the shock absorbers clapped out, draining most of my remaining cash. No matter: we both had jobs; the universe would unfold as it should.

How did the path of true love unfold for others in the fifties . . .?

From the moment university student Lach MacLean sidles onto a stool beside co-ed Barbara Fraleigh at the London Cafe lunch counter, they are a couple – a couple so decent, so stunningly attractive (he, tall and dark; she, rather like the movie star Gene Tierney), who are so much of everything we are or hope to be, that the University of Western Ontario *Gazette* features them on the front page of its 1950 graduation issue. "Dream Team" and "ideal campus couple," it calls them. (They fulfil that promise, marrying and staying married, while Lach pursues a career in business and later as an educator.)

In Vancouver, Ben Robertson, having been booted from pillar to post during the Depression, has found temporary security selling hot dogs at the 1950 Pacific National Exhibition. Lo! Who is that sweet creature peddling ice cream across the way? She is Louise Gjertsen, daughter of Norwegian immigrants. Ten months later they marry. But how to make their four hundred dollars last through the honeymoon? Simple. They drive into the United States in Ben's second-hand Pontiac until they've spent two hundred dollars. Then they turn for home.

Bill Williamson, home from POW camp, has a graphics job with Imperial Oil in Toronto. Sometimes he drives to London on weekends to visit family. One day a friend mentions that a pert young Esso employee, Norma Ritchie, needs a ride. "She can ride with me if she doesn't yap all the way," Williamson says sourly.

The canny Norma rides to London and back barely uttering a word. *What a jewel!* Williamson has found a soulmate. They marry in 1953.

Gildas Molgat, the Manitoba boy who took to the lifeboats on the first day of war, has graduated from the University of Manitoba with an honours degree in commerce and a gold medal. He joins Merchants Consolidated, a retailer-owned wholesale organization, as assistant to the general manager at thirty-five dollars a week.

One day his boss hires a tall, bright young university graduate, Allison Malcolm, for the one-person advertising department. Her father owns a construction business, and they live in Winnipeg's uppercrust River Heights. The assistant manager wants no part of her.

"Don't give me any of these city girls!" Gildas Molgat grumbles. "I want someone who knows how to work!"

Luckily for him, the boss prevails. Gil and Allison marry in 1958. Nowadays, to keep him on his toes, she sometimes reminds Senator Gil Molgat of "the country boy who didn't want a snob from River Heights."

Odile Bidan, newly arrived from France, meets Stan Winfield, lawyer with an insurance company, in that hotbed of romance, a Vancouver apartment laundry room. Stan, a klutz around washing machines, pours too much soap. His socks are billowing out on a tide of suds when Odile, whom he has sighted earlier ("a gorgeous creature with a lovely accent"), comes to the rescue. He invites her to a play. They marry a year later.

The honeymoon is financed on a hundred dollars Odile has thriftily saved from her modest job in the UBC bursar's office. Stan, contrary to his Depression upbringing, has many debts: "I needed that hundred dollars so badly!" Odile likes to say that he married her for her money.

So *many* of our honeymoons are fraught with mishap. After Patricia Wilson marries John "Bud" McLaughlin in 1952, they go, like many other Winnipeggers, to Minneapolis. A colleague of Bud's from the Canadian Wheat Board is staying at the same hotel. They can't shake him. Every evening he says, "Now, where are we all going for dinner?" In a grand gesture he orders a television for their room (in these uncivilized times, TV is *not* included with a room). When they check out, Bud discovers he has to pay for the rental.

At least they *have* a honeymoon. In Edmonton, Hal Sisson and Doreen Young – they met at the University of Saskatchewan, where he studied law and she commerce – can't afford one. Just before the wedding, the groom, a free spirit, gets back from New York, where he has blown his entire savings. He has to borrow five hundred dollars for a wedding suit, shoes, and incidental debts and expenses.

During his absence, Doreen's parents have kept asking, "Have you heard from Hal? What's he doing? Having his honeymoon before the wedding?" The night before the nuptials, Doreen goes to the bathroom and hears her mother weeping. "He doesn't even own a decent pair of shoes!"

But forty-five years later, the Sissons, living in Victoria, are replete with life's comforts, including shoes for Hal.

The meeting and mating of Suzanne Desjardins and Louis Hamel is the very epitome of our generation's sweet and proper courtships. It is Montreal, February 1947. She is in her final year of high school, he, in his last year of college. A big formal dance is coming up, and Louis's regular girlfriend is sick.

A college friend has a sister who knows Suzanne. The friend phones her on Louis's behalf: "Are you free next Saturday?" He explains that Louis is a nice guy and a budding artist (as is Suzanne).

"I must check with my parents first," Suzanne tells the go-between. She is seventeen and would never go on a blind date without their permission. Her father is on a two-week business trip, so the momentous decision falls upon her mother alone. Who is this Louis Hamel? her mother quizzes. Who else will be there? In the end she says, "I guess if they all come together to pick you up and bring you home, it's all right."

They go, they dance, they like each other. Louis gets home at two in the morning, very late for him. Still wearing his tuxedo, he stokes up the apartment-building furnace, one of his regular chores at the time. Upstairs, his mother is still awake.

"How was your date?"

"I tell you," Louis says reflectively, "she is the type of person I'd like to marry." His mother reminds him of these words when he and Suzanne marry four years later.

"A GREAT HONEYMOON"

Gene Rowe and Merle "Ting" Tingley married in 1952. As with most of our generation, the honeymoon was to be their jubilant entrée into wedded bliss. Like all of us, they were short of money. Gene tells the rest.

The wedding went wonderfully. We took off in Ting's new car that I think he was still paying for. Only then did he tell me where we were going: the east coast. The first night we had nice accommodation and a good roast beef dinner. The second night was good. But by the time we got to Quebec City, Ting admitted he didn't have any more money.

Luckily I had about $550 saved up, converted into traveller's cheques. The next day we bought a big cooler for food, maybe a frying pan, and travelled on the cheap. It was just like being on the dole. Except one night I sprung for a lobster dinner.

By the time we got to the Atlantic, I was so fed up with my husband I took off my wedding ring – he couldn't afford an engagement ring – and threw it in the ocean. He ran out before the waves took it away and kept it in his pocket for several days.

One day he took me down to the dry docks for a treat. The fog was so thick I couldn't even see him. That was one of the highlights of the tour. We sort of figgled and faggled back through the States.

Once we ran out of gas.

"You'll have to get more, you've got the money," he said. I said, "There's no damn way!"

So Ting walked to a service station, and when the fellow came back with gas I paid with a traveller's cheque.

We got to Niagara Falls. I must have paid for a cheap room somewhere. Ting had splurged and bought a new suit for the honeymoon. All of a sudden I see him down in the gutter, slapping his pants. What the heck was he doing? Well, he'd put his pipe in his pocket still alight, and burned a great big hole in the new suit. There was no money for another one for a long, long time.

We arrived back at our little apartment in Lambeth [near London] with two dollars. We had some mixed fruit and maybe six tins of stuff. That's all.

Great, wonderful honeymoon. I paid for it.

Be It Ever So Humble

With marriage came babies, the celebrated boomers: 4,322,904 of them in the fifties, more than in any decade before or since. We adored them and did our utmost to give them everything we never had. (And therein lies a story all its own. See Chapter VI.)

Marriage, babies, home. Unlike our offspring, we did not aspire to a monster home with pseudo-stone walls in the style I call Penitentiary Modern, with three or four bathrooms, two-car garage, sauna, Jacuzzi, pool, and noisy youths to tend the lawn.

Children of the Depression, all we asked for was a tidy little bungalow with a picture window, carport, garden, possibly one of those new "barbecues" (serious odours of burnt meat were wafting across the land). Give us this, far from the city's downtown roar, and we would kiss the hem of your garment.

We wanted land, lotsa land under starry skies above. We wanted to stand tall and proud on our own little spread, like Gary Cooper or Randolph Scott. When English immigrants Rose Baines Dyson and her husband bought their first home in Toronto, he said proudly, "We own a bit of Canada now!"

Ben Robertson wanted land so that "if there was another Depression I could feed my family." He and Louise bought ten acres in what is now Surrey, British Columbia, for $3,300. On it crouched an appalling shack, the remnant of a wartime barracks. It was shingled partway up the sides, and the inside walls were brown paper tacked over two-by-fours. There were no cupboards. An outhouse stood at attention to one side.

Ben hitched the outhouse to his Austin and hauled it a respectable distance into the woods. Louise made cupboards out of orange crates. They painted, stained, and cleaned, and lived in the place six years.

Prudent as always, we bought only what we could afford without mortgaging the kids. Near Govan, Saskatchewan, Alice and Art Pearson lived with Art's bachelor uncles for five years before they could afford their own place. In Toronto, I waited six years after marrying before I could afford a three-bedroom dollhouse in far-out Willowdale (but with picture window, yes!) for $17,500.

In far-out Clarkson, Joe and Mary Arnold waited twelve years for their first house. Jack Brown, one of my university classmates, who worked in public relations, also bought in Willowdale for $15,700. "I had $1,500, borrowed $1,500 from the bank, and had two mortgages, one from a dentist for 6 per cent. That 6 per cent damn near did me in, but I paid it."

Merle and Gene Tingley, having survived their honeymoon, rented until they could parlay his wartime credits into a bungalow on a half-acre in a veterans' subdivision. Ron and Vips Laidlaw moved in nearby; their furniture amounted to a baby bed and two packing crates for chairs.

"When the spring rains came, our basement flooded – and we had no sewers!" Gene Tingley says merrily. "The furnace went out, and the washing machine was floating. Our spaniel had a wonderful time swimming round and round the furnace. It was a disaster. Yet we laughed. We were like pioneers."

Pioneers? Persistence? Consider Gil and Madeline Murray of London, Ontario. In 1946, after Gil came home from Australia, where he was an army wireless operator attached to an intelligence unit, he married his wartime sweetheart, petite dark-eyed Madeline Marr. They rented a room in London – with kitchen privileges – at nine dollars a week, while he attended the University of Western Ontario and she worked in an office at twenty-five dollars a week.

One night, talking with two other student couples, someone said, "Hey, let's each build a *house*! We'll help each other." Gil enthusiastically fashioned a cardboard model of House Beautiful. In spring 1948 they looked for property, farther and farther out until they found their price range in a country field. They bought a quarter-acre lot for three hundred dollars from their savings (Gil had already applied his DVA credits to his education.)

The friends weren't ready to build, so Gil and Madeline went on alone. He had never built anything bigger than a model airplane. Madeline's father, a farmer, offered tips, and Gil got the rest from library books.

In June he hired a farmer with two horses and a metal scoop to dig the forty-by-twenty-five-foot foundation. The farmer-artiste squared off a perfect basement in gravel soil, and gladly accepted twenty-five dollars for the job.

Next, the foundation. Gil, clad in shorts and boots, spent six weeks of a blistering summer building wooden forms. Tall, lean, and sandy-haired, he turned black from the sun and lost thirty pounds. "I was down to 138, and almost invisible when I turned sideways."

At last the forms were ready. But alas, there was a cement shortage. Gil finally found a supplier who would let him have a hundred bags by the last week of July. The only problem was the entire construction industry went on holiday that week. Gil couldn't wait; he had one month to close his hole in the ground before classes resumed. Madeline's family agreed to help.

Next problem: no water on site for mixing cement. Murray had to act fast; a hundred bags of cement were now stacked in the open beside a mountain of sand and gravel. If it rained he would own a hundred bags of hard stuff.

Gil found a five-hundred-gallon drum across town, wrestled and roped it aboard the "pickup truck" he shared with a friend: a 1932 Chev sedan with the back end cut out for haulage. He drove the monstrosity through downtown London to the smirks and jeers of men in suits and white shirts. Safe back in his rural retreat, he rolled the monster drum off the truck. God smiled on Murray that day: the drum landed right side up near the hole in the ground.

The nearest abundant water was the Thames River, two miles away. The unsinkable Murray drove his truck bearing four fifty-gallon drums to an embankment fifteen feet above the river. He ran up and down, up and down, filling the drums with pails; trucked them back, then did it all again. It took most of a blazing day to collect five hundred gallons.

On B-for-Basement Day, the relatives arrived promptly at seven a.m. Another fiery, cloudless sky. They were still working at nightfall. Along the way they ran low on cement, so Gil hastily improvised two big basement windows. They used every scrap of cement, sand, and gravel, and emptied the five-hundred-gallon drum. The little crew stood in the twilight, quivering with fatigue, admiring their handiwork. Then Madeline's relatives drove sixty miles home to Brantford.

When the foundation cured, Gil and Madeline stripped away the wooden forms. Future generations would have thrown such wood in the garbage. The Murrays salvaged the one-by-six tongue-and-groove lumber, pulled the nails, and reused it to close in their house.

Their savings were gone. Madeline's twenty-five dollars a week was keeping them in food. They applied for a bank loan.

"What collateral do you have?" asked the banker.

"We have a foundation to a house."

The banker fell down laughing.

They turned to local lawyer Leo Gent, who had money-men connections and liked to help veterans. He got them their loan. Gil kept building. By autumn 1948 the house had walls, boarded-up windows (glass was not yet in their budget), and a half-shingled roof.

It rained hard the night they moved in. They slept in the living room to dodge water pouring through the roof. The rest of their running water came through a plastic line across a neighbour's field.

The lawyer's loan helped install a bathroom, but they had to fill toilet tank, bathtub, and cooking pots by pail. Gil spent the Christmas holidays digging trenches to lay pipe. By mid-January a waterline ran into the house.

Slowly, painfully, a two-bedroom house emerged, with a brick fireplace Gil built himself, insulation Madeline helped install, and electrical wiring courtesy of her brother. By 1950 it was finished except for hardwood flooring.

By then Gil had graduated and was a *Toronto Star* reporter. As soon as Madeline could join him in Toronto, they sold the house for about eight thousand dollars. It paid off their debts and loans and left a $1,200 profit.

Forty-six years later, from their handsome home in Burlington, Ontario (built by someone else), Madeline Murray says, "It was a lot of fun."

"Yeah," Gil says, ". . . but we'd never do it again."

The saga of Chez Murray was an extreme example of a nation-wide craving to Do-It-Ourselves. That, in part, was a hangover from our Depression ingenuity, but it had gone beyond such rudimentary tinkering. Though not yet affluent, we could now afford real tools and materials. No longer did we cobble together crude repairs with twine or baling wire. Significantly, one of the most popular shows of early Canadian television was "Mr. Fix-It." Its host, a cheery, rumpled fellow named Peter Whittall, became a bona fide star.

We liked to work with our hands in our wee new homes, and fifties magazines catered to our madness. "Of Course You Can Make Your Own Draperies" cried our cheerleader, *Canadian Homes & Gardens* (CH&G). *Canadian Hobby-Craft* magazine assured us that "Tin Cans Can Be Beautiful" and that hurricane lamps made from coffee jars, pictures made from plush, felt, or seeds, and almost anything created from seashells would enrich our lives. These grotesque concoctions, unlovely but loved (because we had *made* them), hung around our homes for years.

For a while we were addicted to homemade lampshades. CH&G carried *four* articles on do-it-yourself shades in one year. I built one such monstrosity with coloured wool wrapped snugly around a wire frame. It was a formidable dust-catcher, but I was intensely proud of it until my wife winkled it into the garbage.

CH&G was tailormade for a decade of home adulation. For two years I worked on its staff as a junior editor, absorbing its zeal and cutesy prose ("Give Your Indoor Air a Drink" and "Liquid Magic from Your Paint Can") and its penchant for the exclamation mark ("Check Your Insurance!" or "Have a Square Dance in Your Own Home!")

Around about this time, Cyril and Lillian Flint moved into "a glorified shack," vintage 1912, near Paradise Valley, Alberta. The bathtub, filled by pail, sat in the living/dining room. "With a wooden top on it, covered with an old spread: *voila!* a couch," Lillian says now. That would have been a perfect CH&G title.

"Where there is a real water problem," CH&G once said, never backward about stating the obvious, "that is, the basement actually floods, particular pains must be taken." Having had basements that actually flood, I can confirm that pains *must* be taken; namely, sell that turkey fast and hope the new buyer doesn't notice the high-water mark on the walls.

The magazine piloted us through many another shoal, such as turning one's basement into the fashionable new thing called a rec room or rumpus room. I spent one long sweaty winter building just such a room, *à la* CH&G, in my Willowdale bungalow. I nailed miles of one-by-two stripping into the concrete walls with an ordinary hammer (experts used a heavy one), coming away with smashed thumbs and wrists like Arnold Schwarzenegger. I added knotty-pine walls, an acoustic-tile ceiling, and an asphalt-tile floor.

After that we rarely used the damn thing. The floor was too cold in winter for children's play. And getting to it required a long unlovely trek past the furnace. But I had Done-It-Myself and was overweeningly proud.

We were obsessed, as well, with gardens. The *Financial Post* in 1952, noting that the annual spring sales of gardening paraphernalia had quadrupled since the war, sought explanations from a professional.

"I suppose you would call it a new scale of values," intoned this Solomon of the topsoil. "The average Canadian today is spending a good deal of his pay cheque in creating and maintaining an attractive home setting more than ever before. Part of it just reflects an attempt to keep up with the Joneses but there also seems a growing awareness of garden beauty and the peace of mind that often comes from working at this hobby."

Again, CH&G had wisdom to impart, on garden shade and sun, gardens in barrels, large gardens, miniature gardens, rock gardens, terrariums. Worried about crab grass? We all were, and CH&G offered solace: "Don't Let Crab Grass Strangle Your Lawn." Pride of lawn consumed our waking hours. CH&G churned out several pieces every year on how to nurture your lawn before, during, and after the season with titles like, "Your Garden's Winter Overcoat" and "Your Lawn an Outdoor Carpet."

I confess, with chagrin, to writing that latter title. But in the days of do-it-yourself, a man hadda do what a man hadda do.

THE LUXURY OF BED AND DRAIN

Marianne Linge and Wilf Harvey became engaged in the early fifties. He worked in, and lived behind, his father's electrical shop. She lived with her sister and brother-in-law in their garage while they built a house in the Toronto suburb of Willowdale.

As soon as my sister and her husband got the roof on their house and walls upstairs – not plastered or anything – Wilf and I got married and moved in. We paid thirty dollars a month to live upstairs.

I had an old studio couch and an old chair. That was our living-room seating. We bought a kitchen table and four chairs for ten dollars. The stove, only two burners worked, but I was thrilled with that. Wilf ran a tap up to the second floor so we had water, and a hose down from under the kitchen sink for a drain. I was delighted. You know, that hose lasted the whole five years we lived there.

The first thing we bought when we got engaged was a bedroom suite. It was four hundred dollars. Everybody said, "Oh, that's all you're thinking about is a bed!" But it was nothing to do with sex. I was sleeping on a studio couch in my sister's garage. He was sleeping on a studio couch in the kitchen behind his father's store. The apartment above the store only had two bedrooms, so Wilf's sister slept in the dining room, his two brothers had one bedroom and his parents had the other. So all Wilf and I could think about was actually having a real bed.

I thought it was all wonderful. At first we didn't have an icebox, so I paid my sister fifty cents a week to use part of hers downstairs. Then we bought one for twenty dollars. We had to empty the water [melted ice from a drip tray] every night. It was a nuisance. I'm glad we had the drain hose.

After five years we bought our first house for $12,500. We borrowed $1,500 for the down payment – $500 from my dad and the rest from the bank. It was just a long narrow room; a living room, and you stepped down into a tiny kitchen and along the side was a bedroom wide enough for a pair of bunk beds. We were able to put a crib in there for our little girl. And there was room for a dresser.

It had a small basement with a bathroom down there. Well, just a toilet, no sink. And a bathtub in the middle of the floor over the drain. But it was on a beautiful piece of property. I thought it was the most wonderful thing that ever happened, because I never thought I'd own a real house.

We had trouble keeping up the mortgage. But we were able to sell after a year because it was commercial and land was becoming popular. We sold it for $18,500.

"What's This Dishwashing Magic?"

So spake *Canadian Homes & Gardens* in August 1952. The magic lay in a device called a "dish washer," a "gadget that washes and dries at the flick of a switch." It was one of the many new marvels that assailed our wondering eyes in the fifties.

At the time only about 4,500 of the 3.5 million Canadian households had dishwashers, and nearly all were American models. But now a Canadian product was available at $472. It washed dishes *and* clothes. Clever housewives had only to remember to separate the underwear from the Spode.

Postwar industry – its muscles toned from producing the stuff of war – poured out one labour-saving device after another. Most, like the dishwasher, although miraculous to us then, are commonplace today. (In my house I still hand-wash my dishes, to my daughters' despair. A nineties father with no dishwasher is like a fifties daughter with no husband.)

In 1952, 86 per cent of Canadian homes were electrified, better than the 69 per cent of 1941, but light years away from modern yuppie heaven. Only 57 per cent of our households had inside hot and cold water; 42 per cent had vacuum cleaners. More than half of us still cooked and heated with wood or coal, only 29 per cent of households had electric stoves, and another 21 per cent cooked with gas. Nearly half of all households – 1.6 million – had electric refrigerators, but another 662,000 clung to the venerable icebox.

"Once a population is given to an appliance age the people are ready for more and more conveniences," concluded a patronizing article in the *Financial Post*. "It is much easier to induce a home-owner with electric lights to buy a pop-up toaster or garbage dis-posal unit than it was to convince the old lady with an oil lamp that she should instal one of those new fangled contraptions – a bathtub."

True enough. In five years the ownership of washing machines, refrigerators, vacuum cleaners, and electric stoves had soared. The *Monetary Times* reported that Canadians could buy seventy types of electrical appliances. We were spending about $225 million a year for electricity and $525 million on electrical products.

There were *so many* new delights. Window air conditioners, for instance, and the heady news that all new homes might have air conditioning built into them. (They didn't, of course.) Then there was frozen food and frozen-food plans. In a plan, you could, for a fee, join a frozen-food club, buy a home freezer, maybe at discount, and get a cut rate on slabs of beef, pork, lamb, poultry, fish. Regular bulletins would explain how to freeze home produce.

It was an appealing idea – and like many eager new house-holders, I bought into it – but it was like riding a Brahma bull; once aboard the plan, you had to hang on or be badly bruised. To make the great lumpish freezer in your basement eco-nomical, you had to stock it with never-ending supplies: a side of beef purchased from some sly farmer, or quarts and quarts of peas, corn, strawberries, that only a genuine earth-mother would willingly prepare. Earth-mothers were still among us, but my wife was not one, and I couldn't blame her. This was not 1930, when hours of slave labour over a hot stove were essential to the winter's menu.

Our freezer soon went unused. It was just too much bother and expense to keep it stocked unless you were feeding a soccer team. Frozen-food clubs lingered until the boomers grew up, but by then it was easier and almost as cheap to dip into the infinite variety of a supermarket frozen-food locker.

Our generation also welcomed, uncritically, the coming-of-age of plastic. Early on, *Canadian Homes & Gardens* told us that "plastics are now recognized as the key to a better way of life in

Canada" and that "the proving ground of plastics is the home." We believed it. Merchandisers boasted that in a couple of years we wouldn't be able to find an unwrapped carrot anywhere. We thought that was progress.

For a time, when I was editor of Imperial Oil's *Review*, the company sent out its public-relations representatives to schools and service clubs, extolling the glory that is oil-and-grease. One of their visual aids was "The Magic Suitcase," full of products made from the derivatives of petrochemicals.

There were even rumours that some fifties couples used Saran Wrap in lieu of condoms. Given the unlikelihood of fashioning leakproof birth control from a piece of plastic film in the heat of the moment, Saran may actually have accounted for the baby boom.

Canadian Plastics magazine in 1957 reported the ultimate: an all-plastic house built in, appropriately enough, Disneyland. Monsanto, the manufacturer, called it the House of the Future. Every mother-loving scrap of this dwelling was plastic. Viewed from the vantage of the nineties, it seems an appalling concept, and, fortunately, it never caught on except in futuristic films.

Throughout this decade there was virtually no thought of the environment. The notion of conservation was voiced almost entirely by such publications as *Forest and Outdoors* or *Canadian Nature* – and not always by them. In 1951, the former ran this article: "Cyanide – Coyote Killer Extraordinary." A 1945 photo in *National Geographic* showed children playing merrily on a beach while a sprayer sent up billows of DDT around them (in a mosquito-control program).

The *Financial Post* in 1957 carried a glowing report on the phenomenal growth of aerosol containers: in 1951 the hair-lacquer business was worth two million dollars per year; five years later, driven by aerosol, it was a sixty-million-dollar business. The article told how aerosols could be used for dispensing paint, pharmaceuticals – "the range is exciting and long." We had no idea that such things could damage the life-protecting ozone layer over our heads. Nor did it occur to us to ask.

A Passion for Work

Hard work had been our way of life from birth. We eagerly embraced it now to pay for our bungalows, washers, and slabs of frozen beef, and to make up for lost time. Most of us with war service were two to six years older than young people who came directly into the job market from school.

Luckily there were plenty of jobs. By mid-1947 only 1.6 per cent of the 950,000 men and women who'd left the armed forces were on unemployment benefits. From 1946 to 1959, the average unemployment rate was 2.9 per cent.

Our outlook, said *Canadian Business* magazine, was "based on a philosophy of getting places, reaching for the top, stepping on the gas and at all costs keep going." For example, Olive McConville of Frobisher, Saskatchewan, was such a dedicated teacher – at one time she taught thirty-eight students in four different grades – that when Jim Hannah, local barber, brought over an engagement ring one night, she made him wait an hour or so before he proposed. "I have to finish my schoolwork," she told him.

At age forty-eight, predicted *Canadian Business*, we were likely to drop dead, having achieved success over everything "except the demons that drive us on." While most of us lived beyond forty-eight, the effect on our families was almost as lethal.

"I had a terrible work attitude," admits Ben Robertson of Surrey, British Columbia, a cheery, open fellow with a crew cut and biceps bulging through his T-shirt. "I almost ruined our whole family life." He was a heavy-duty mechanic in the fifties, on the road much of the time. Louise raised the children. "Work came ahead of everything, partly because of those 1930s, but, anyway, I always *loved* to work."

So did Stanley Westall, English immigrant employed on major Canadian newspapers and, later, federal-government agencies. "Work was my pleasure. My children apparently complained to their mother that they didn't see much of Dad when they were growing up. I wasn't conscious of that."

Stan Winfield's "greatest regret" is of not spending more time with his first-born son in his early years as a lawyer. "I was a worry-aholic and a work-aholic and probably didn't have the confidence in myself that I should have had. So I spent more time with the clients. There were many a dinner and many a night that I didn't get home until very, very late. And I know that my wife and my son suffered greatly as a result."

Add Bill Finnbogason to the list. "My kids used to raise hell with their mother for having to wait for me to come home from work," he remembers of his days with Winnipeg's civic government. "The staff would leave at four-thirty, and I'd work for an hour and a half. Push, push, push, trying to get ahead."

Other families fed their children by five, then released them to the streets. The Finnbogason brood fretted and looked longingly out the window until after six (dining with both parents was a family rule). It did not scar them for life, but Finnbogason regrets it.

Sometimes it was not the demons within us but those in the corner office that drove us to exhaustion. Steve Walbridge, now of Pointe Claire, Quebec, worked seven years without missing a day for the Canadian affiliate of an American plate-glass manufacturer. He says the parent company made it clear that if he missed one accounting deadline, he was out.

"I made damn sure I didn't lose my job. I'd phone Shirley and say, 'Well, I'm not going to make the 5:19 train.' 'When will you be coming?' 'I'll get the 9:15.' I'd get home at ten o'clock and have my supper, which was a burden for her, and the kids were in bed. When I left that job they hired two people in my place."

The fruits of those labours seem laughable today. In 1953, doctors, our highest earners as reported by Revenue Canada, averaged $11,258 per year. Consulting engineers were next, averaging $10,289. After them came lawyers and dentists. Agricultural workers averaged $1,854 a year. For Canada as a whole, the average income was $3,383 a year, or $65 a week, and the average income-tax paid in 1953 was $338.

Many professionals earned far less than the average. In Manitoba, Alan Cooper came out of university qualified as a social worker but discovered he could make twice as much money selling sewing machines door to door, which he did, until he built up a nest egg. Marion Pratt earned two hundred dollars a month as a nurse at Toronto's Mount Sinai Hospital. In 1956 Charles Smith emigrated from Britain and landed a job with the *Oshawa Times* at fifty dollars a week. A few months later, his boss announced jubilantly, "I got you a raise – four dollars a week!"

Yet we were doing well by the standards of the day: between 1946 and 1953, the average income of all taxpayers went up by 65.5 per cent, while the cost of living rose only 37 per cent. Vacations with pay, the working man's dream not long before, were available to 98 per cent of Canadian industrial wage-earners. In all provinces west of the Maritimes, provincial laws stipulated that all employees get at least one week's vacation with pay. Many companies voluntarily offered two weeks' holiday after one year of service.

Office dress codes were rigid: dresses or skirts for women (no slacks), always with stockings; suits for men. When I joined Imperial Oil, sports jackets were forbidden. A pseudo-handker-chief provided by the dry cleaners – three triangles of white stitched to a slip of cardboard – peeked from my suit breast pocket and a thousand others. Before the fifties ended, we were loosening up with patterned waistcoats and shirts. The synthetics revolution gave us wash-and-wear suits and drip-dry shirts, although most looked as though they'd been slept in.

Our working tools changed more rapidly than our wardrobes. Photocopiers were appearing. In 1951 the *Financial Post* described a wonder of the future: a "telemagnet" that "answers a telephone with a recorded message while you are out and takes the caller's message from magnetic wire." It sounded remarkably like an answering machine. As late as 1959, advertisements were touting a teleprinter: "Your branch office is just seconds away; your messages come and go at up to 100 words a minute." Don't laugh, boomers, that was faster than a speeding bullet in '59.

One year the Canadian National Exhibition displayed steel sections that could be bolted together to create instant office walls: what my daughter a generation later called "cubicle land." That's just another of our many legacies, and we hope the millions of boomers and Generation-Xers, compartmentalized like cookies in cubicle land at this very moment, will thank us for it.

The business bombshell of our time was "automation" in industry and what the press nicknamed the "electronic brain," alias the computer. The earliest models were filled with vacuum tubes and bristling with wires. One company produced a monster called Univac 120 that could do 6,000 additions and subtractions or 1,200 multiplications and divisions per minute – beyond belief in 1955. You could buy it for $115,000 or rent it for $800 to $1,300 a month.

"As yet there are only a handful of electronic computing devices in Canadian offices," said the *Financial Post*. "The industry confidently expects there will be a good many more in the near future."

Universities began devising instruction courses for businessmen ("THEY'LL LEARN COMPUTER MAGIC," a headline shouted). The rest of us began to worry: when the push-button machines learned to push their own buttons, would it mean more leisure or more unemployment?

Those concerns, coupled with our headlong work habits, contributed to what the *Post* in 1956 dubbed "executive fatigue." Ah, but there was already a better word for it, a term that would become the nation's byword, a crutch for every real and imagined ill. Our generation invented "stress."

More accurately, the brilliant Dr. Hans Selye made it part of our language. In 1950, when Selye, forty-three, was at the University of Montreal Institute of Experimental Medicine, his stress theory was relatively new. *Canadian Business* said it had "the medical world gasping."

Since nearly everyone today claims proudly to be stressed, you might like to know the physiology. In the stress cycle, as Selye hypothesized, an alarm reaction came first: temperature and blood pressure fell, muscles went limp, and the victim had shock symptoms similar to those in motor accidents. If stress continued, a second stage kicked in: blood pressure and muscle tension rose, internal organs enlarged. In phase three, exhaustion was followed by weakened organs, followed by death.

Selye's theory revolutionized our lives. If we weren't sick before, we felt like it now. It struck at the heart of our work ethic. Was the compulsive worker, once prized by management, a hazard to himself and – by bringing destructive tendencies (aggression, hatred, rivalry, resentment) to work – to the office?

More companies opened medical departments. More of them urged employees to take company-sponsored physicals. According to Dr. F. R. Griffin, then the national director of the Canadian Mental Health Association, mental illness was the biggest health problem in Canada at the time. The Dominion Bureau of Statistics (the precursor to Statistics Canada) calculated that one in every ten Canadians would visit a psychiatrist in his or her lifetime.

What? A shrink? It ran counter to everything we tough Depression graduates believed in: solving our own head problems, if we even admitted to having them. The idea that mental illness was a disease and its sufferers deserving of compassion was not universally accepted. Nevertheless, such companies as Bell, Lever, Ontario Hydro, and Canadian General Electric installed staff psychiatrists or psychologists. In the United States, "analysts" were already a hot ticket, although their costs were high, reported *Saturday Night*: as much as fifteen to twenty-five dollars a session. In Canada, however, the magazine said, "the number of psychoanalysts may be counted on the fingers of one hand." We just didn't like the idea of therapy.

"We didn't know as much about it then," says Douglas Gardner of Toronto, one of our generation with a master's in social work. "In the fifties, if your marriage was in trouble and you needed help, an awful lot of that was being done by the clergy. And it still is, to good or bad effect. Some are good at it, some are terrible."

Some among us, the Columbuses and Magellans of their time, did try therapy. Gene Tingley was one.

"I've always had great self-esteem," she says, "but at one point I was pushed down. Therapy was a wonderful experience, wonderful. Without it I might still be bewildered."

On the other hand, Chick Childerhose of Sooke, British Columbia, is not a believer. "I read a book called *The Age of Narcissism*," he says. "I thought, 'Well, I should look inward and find the inner man.' So I did. I looked inward and found a horse's ass."

A WORKING MAN, I AM

Stan Hoffman of Moose Jaw is a big, bulky man with a broad, friendly face. He is courteous in the extreme — a vanishing trait — and speaks in exuberant gusts. He has few friends, is sometimes lonely, but adores his two grown children and his grandchildren.

Hoffman is forever putting himself down ("I'm not smart enough . . .," "Was just a dumb farm kid . . .") yet he reads extensively, writes poetry for his grandchildren, plays the guitar and keyboards, marvels over the galaxy, collects rocks, is angered at the rape of our environment.

Above all, Stan Hoffman is a virtuoso with his hands. He can fix almost anything, from cars to watches to TV sets to refrigerators. He is proud of his work. As such, he is the embodiment of our generation.

Working with my hands, that's all I know. There's nothing up here [tapping his head], so I have to do something with my hands. Oh, I made the kids cradles, big wagons, airports that had lights and switches. Good toys that you couldn't buy for several hundred bucks. I made them because I loved doing it.

I've got washing machines out of the garbage – I don't mean the garbage heap, I mean people's backyards, some people throw away pretty good stuff – and overhauled them, and they're still running. For a few dollars. People say, "Hey, Stan, I've got a dryer. Do you want it?" "Well, is there much wrong with it?" "Not really, but I don't want it." So my kids have both got a washer and dryer and one has a fridge that cost practically nothing. Changed the compressor myself.

At home on the farm we got an old tractor. The blasted thing damn well broke down the first summer we had it. The governor [controlling engine speed] broke, so I took hacksaw blades and made a governor better than the original. We fixed whatever we could. One guy says, "Well, what can't you fix?" I says, "Well, I can't fix a broken heart."

I'd like to be a professional at something. I'm just a master of Mickey Mouse stuff. But I've always kept busy. I could always find a job. Not a big paying job. But I got the kids through school, university, and I don't owe anything.

Yeah, we worked hard. I think we built a foundation for the people that are growing up now, that have it pretty darn good. I'm proud of being in Canada. And I'm proud of the work I've done, because it's honest work. I didn't get rich at it, but it was honest work. Like a lot of others, I did my best.

You can't ask for anything better than a man or a woman that has done their best for their family or for the good of their country or whatever. I guess it's kind of a heritage or something.

Not all of our working lives had happy endings. After fourteen years in his perfect job with Brinco, Peter Marchant got caught in the crossfire of a management takeover. Being left in "a position with no pizzazz and little future," he moved to another construction firm. Four years later, a recession hit, and Marchant was laid off.

He started again with a chartered accountant. After four years he was let go. "My gut feeling was that the age factor – I was fifty-seven and turning grey – was responsible." He admits that maybe he was not aggressive enough for a dog-eat-dog business world.

He sent out 150 resumes. Several prospects showed enthusiasm but no follow-through. "Then I had a blinding flash of the obvious: I *knew* that the age factor was at work. I had a degree. That didn't matter. I had the service background. That didn't count. I was over the hill."

Not too proud to try anything, Marchant got a series of odd jobs – commissionaire, selling real estate, in the post office. Then he was sixty-five, and the former lieutenant commander was just another retiree, but with no pension or prospects.

Last of the Simple Times

The fifties probably don't sound like much fun to today's young people. We were focused on work, mortgages, and getting ahead. While the men were out slaying corporate dragons, young wives in pedal pushers and tube tops – mired in the subdivisions with babies, low incomes, and gumbo – clung together and devised a culture.

"We were starting to understand that housework was work even though it wasn't paid," says Gwyn Griffith, who spent many years with the YWCA. She went to Don Mills, the newly formed perfect community, on a YWCA research project. "I remember those young housewives struggling in the suburbs – the mud streets and isolation. If their husbands were at work, and they only had one car in those days, they had no way of getting out." Ultimately the YWCA launched a "Take a Break" program for suburban mothers marooned in the midst of a great city.

Many of them, mind you, were coping nicely among themselves. They swapped recipes and gossip at the morning or afternoon coffee klatch. "In the fifties, canned soup was often the secret ingredient of a cherished recipe," reports writer-broadcaster Helen Gougeon in *A Century of Canadian Home Cooking*, who also collected recipes for "jellied concoctions and 'candle salads' [a banana set like a candle in a slice of pineapple.]"

They held Tupperware parties, where the sale of plastic containers was sometimes incidental to the sociability. A steady procession of tradesmen and service people brought products and the outer world to their doors: the bread man, the milkman, the Watkins man, whose wares included toiletries and spices.

"Eaton's would come twice a day if you needed them," says Pat McLaughlin of Winnipeg. "They'd even bring a spool of thread."

To newcomers such as Stan and Patricia Westall from England, the community spirit was like a surprise embrace. In England one might barely know one's next-door neighbours, and never on a first-name basis.

"Yet immediately we moved into Oakville [Ontario] we were members of a community," Westall says. "The whole crescent was a social club. We were invited by the bank manager who lived opposite to come and play bridge, frequently around eleven o'clock at night. When my sewer backed up, my next-door neighbour was the first one at the door with his eleven-year-old son and a plumber's helper in hand. This feeling of *membership*, you were all in this thing together."

One of our simple pleasures was taking family and car for a mindless Sunday drive. Traffic was not the exquisite kind of hell that it can be today. Most of us, being who we are, drove second-hand clunkers. We refused to go into hock for a new model. When Cyril Flint of Paradise Valley met his future bride Lillian Dunn in 1949, he was driving a 1938 Ford half-ton truck with one hand, and holding the door shut with the other. Jim Hannah of Frobisher courted Olive McConville in a 1929 Chev with no floorboards. Joe and Mary Arnold's first car, eight years after marriage, was a four-year-old Pontiac coupe.

"It cost $1,050," Joe remembers. "A fortune! And I paid thirty-five dollars extra to have it painted two-tone, a darker roof. I never slept that night, I just tossed and turned. That extra thirty-five dollars really bothered me."

Home entertaining was good cheap fun. We'd lead our guests into the rec room (well, not into *mine*, not with that ugly stroll past the furnace) and lay out rye-'n'-ginger or rum-'n'-Coke, chips-'n'-dip (Lipton's Onion Soup dip was a front-runner), meatballs on toothpicks, and something concocted from cream cheese, such as little balls of cream cheese rolled in nuts, cream cheese stuffed into celery stalks, or olives in cream-cheese overcoats.

A big night out was a movie. In 1951 Gallup said 50 per cent of us went to the flicks anywhere from one to six times a month. Drive-in theatres were catching on across the country, and to those of us with children they were heaven-sent, saving – who knows . . . a dollar, two dollars? – on a babysitter. Average admission was fifty cents for adults; kids got in free. With popcorn around twenty-five cents – and stolid Alan Ladd in his platform shoes as Shane the noble gunman, or Bogie breathing cigarette smoke at Ava Gardner in *The Barefoot Contessa*, or the elfin Audrey Hepburn in *Funny Face* – a drive-in was the best seventy-five-cent bargain in town.

"I was Audrey Hepburn until I got married," Bernice Quinto Holmes reports. "She was gorgeous. She was sophisticated. She was slim. She had her heartaches in every movie of hers I ever saw. I associated with her. Under the blood and under the skin I *was* Audrey Hepburn. Except that I looked like I do and she looked like she did. That was the only difference."

The raunchiest movie I recall from that period (actually a forties film) was Howard Hughes's *The Outlaw*, in which the magnificently endowed Jane Russell nearly spilled out of her bodice while frolicking on the hay. (Later she modelled brassieres on TV, a classic case of everything falling into place.) The raunchiest book extant was *Lady Chatterley's Lover*, in which the gamekeeper and the lady indulge in explicit sexual dialogue (along with exuberant sex).

For all of our wartime experience, our sexual mores were still anchored in the past. Many of both sexes were just realizing that it was okay for women to enjoy it, and that there were positions other than the missionary. In 1950, Alfred Kinsey's first book on sexuality of the human male created a mini-tempest. *Health*, the organ (no *double entendre* intended) of the Health League of Canada, tried unsuccessfully to have Kinsey's book suppressed. As a *Saturday Night* writer observed, however, Kinsey's statistics might or might not have been accurate, but "a statistic, even of orgasms, can hardly be described as obscene."

Three years later Kinsey's second report on the female's sexual habits drew another response from *Saturday Night*.

"Fifty years ago it was still widely believed that only depraved women enjoyed sexual experiences," a female Ph.D. told the magazine. "Physicians and clergymen asserted that this was so." But doctors already knew "that a large number of women are masturbators and that some of them continue in this habit to advanced ages; that a large number of them have sexual experiences of some sort during childhood . . . that in adolescence a large number of them have homosexual relationships with other women."

Startling news for a generation that was not yet sure whether sex should be fun. Yet we indulged in other habits that today's young people consider beyond the pale. We drank to excess, smoked our brains out, and punished our stomachs and arteries with the wrong food.

A learned publication, the *Economic Annalist*, reported in 1954 that Canadians spent about $3.5 billion a year on food. Since wages were rising more rapidly than food prices, we were getting more for our money than in, say, 1939. But we were also eating fewer cereals, potatoes, and vegetables, and more meat, eggs, milk, and cheese.

By the end of the decade, each of us was eating on average seventeen imperial pints of ice cream. Not as much as in the United States, where each citizen gobbled 25.9 imperial pints, but American blimps were hardly role models. Before the war we as a nation ate 1.3 million pounds of red meat per year. In 1958 it was 2.3 million pounds. That was not because of a growing population. The *Financial Post* reported in 1957 that we were each downing 154 pounds of meat per year, compared to 118 pounds per head before the war. Again, less than the

Americans (who consumed 165 pounds per person per year) but who wanted to be *that* fat?

"When you put on a meal you always had dessert," says Pat McLaughlin. "It was *important*." Carol Ferguson and Margaret Fraser elaborate in *A Century of Canadian Home Cooking*: "New product promotions [in the fifties] convinced homemakers that the ultimate in culinary chic was producing four-layer cakes covered with fluffy frosting mix, glazing Klik or Prem with pineapple and calling it 'Hawaiian,' topping sweet potatoes with marshmallows and adding canned soup to every casserole."

Everywhere, we were eating wrong. Quebec, supposedly the cradle of fine food, was (according to *Maclean's*) deadening its palate with white bread. Bad teeth and gum disease were rife in Newfoundland because of bad diet, said *Saturday Night*. Across the country, children were often undernourished because their mothers were boiling the life out of potatoes, cabbage, and other vegetables.

Why? Two reasons: we were diverting more of our disposable income to homes, cars, refrigerators, and TVs instead of good groceries; and we weren't particularly savvy about food. The influx of European immigrants had not yet made their mark on our eating habits.

A couple of indicators to our primitive ways:

First, the Canadian Periodical Index, which lists the contents of scores of Canadian magazines. Throughout the 1950s the Index had eleven entries on the cooking of fish and game (including "How to Cook a Bear") versus one on French cooking.

Second, *Saturday Night's* 1950 list of some of Canada's so-called best restaurants. One was a hotel in Thessalon, Ontario, frequented by future prime minister Mike Pearson whenever he was in the area, and specializing in "steaks and chops and the best lemon pie you've ever tasted." (Pearson subsequently won the Nobel Prize, but not for eating.)

To be fair, *Saturday Night* also recommended Quebec City's Chateau Frontenac with its onion soup (the magazine spelled it in French to impress us), partridge with cabbage, and vichyssoise (which, the article explained helpfully, was a cold soup).

Given those drop-dead eating habits, and our penchant for booze and cigarettes, it's a wonder we made it into the sixties.

Many of us learned to smoke during World War Two; the rigours of battle and the almost unlimited supply of free cigarettes strongly encouraged it. Fifties movies did nothing to dispel our belief that smoking was chic. Humphrey Bogart appeared to have been born with a cigarette in his mouth (and, of course, died in 1957 following an operation for cancer of the oesophagus). Bette Davis and Barbara Stanwyck were generally seen through palls of smoke. "I look at those old movies now," says Elizabeth Murray of Halifax, a former nurse and reformed smoker, "and it makes me cough!"

Many of us, relatively penniless going into the fifties, bought cigarette-rolling machines. My wife and I had one: a hand-cranked gadget that – when fed a cigarette paper and a dollop of bulk tobacco, combined with a flick of the wrist and a lick of the glued paper – turned out an acceptable smoke that, with practice, did not fall apart when you lit up.

By 1954 we were smoking twenty-one billion cigarettes a year. A classy gift was a Ronson cigarette lighter; even classier, a slim, silver cigarette case. About two-thirds of the population – 15 per cent more men than women – puffed, coughed, and smelled like dead ashtrays. It was a bonanza for the industry; Canadian cigarette sales for 1954 to 1955 were estimated at $25.01 billion. By then, according to the *Monetary Times*, doctors were seriously examining the relationship between smoking and lung cancer. *Maclean's* in 1954, questioning whether cigarettes could kill us, reported lung-cancer deaths had increased from

183 in 1931 to 1,503 in 1952. Smokers were not immediately convinced, but a decade or two later most of us saw the light and kicked the habit. And so here we are still, to brighten the lives of younger generations.

BAKED BEANS AND BEER

Gene Tingley remembers married life in their early fifties Ontario subdivision. She and husband Merle now live in a London condominium.

Our husbands' pay went into the bank every two weeks. So we women all met at the bank. We sort of dressed up for that, and we took the little kids with us. We'd stand back and wait, and have a little visit, and the tellers would signal when the money was in. Then I'd take out our grocery money – I had fifteen dollars in my household budget to feed us – and maybe buy little scraps of material to make clothing for myself and the kids.

In the winter we used to go out on the ponds and take shovels and clean a rink. We'd take a crock of beans, and celery and carrots, hot chocolate for the kids, and beer for the parents. Then we'd play hockey. Often they'd put the mothers in goal, we were so bad. They'd give us snow shovels for goal sticks. We could stop a few pucks that way.

At Easter we all went to Woolworth's, because everybody had to dress up at Easter whether they had money or not. We would find flowers and feathers and stuff, and cheap white gloves, which you always wore. And we laughed ourselves silly. The outfits were pretty terrible, but we thought we were smart.

We were so poor and didn't know it. And we had *so* much
fun, 'cause we shared. And we looked after each other.

Wrestling with the Demon Rum-'n'-Coke

As with smoking, most of us learned to drink during the war,
and for much the same reasons.

"I drank because it was there," says Larry Holmes, who spent
seven years in the navy. "Every man got two ounces of rum daily.
Officers could save theirs up. You'd get into harbour, collect your
mail, break open your jug from your locker, sit on the floor and
drink and read." By war's end, Holmes says, it was habit.

We drank for another reason: we had discovered it was not
Original Sin. It could, in fact, be a sociable habit if handled with
moderation. In the Canada of the thirties, forties *and* early fifties,
public drinking in the dank, depressing beer parlours was
freighted with censure and guilt. Men huddled around small
beer-slopped tables topped with tin or formica, shouting over
the din and getting sullenly drunk. Waiters, thick billets of men
with scars over their eyebrows and forearms like beer kegs, cir-
culated with trays of draught. Every table had a salt shaker, to
liven up the bland draught beer.

"Women and Escorts" were banished to slightly less dreary
rooms so-named next door. A few restaurants permitted us to
smuggle a mickey (twelve-ounces) of booze under the table in a
brown paper bag. Naturally the drink of choice was rum-'n'-
Coke or rye-'n'-ginger. Wine? No one in his right mind would
touch that cheap sweet bingo that down-and-outers drank under
bridges.

But when we travelled abroad, courtesy of His Majesty, we

discovered in continental bistros and cheery English pubs that wine need not taste like shaving lotion, and a mug of Guinness with darts, song, and cheddar cheese, did not invoke a deal with the devil. Canadians, Aussies, and Yanks monopolized British pubs, singing too loudly, drinking too much, sometimes behaving badly.

The civilized Brits tolerated us. Our money was good, we would – they prayed – go home some day, and meanwhile we were helping beat Hitler. (Once, just after war's end, two gentle elderly Yorkshire women accosted me on a train to thank me for Canada's help in winning the war. I accepted their thanks, on behalf of the Dominion, and we parted on a wave of goodwill.)

Back home – except in enlightened Quebec and, eventually, in Ontario – we rediscovered the puritan disapproval and the same execrable drinking dives. Canadian society still required opaque windows on beer parlours, liquor-permit books that patrons had to proffer before buying a bottle, and, even after 1957, permit cards. Until 1960, in the ultimate absurdity, Ontarians could not *legally* carry a bottle home from the liquor store. Once you smuggled it home, it became legal.

To immigrants this was shockingly inane. Stanley Westall, arriving from Britain with sidekick Gordon Donaldson, checked into a Halifax boarding house.

"Do you drink?" demanded the landlady, threateningly.

"Yes, please," said Donaldson.

We drank on, in our crude fashion. Like Joey Smallwood, then-premier of Newfoundland, most of us in our formative drinking years had little use for cocktail parties.

"Until I went to Ottawa I had never been at a cocktail party in my life," the ebullient Joey once told *Saturday Night*. "Of all the boring experiences a man can be called upon to endure, cocktail parties are the worst. Personally, I do not drink anything stronger than chocolate milkshakes but I could endure cocktail

parties a bit more if they provided chairs. The business of standing around for an hour holding a full or empty glass and pre-
tending that you are enjoying yourself is my conception of the
last word in futility."

But give us a case of beer, a mickey of rye whisky, and a bowl
of peanuts, and we'd be happy for hours. Gallup in 1951 found
that 53 per cent of us admitted to imbibing more than ever
before, and that 64 per cent of the adult population (and 75 per
cent of all men) drank. We drank and drove and thought little of
it. When Gallup's pollsters asked Canadians what changes they
wanted in the issuing of driver's licences, they called for stricter,
more frequent tests, medical examinations, age limitations – but
only 4 per cent demanded greater punishment for drunk drivers.

By 1954, Canada had 1,804 alcoholics per 100,000 of the population – not the world record, but enough to put us in sixth
place. A twenty-nine-page report from the Addiction Research
Foundation of Ontario revealed that each of us, on average,
drank 1.48 gallons of alcohol per year. British Columbians were
the biggest toss-pots, with 2,532 alcoholics per 100,000. Quebec
came second. Newfoundlanders were the most sober.

Statistics don't convey the misery of lives marred by alcoholism. In the course of this research, I met many men and
women who had been sorely tried by the bottle.

"In the law practice, clients would come in from the east, and
to those guys in those days business was lunch," recalls Stan
Winfield. "Boy, you'd drink martinis. I loved martinis. But we'd
drink through lunch and on into the afternoon." Winfield recognized the problem and eased into moderation. Others had to
take the cure.

"Lordy, lordy, what a plague alcohol is, and how little we're
taught about it or know about it," says Elsie Sheane Towson of
Scarborough. Her marriage began to fall apart when for both
spouses a social drinking pattern became more than that. "What

really upset the apple cart was in 1974 when I fell down stairs after drinking. I thought, This has got to stop. This is utterly ridiculous. So I went to Al Anon for four years. I feel impatient with people who say it's not a disease. It sure as hell is an addiction."

"Nobody knew he was an alcoholic," says Marianne Harvey of her late husband. "He could hide it. That's what makes an alcoholic: somebody who can drink everybody under the table and not show it."

Helen Margison, who spent many years with the United Way, says it was "almost a cliché that women in their forties were going to turn into alcoholics." They were trapped in suburbia, often getting no thanks or respect for their wife-and-mother role. "And so they retreated into alcoholism," says Margison. "The number of women that we saw in this situation was ghastly."

It was probably no comfort to the families of alcoholics to see, by decade's end, liquor laws relaxing across the country. In most provinces, wine and spirits could now be served in licensed restaurants and in authorized cocktail lounges. Hoteliers, restaurateurs, and patrons were ecstatic. The *Financial Post* reported that Vancouver had hosted only fourteen conventions in 1952, but had eighty-five in 1958 with the new laws. A failing Edmonton restaurant tripled its business under the new regulations. In Manitoba under the first two years of relaxed laws, hotels, restaurants, and lounges reported a capital outlay of $5.6 million.

At last Canadians could drink without opprobrium. Before the change, wrote Alexander Ross in *The Booming Fifties*, women could not drink in public anywhere in Saskatchewan or Manitoba, apart from in a few private clubs. Did the increase in watering holes and their improved ambience exacerbate our drinking habit? Not necessarily. "The evidence for a cause-and-effect relationship is mixed and a clear conclusion is difficult to make," say Reginald G. Smart and Alan C. Ogborne in *Northern Spirits: Drinking in Canada Then and Now*. In Edmonton the day after cocktail bars were first opened, Ross reported, not a single drunk turned up in magistrate's court – for the first time in court officials' memory. Tragic though alcoholism was and is, it is too complex an illness to be blamed on liquor laws alone.

DRYING OUT

The narrator of the following account, a retired executive in Regina, cannot be identified, in keeping with the rules of Alcoholics Anonymous.

As my craving for alcohol progressed, it became a major disruptive force in the family. My brother, a psychologist, tried to intervene. I stopped for a while – which was odd, because my normal response to any mention of an alcohol "problem" was hostility. (I was not only addicted to alcohol but also to prescription drugs; namely, Valium. This made my drinking highly unpredictable. I might drink great quantities without visible effects, or a drink or two would send me into orbit.)

Finally, the crash came when I had been sober for about three months. Everything was in control in my little world. I was going to a meeting in Toronto on a Tuesday. The Friday before, I played in a golf tournament. After the game I ordered a tonic and lime. On the second round, I said without a thought, "Put a shot of gin in it," and I was off.

During the next few days I pleaded illness, cancelled the trip, and don't remember a damn thing about it. I was wandering around drunk but appeared sober. I went into the office to tell people that I changed my plans because of a flu bug. They told me later that I appeared perfectly normal. But between Friday and Tuesday night I went through eleven bottles of booze.

By Tuesday night I was hyperventilating, and my son and nephew knew something was seriously wrong. I wound up in Plains Hospital in intensive care.

My wife, down east visiting her mother, who was ill, hurried home to find me still there. She asked the nurses to recommend a doctor who knew about alcoholism. I, too, was looking for some way out of this mess. The flu excuse had run its course, and when the doctor recommended a treatment centre in the States, I agreed to give it a whirl.

That was twenty years ago. I have not found the need to take a drink since. I still go to three AA meetings a week. During the drinking, I told my wife she could pack her bags and leave, which thankfully she did not. Instead she got involved in a sister organization of AA for wives and friends of alcoholics.

When I went back to work, I called my department heads together and told them exactly where I had been and why. After all, you can't really write off an absence of eight weeks as some sort of bug. I said that if anybody asked about my absence, they should tell them the truth. If they weren't comfortable working for an ex-drunk instead of a practising one, they knew where the front door was.

I also said that anyone who might need help should come to me. Before I retired, twenty-three employees either came forward on their own or were steered my way.

Earth People Meet One-Eyed Monster

One summer day in the early fifties, Bernice Quinto got a phone call from her brother-in-law, Pat, in suburban Willowdale.

"Come on up," he said. "We have a surprise!"

Bernice, her parents, and brother drove up from downtown Toronto that very afternoon. Garden chairs were arranged in orderly rows on her sister Marie's front lawn, facing the window of the den. All the neighbours were there.

In the window, facing the assembled throng, a tiny screen embedded in a vast wooden case blinked its flickering blue eye. Marie and Pat were the first on their block to have TV.

"My God, you could hardly hear it; you could hardly *see* it!" Bernice recalls. But the little crowd was enchanted, as thrilled and awestruck as early man discovering fire.

By the time the CBC launched its television service on September 8, 1952, Canadians already had 146,000 sets within tuning range of the U.S. border. But perhaps it was just a flash in the pan. Writing in *Maclean's*, the erudite Toronto critic Nathan Cohen asked his readers, "Are plunging necklines to be the main TV attraction? Will Canadian telecasting schedules consist mainly of antiquated movies, sadistic mysteries, mental-case melodramas, hoked-up wrestling matches, quiz shows making boobs out of contestants and prizefights where has-beens and newcomers punch each other to exhaustion? All for the glory of the sponsor and the glee of the TV set owner?"

Not if the recommendations of Vincent Massey's Royal Commission on National Development in the Arts, Letters, and Sciences were heeded, said Cohen. Massey recommended that Canada bend its back to maintain the Canadian character and identity in many ways, including broadcasting. (His recommendations to aid universities and subsidize Canadian creative and scientific endeavours also resulted in the Canada Council: the beginning of a long line of useful grants and assorted boondoggles.)

"Regulated by CBC officialdom every step of the way," Cohen continued, "kept under constant guard of groups apprehensive of the medium's influence on susceptible children and teenagers, Canadian TV promises to enter in auspiciously and after the first excitement will make only a moderate impression on the Canadian cultural and entertainment topography."

Nathan, Nathan, how could you have been so wrong?

By January 1955, sets were poised in more than a million living rooms. By 1956, more than *two* million Canadian households had TV. They were not cheap, especially with our Depression ethos (meaning, if you couldn't afford it flat-out, you were loathe to buy on credit). In 1954, Admiral's TVs started at $249.95 for a seventeen-inch set, up through a twenty-one-inch set in a limed oak console for $449.95, to a top-of-the line $649.95 (not merely entertainment but a fashion-statement in furniture). Those who couldn't afford TV lined up outside appliance-store windows.

It was all very well to say, as many did, that they would not be rushed into ownership. Social pressure forced them. In Clarkson, the Arnolds bought in self-defence. When Joe, a printing salesman, discovered that all his clients and cohorts in Toronto were talking on Monday morning about the Ed Sullivan show the night before, he felt like some tribesman just in from the Orinoco. One Hamilton couple laid down the law. There would be no TV in the house until they bought the new carpet. Fair enough. Their children simply left home every Saturday morning to watch at the neighbour's.

It was addictive, although the reception could be a maddening blizzard of snow or a shrinking image. More than one outraged viewer, like Wilf Harvey of Willowdale, flung a shoe at the set when the picture dwindled to black just at the climax of a favourite show. For a while we watched shows that we blush to remember now. In Orillia, newspaper publisher Jim Lamb found himself staring at a puppet show, "Uncle Chichimus" (his excuse: his sons watched too). Diane Bickle of Regina remembers her father sitting through five straight hours of television, dying to go to the bathroom but unwilling to yield even one precious moment away from the tube.

In Victoria Stan Winfield phoned his new bride daily from the office. One day he heard strange background noises: a hoarse voice croaking, "I yam wot I yam," accompanied by the *Ka-pow!* sounds of (could it be?) a skinny sailor with huge forearms beating the pulp out of a bully.

"What are you watching?" Stan asked suspiciously.

"Popeye," said his sophisticated wife, putting a lyrical French spin on the word.

Ian Bickle, husband of the aforementioned Diane, was one of Saskatoon's first TV stars. On December 6, 1954, after eighteen months of radio broadcasting, he had delivered the first newscast on CFQC-TV. There had been weeks of rehearsal, with coaching from an imported American, and a dry run before a live audience. The neophyte announcers were advised to look happy. Bickle – tall, lean, with a thatch of well-barbered hair – delivered a multi-megawatt smile with his sign-off. He became an instant hit.

Suddenly he found himself stared at in public and pestered for autographs. One viewer wanted him to meet her daughter: object, matrimony. Another told CFQC that she wanted Ian Bickle for Christmas. Bolder women invited him to parties – sometimes very private parties.

Bickle avoided the overtures, being engaged, and also keenly aware that a TV person's every move was under scrutiny. When he and Diane married in 1955, a fellow announcer led off the nightly news with, "Ian Bickle is gone." Later, a man phoned Bickle at the station.

"Why don't you quit that smiling now?" he demanded grumpily. "You're married!"

Within three years, Canadians were as firmly glued to the tube as Americans. We clung to daytime radio – our TV stations didn't go on air until afternoon – but for every radio listener there were ninety-seven TV watchers. Fathers (well, not me, nor anyone I knew) began calling their prepubescent daughters Duchess, Princess, and Kitten, like the TV daddies.

Families began sitting down to eat meals in front of the television, the beginning of the end of civilized conversation and family togetherness around the dinner table. The TV table, a wretched, precarious little tray on folding legs, insinuated itself into living rooms. The frozen-food people quickly cashed in on the craze with TV dinners, watery excuses for a real meal, but handy if you were in a rush to watch "The Honeymooners" or "I Love Lucy" or "Don Messer's Jubilee."

Canadian publications gave inordinate space to the medium that would soon take huge bites from their advertising. In 1953, *Saturday Night* assigned author and curmudgeon Hugh Garner to find out what we were getting for our tax money. Garner watched sixty hours of CBC television for a week: from cowboy films and puppet shows to comedy and variety.

"Of these totals, only twelve and one quarter hours could be called by any stretch of a Parliamentarian's imagination cultural in the general accepted meaning of the word," he grouched. "Of those twelve and one quarter hours, at least seven hours were from private networks in the U.S."

Not to be outdone, *Maclean's* plunked the gentle humorist Robert Thomas Allen in front of *his* TV. He reported on it in exhaustive – and, for today's reader, boring – detail. But it was fascinating then. What if most of it *was* candy floss for the mind? We gobbled up the Sullivan show, Milton Berle and "Holiday Ranch" hosted by hefty Cliff McKay. A young, dark, flashing-eyed Robert Goulet, a blonde singer known as "Our Pet" Juliette, Percy Saltzman, the thinking viewer's weatherman, singers Wally Koster, Joyce Hahn, and Billy O'Connor, all were "names" then, now lost in the mists of time.

Maclean's permitted American writer Gilbert Seldes to utter the definitive words. "The fatal weakness of all the efforts to control the excesses and correct errors of TV in the United States was the attitude of people who thought themselves untouched because they never looked at offensive programs or never saw TV at all," he wrote prophetically. "There is no immunity – there is no place to hide."

IV

THE SENSE OF A WOMAN

A Woman's Place in the Fifties

NOT ENOUGH "GOOD" GIRLS
— *Financial Post*, Oct. 8, 1955

I t was not a lament for chastity lost. The *Post* headline meant, in fifties' male-speak, that there were not enough good secretaries. In business Canada, men were men but women were still girls.

They had proved in uniform and on the assembly line that they could do the same jobs as well as, if not better than, men. They had painfully won the right to vote – even, by 1940, in Quebec. Yet now women seemed in danger of being pushed back into their subservient prewar past.

Many had yielded their wartime jobs to homecoming servicemen, which seemed fair. Many were glad to go home and start families. As the *Post* lamented, "Because so many women are interested in marriage, high salaries seem to have little effect in boosting the supply of secretaries, stenos and typists." The "high" salaries, incidentally, were two hundred dollars a month for a "top-notch" steno (who could take dictation as well as type), and up to four hundred dollars for secretaries (who had grander duties, including fetching coffee and sticky buns for the master).

Going into the fifties, the National Employment Service had 4,296 office vacancies for women in Toronto alone, and only 2,453 applicants. Charlotte Whitton, at the time a leading welfare expert and later the feisty mayor of Ottawa, put it this way: in a typical year, only 250,000 Canadian girls over sixteen were attending school, and 150,000 to 175,000 of them were needed for "marriage to retain anything like our present balance." She did not mean to make them sound like brood mares; stay-at-home motherhood was still a prime and honourable female career.

"That was the way we were raised," says Elizabeth Rudge Tucci of Toronto. "The white prince was going to come along and carry us off and look after us." When she was fifteen, Elizabeth announced, "I'm not gonna work after I get married."

"I certainly hope not!" her mother said. A married daughter of their acquaintance *was* still working, and it was considered pathetic and distressing. Her place was at home. If her husband couldn't support her, he shouldn't have married her.

But more and more women felt cheated and frustrated. They knew they could do better than muck out diapers or bake an angel food cake.

"If I could change anything, I wouldn't have let the dictates of society as to a 'woman's place' take away my career and ambition," says Marilyn Chandler McFadden, now widowed and living in London, Ontario. Before marriage, McFadden worked briefly as a reporter on the *Winnipeg Free Press*. "I wish I had been smart enough not to fall into the all-consuming role of homemaker and mother and followed the emerging female trend towards sharing energies between home and career. My husband wouldn't have liked that, but my kids might have been less spoiled and I might have become a more interesting person."

Fifties women were, to many fifties men, not to be taken seriously except as homemaker, mother, and, possibly, in bed. "It was a disaster to have female offspring, who couldn't be of any use on a Prairie farm," Olive Thorne of Edmonton says with a tinge of bitterness. "Women were useless except to get married and be wives."

Rarely were they regarded as professional or intellectual equals. "You'd go out with a guy, knowing you were a helluva lot brighter than he was," says Hope Morritt of Sarnia, who was in those days working for a radio station in Whitehorse, "and yet you tried not to be. We actually played down our intelligence."

The media perpetuated the myth of the airhead wife. *Canadian Homes & Gardens*, edited by a woman, once suggested: "A mirror on the wall or inside of a cabinet door makes a handy place for you to dab on some lipstick before answering the door." Of course. Only the most slovenly housewife would dream of facing mailman, milkman, or garbage collector without "putting on her face."

An article in *Saturday Night* warned that "Careers and Marriage Don't Mix." Even back in 1950 such an author would have been boiled in oil (preferably Crisco) by some progressive women, except that she – yes, *she* – hid behind the byline "Anonymous." She was in advertising. She earned ten thousand dollars a year, twice as much as her poor chump of a husband. But it was a hollow triumph, Anonymous wrote, because "there is, you see, that all important matter of a man's ego. To my way of thinking any self respecting wife worth her salt will awaken sooner or later to the fact that all the gold in the U.S.A. is not worth the multitude of little pricks her husband's ego receives simply because he happens to have a working wife. These nasty pricks can come in a dozen different ways, none so difficult as feeling within himself that part of his living comes through his wife."

There was more, a veritable Niagara of feminine treachery.

"The reason why most men endure . . ." *Endure!* ". . . a career wife at all," Anonymous continued, "is that they are prepared, so they think at first, to put up with certain inconveniences for greater gain to get started sooner, mostly for their wife's sake, with owning their own home, buying a new car, and getting a place in the country. But try to stop this mad whirl, this bird-in-a-cage act, once you get started! It is not easy for any career woman to adjust to a lower standard of living. Until she sees the light." (Does anyone besides me wonder if Anonymous was really a man?)

Never mind the working wife. Was homebody wife an asset or a liability to her upwardly clawing husband? According to *Canadian Business*, she was neither. Canadian corporate honchos had not yet gone the American way (establishing finishing schools for executive wives, sometimes having the hapless wife screened by a psychologist before the company granted her husband his top-floor aerie with private washroom, blue-rinsed executive secretary, and fake Renoirs on the fake-oak walls). As the magazine put it, "Canadian executives by and large believe that woman's place is in the home. If the wives do not agree with this proposition completely at least it is certain that they are not in the company councils."

To further its depiction of wife as dimwit, *Canadian Business* cited an alleged conversation between two captains of industry:

"My wife and I are very concerned about the future as far as our firm is concerned."

"Your wife is *concerned*?"

"Certainly, isn't yours?"

"My wife doesn't know what business I'm in!"

Such was the climate of our time. All the people of my generation interviewed for this book were asked if they felt they had fulfilled their life's objectives. Would they change anything, given the chance? Virtually all of the dissatisfied were women: "I could have done more"; "I would have retrained to get back into the work force"; "Wish I'd had a career."

"Higher education was considered really strange, especially for women," says Marion Pratt of Tillsonburg, Ontario, who wanted to be a librarian, but, faced with the stereotypical choices of the day – teaching or nursing – chose nursing. Nearly always, women's dreams of university or a non-traditional career were thwarted by a father with attitudes anchored in the past.

"My dad, bless him, in his old English way did not believe in women getting a university education," says Marilyn McFadden. Nevertheless, he grudgingly agreed, and afterward "seemed to be delighted and satisfied with his investment in me."

Jean Marie Danard, the patriotic young navy veteran from Kirkland Lake, got through university, but, in the job market as in the military, ran head-on into the male establishment. In the navy she had hoped to get into operations, perhaps plotting ships' locations at sea. But when she told the recruiters she could type, "my fate was sealed." She fought the war with her type-writer in Halifax, Toronto, and Ottawa. Her applications for overseas postings were regularly shelved. In spite of that she moved up to chief petty officer and became secretary to the head of all naval divisions across Canada.

Along the way she learned to fend off wolves in officers' clothing, including the commodore and commander who one night flipped a coin to see who'd escort her home ("Luckily the nice guy won"), and the commander who impulsively seized her hand during dictation. "I looked at the gold rings on his sleeve and kept writing with my other hand." Bewildered, the com-mander let go.

War over, with her crisp new economics and political science degree in hand, she applied to External Affairs. No jobs for women in External, the Ottawa mandarins told her. She settled for more typing at *Maclean's* magazine and the University of Toronto, then for a long stint in public relations with Imperial Oil. Some twenty years after the war, her persistence paid off: she became the travel editor of the *Financial Post*.

Gene Rowe Tingley, then of St. Thomas, wanted to be a lawyer. "I have absolutely no use for lady lawyers," her father announced. "You can be a schoolteacher, a nurse, or a missionary."

Gene rejected all of those and went into advertising sales. Her father was appalled, but she loved it.

"My father insisted that I take teaching," says Fran Murray Peacock, who grew up in Fredericton. "He said, 'What good is a B.A. going to be to you when your husband leaves you a widow with four children?'" She qualified as teacher *and* got her B.A. in history, but married and never used either.

A fifties report from the UN secretary-general, obviously written by a man, said the working world was good training for a wife or mother: "It may make her more conscious of her looks, deportment and speech." All the same, many employers were wary of married women. They had bothersome habits, such as getting pregnant, leaving the job because they couldn't find babysitters, wanting to take holidays at the same time as their husbands. Some employers, including certain school boards, actually forbade married women on staff. Couples desperately needing a combined income sometimes concealed their marriage, wife living with her parents, husband living with his.

"It's the way it was," says Madeleine Townsend Cranston of Victoria, explaining why she gave up her nursing career to marry Peter, a civilian pilot. "If I'd had more of a feminist attitude, I suppose I could have been upset about that. But, well, I was pretty desperately in love, and wherever Peter's work was going to take him, that's where I would be. There were lots of things that women should have expected in those days, and didn't."

Lillian Dunn of Calgary bucked the trend, getting a B.Sc. in honours math and an M.A. in meteorology. However, along the way she visited a farm for the first time ever and fell in love with her girlfriend's brother, Cyril Flint. She worked a year at the Edmonton weather office, then married. "My guiding principle had been, never marry a farmer. So much for life's hopes and objectives!" But she raised seven fine children, a lot more rewarding than making weather maps.

Elizabeth Rudge Tucci tried to break the mould. Her father allowed that university education was not "wasted" on a girl, because it made her a better mother. With no imminent plans for motherhood, Elizabeth studied modern languages and literature at the University of Toronto. She came out with French, Spanish, and Italian, spent eighteen glorious globetrotting months as a stewardess for American Airlines, then married and quit. "My husband didn't like the idea of my flying away for two weeks with eight men. I can't imagine why!"

Mary Matthews majored in psychology and worked for the Metro Toronto Children's Aid Society. "Then I got married and, of course, that was the end of the career," says the now-divorced Mary Greey, a successful psychotherapist. "At the time it was perfectly logical. It's what all my friends did. I never had envisioned myself working and being a mother, and I certainly wanted to be a mother."

Dr. Mary Wright, from an accomplished Ontario family (a brother is Don Wright, who in 1957 founded and led the famed Don Wright Singers), deliberately *didn't* marry, because "I couldn't bear to lose my freedom." She had spent two engrossing wartime years in England with the Canadian Children's Service, helping train teachers for nursery and early-education classes. Back home, she earned her Ph.D. and headed the University of Western Ontario's department of psychology for ten years.

Her father mentioned marriage only once, when she was setting off for graduate school. "I don't know why you're doing this," he complained. "It seems to me you're going to get married to one of these guys coming around. I'll give you a thousand dollars now and you get a hope chest." Mary said she'd rather have the thousand dollars for education.

"If you married, you became your husband's wife and lost your identity, and you really had to love a guy one *hell* of lot," she says. "The ones who wanted to marry me were not that interested in anything I was doing."

Despite all the road blocks, working women were a steadily increasing presence. In 1951, said the *Labour Gazette*, 23.6 per cent of Canada's nearly five million females over fourteen were in the labour force, a modest increase over 1941. But they earned only 50 to 60 per cent as much as the men.

Around the beginning of the fifties, the average man in manufacturing earned $45.73 a week; the average woman, $25.91. Gene Rowe, before quitting her job in advertising to marry Merle Tingley, earned sixty-five dollars a week – but men she trained on the job were earning eighty-seven. Elizabeth Rudge Tucci, before joining American Airlines, worked for a life-insurance company. At the time, a Bachelor of Arts degree was prized. "I was paid thirty dollars a week, a whole magnificent two dollars more than girls who'd gone through secretarial school and actually had business skills. Boys right out of high school got forty-five dollars a week – for being men."

Equal-pay acts were passed in some provinces in the early fifties but a writer in *Saturday Night* commented, "It did not usher in the millennium. Some school boards still advertise for men and women teachers at different rates. The labour unions still sign agreements providing for different wages with the higher scale in favour of the men."

But as *Canadian Business* summed it up with ill grace in 1954, "Whether working wives are a good or a bad thing is a moot point. In today's tight labour market, the working wife, whether she is liked or not, appears to be a built-in feature of our economy."

By late 1956, *Maclean's* was a trifle more generous: "Today even the most reactionary has come however reluctantly to understand

that a woman is much more than a wife or privileged domestic."
She may also be mayor of a large city, senator, prospector, engineer, scientist, labour leader, or even a cab driver or professional
wrestler, the magazine said.

Or, they might have added, bookseller. In Calgary, Evelyn
Orser de Mille worked in Eaton's book department for eleven
years, decided she could do it better than they did, opened her
own store, and became a local legend. In 1997 she and De Mille
Technical Books were still going strong, in one of the most merciless kinds of retailing.

But the working woman had another cross to bear.

Woes of the Working Mother

Marilyn McFadden thinks that working mothers of her generation carried "all sorts of guilt loads." Indeed, the load was colossal compared to the guilt of today's mother in the workforce.
Her fifties counterpart was much more of a rarity; even in 1960,
Gallup found that only 4 per cent of men and 5 per cent of
women approved of women working outside the home if they
had children – and they had fewer support systems.

Daycare as we know it was non-existant. Working mothers
would scrabble to find a nursery school, friend, or relative
willing to take the children all day, or had to risk farming them
out to unqualified strangers. Some placed newspaper advertisements seeking a "boarding home" for their kids. Some of the
landladies of those places so badly neglected their little charges
that the Children's Aid Society became alarmed.

Bone-weariness from a double career and the resentfulness
of mates is not an eighties or nineties phenomenon, either.
Working women, Sidney Katz reported in 1951 in *Maclean's*,
were often exhausted from coming home to a second full job

of housekeeping, and some husbands were bitter because their wives were challenging the Big Enchilada's role as primary breadwinner.

"I often felt that I probably wasn't as good a mother as I should have been," says Marion Pratt of Tillsonburg. She worked part-time as a nurse around two pregnancies and went back full-time in 1972 when her daughter and son were ten and eight respectively. Husband Bill was supportive, but "people were very quick to tell you that you shouldn't be working if you had children. So you carried that kind of guilt all the time."

Elizabeth Tucci is glad she stayed home when her children were small. "It's much better for them. What I regretted later was that nobody clued me in to the fact that I might have to earn my own living some day. That if the marriage didn't work . . . well, you didn't even think that if it didn't work you could leave."

When she did divorce after twenty years of marriage, she paid a price – as did many of her fifties contemporaries – going back to a workplace revolutionized by technology.

"I was like a dinosaur," Tucci says. "I came back to offices with phones that I didn't know how to work. The last time I'd worked in an office, they had the old plug-in switchboard, like Lily Tomlin's Ernestine routine."

STAND BY YOUR MAN
(OR KNEEL, IF THAT'S WHAT HE LIKES)

This excerpt, from a 1950s home-economics guide for Ontario schools, demonstrates how budding "homemakers" were taught to greet a husband – should they be so lucky as to land one – upon his daily return from work.

– Plan your tasks with an eye on the clock. Finish or interrupt them an hour before he is expected. Your anguished cry, "Are you home already?" is not exactly a warm welcome.

– Plan ahead, even the night before, to have a delicious meal – on *time*. This is a way of letting him know that you have been thinking about him and are concerned about his needs. Most men are hungry when they come home and the prospects of a good meal are part of the warm welcome needed.

– Take 15 minutes to rest so you will be refreshed when he arrives. Touch up your makeup, put a ribbon in your hair and be fresh looking. He has just been with a lot of work-weary people. Be a little gay and a little more interesting. His boring day may need a lift.

– Make one last trip through the main part of the house just before your husband arrives, gathering up school books, toys, paper, etc. Then run a dustcloth over the tables. Your husband will feel he has reached a haven of rest and order.

– Take just a few minutes to wash the children's hands and faces (if they are small), comb their hair and, if necessary, change their clothes. They are little treasures and he would like to see them playing the part.

– At the time of his arrival, eliminate noise of washer, dryer, dish washer or vacuum. Try to encourage the children to be quiet.

– Greet him with a warm smile and act glad to see him.

– Don't greet him with problems or complaints. Don't complain if he's late for dinner. Count this as minor compared with what he might have gone through that day.

– Have him lean back into a comfortable chair or suggest he lie down in the bedroom. Have a cool or warm drink ready for him. Arrange his pillow and offer to massage his neck and shoulders and take off his shoes. Speak in a soft soothing pleasant voice. Allow him to relax – to unwind.

– You may have a dozen things to tell him, but the moment of his arrival is not the time. Let him talk first.

– Never complain if he does not take you out to dinner or to other places of entertainment. Instead, try to understand his world of strain and pressure, his need to be home and relax.

Making It in a Man's World

Over the past two years I have met many remarkable women of our generation. Many pursued the honourable occupation of wife and mother, although not always by choice. Some tackled the male establishment on its own turf. These three made it with drive, talent, and another advantage that many of their sisters lacked: supportive parents and, particularly, a father who believed women were people.

At eighty, Helen Margison still shows the fire and vigour that took her into some of the highest boardrooms in Canada. She needed it.

"It was very, very tough for young women in the forties and fifties," she says in her Toronto condominium. "I don't remember any of us having ambitions aside from hoping desperately that we would be able to support ourselves." But Margison's father, E. Percy MacDonald, differed from the norm. "He just assumed I would do well," she remembers fondly.

A middle manager with a large manufacturing company, MacDonald told his five children, "Every one of you will get the education that you can handle. Wherever you want to go, that's fine."

At university Helen studied political science and economics with extra courses in sociology. With other students she did legwork for an inquiry into Toronto sweatshops that employed young women in the needle trade at long hours and in shocking conditions. "It was an eye-opener. Young women of my age, practically chained to their sewing machines, arms covered with rashes from the material they were working with." Out of the project came a "white label" designation for clothing made in factories certified as having decent working conditions.

In the mid-thirties she helped research a Toronto slum-clearance project. She found families in downtown Toronto living on dirt floors. "They defecated in one hole and had fire in another. A hole in the ceiling took the smoke away. There'd be perhaps an orange crate for furniture." From this, ultimately, came a public housing project known as Regent Park.

From then on, although she started out in personnel with Canadian Industries Limited, the love of Margison's life — aside from her children — was social work. She spent years with the YWCA, ultimately as vice-president, then with the United Way, where she ended up as vice-president for Canada. Her energy and drive brought her onto as many as six boards of directors at a time, including the Industrial Acceptance Corporation.

"There were certainly men who would just as soon not have had a woman around. But the big thing I brought was my experience with the social-services scene."

She once was offered a seat on the board of a leading bank. Plenty of men in her previous posts had been twitchy about taking direction from a woman. But, Margison says, the bankers just didn't listen. They seemed delighted to have a woman on board, as an adornment.

When she attempted to advise on an important issue, her opinion was not enthusiastically received. So she quit. Activist friends asked, "Why would you get off when it was so hard for a woman to get on?"

"I won't be a token," Margison told them. She joined Bell Canada's board, then became a founding director of Bell Canada

Enterprises. It was a happy fit. Bell was welcoming women into its higher echelons. She stayed until she retired at the age of seventy-two. At eighty she still receives, and enjoys, books on management for Christmas and talks over business problems with her sons.

"I am now doing what the Chinese say you do at this stage," concludes Margison. "Which is 'make your soul.'"

For Lillian McGregor, who is Ojibwa, the hurdle was not so much a man's world as the *white* man's world. She forced herself to enter it, and succeeded at a time when resources for and understanding of native people were virtually non-existent.

Lillian spoke no English until she started grade school at age seven. She was an apt student in all subjects, in part because of her remarkable father's example. She "always wanted to know things," and her father always found time to answer her questions.

Augustine McGregor was never idle. He obtained the postal franchise for Birch Island, site of the Whitefish River Indian reserve. He started a small store, selling such staples as flour, sugar, lard, and candy. He operated a couple of gasoline pumps for the summer tourist trade and sold worms and tadpoles for bait. He ploughed a field on their rocky island and raised vegetables for the winter root cellar. He took a correspondence course in electricity, wired their house, and lit it with wind power. In the evenings he was always whittling toys for the children or reading.

Lillian and her nine brothers and sisters were cast in his mould. "That's what he instilled in us; that you have to work for a living." Native children had a tendency to shyness; her father encouraged her to speak up when asked. "Don't tell a lie," he said. "Speak the truth. If you don't know anything, say so."

She was one of the first in her community to finish grade eight. Augustine drove her and her cousin the eighteen miles to Little Current to write the high-school-entrance exams. She passed with honours. To go on in high school, she would have to commute from home each day or enter a residential school. Neither was appealing.

During summer vacations Lillian had worked as a maid at a neighbouring summer resort. Now a vacationing couple hired her as a nanny for their two small sons. When summer ended they invited her to live with them in Toronto, care for their home and children for pay, and go to school.

It was a wrenching decision. The McGregors were a devoted family, and Toronto seemed as distant as the stars. They would not be able to afford frequent visits or phone calls. But Lillian desperately wanted more schooling.

Her parents checked out the Torontonians – lawyer George Gale (later to be a chief justice of Ontario) and his wife – and liked them. That autumn she made the long, frightening pilgrimage to the city. She was very lonely but, being Augustine's daughter, always busy. The Gale home was full of wonders: gleaming appliances, water from taps, flush toilets. She learned to prepare and serve meals in city fashion. At the children's bedtime she read them stories and nursery rhymes (which she'd never heard before), improving her English vocabulary.

At school, being relatively light-skinned, Lillian had only one nasty racial encounter. In the gym changing room one day, a girl said, "Your hair is so black!"

"Yes, because I'm Indian." Instantly Lillian regretted using the word that she has come to abhor.

"You mean you're from India?"

Lillian explained.

"Get away from me!" the other squealed. "We don't like Indians!"

The class seemed about to turn against Lillian, but a wise teacher sat the white students down for a talk about races and nipped their prejudice in the bud.

"It was such a tough lesson for that generation to accept that there were [races] other than white people in the world," Lillian says now.

Twice in four years, Augustine and Victoria managed visits to Toronto, at great expense to them. (The Gales took them into their home and showed them the city sights.)

Lillian's sister June also came down for school and to work for a white family. Sometimes the sisters walked downtown on their days off. Once, wearing their dark hair braided and coiled atop their heads, they encountered a gang of young people who, in a peculiar twist of prejudice, yelled, "Get away!"

"Who? Us?"

"Yeah, you Jews!"

They met other native girls, began rendezvousing in a local restaurant, then rented a meeting room in the YWCA. In time they had a club for lonely native people, the nucleus of today's thriving Native Canadian Centre in Toronto.

On Saturdays Lillian began volunteering as a candy-striper at Toronto General Hospital. She decided to be a nurse, despite the prospect of four more rigorous years of training. She chose St. Michael's Hospital, because she liked the name ("St. Michael was the big angel," she told Mrs. Gale, who helped guide her into the career).

During her second year of training, she went home for a visit. She'd had her long black hair cut and permed. She wore red nail polish and lipstick. When she got off the train, her father exclaimed, "Lillian, is that *you*?"

He waited until they were home to get the rest off his chest:

"Why did you cut your hair?"

"It was hard to wash."

"Nothing's too hard," her father said sternly. "Look at your mom. She's never had her hair cut!" Victoria wore it wrapped in a bun.

"Well, I can't be like Mom."

"You're right," Augustine said, "but we wanted you to keep a little bit of what you are!"

He needn't have worried. Lillian went to church every Sunday. For a long time she wouldn't dance close to a man for fear it would make her pregnant. Ultimately she married a white man and had three sons. She had a long, successful career as a visiting nurse with the St. Elizabeth order, later worked in a nursing home for seniors, and retired at sixty-six.

Now, at seventy-three, and despite angina, she's a director on the boards of Nishnawbe Housing and the Native Canadian Centre in Toronto. She's a member of the centre's Elders and Traditional Teachers Council. She's involved with the native people's parish of St. Vincent de Paul Church and is elder-in-residence for native students at the University of Toronto. (She dislikes the term "elder," preferring "Grandmother" or "Auntie.") She talks to the students about sexuality, abuse, drugs, alcohol, health – anything that worries them. She answers their questions the way her father answered hers, sixty-odd years ago.

And in 1996 she won one of four Outstanding Achievement awards for volunteer service, sponsored by the Ontario government. Lillian McGregor did her father proud.

The day in 1928 when Barbara Cumming was born, her father took out an insurance policy that guaranteed her university education. In a generation where most fathers regarded educated daughters as excess baggage, Robert McIntyre Cumming, a Scot who revered learning, was treading where few men had gone before.

Barbara grew up as tall as most men, with a level gaze and a sprightly sense of humour. Her father, also tall, told her that tall people got better jobs.

"People *do* hire in their own image," Barbara Cumming Gory agrees. "You judge and evaluate someone on how they look when they walk into the room. That's one form of discrimination." She's become an expert on discrimination.

She graduated in commerce from the University of Toronto, one of eight women in a class of hundreds. As in every graduating year, recruiters from business and industry came looking for prospects. "It really shocked me that nobody wanted girls. It got to the point where we'd raise a hand and ask, 'Would girls be eligible for this job?' 'No.' Just flat out 'No.'"

She finally landed a job in Eaton's as assistant to the company economist. She earned twenty dollars a week, lived at home, and ate the fifteen-cent cheese-and-macaroni lunch in the company cafeteria. It was cosy and paternalistic. "When John David Eaton came through at Christmas, people would practically curtsey." She joined the in-house bowling league and bowled against the store detectives, who "all wore their hats and looked very ferocious." There were cheap country vacations for employees. "You could live your whole life under Eaton's umbrella."

She wanted more. "I want to be an accountant," she told her former U. of T. accounting professor.

"Forget it," he said. "It's impossible for a woman."

"Well, let's figure out a way," said Barbara, a phrase she would use often through life.

They did. She took a correspondence course without having to article with a firm (chartered-accounting firms wouldn't hire females), came out as a certified public accountant, and "ended up with a gold medal just to show them."

Along the way she met and married Hungarian immigrant Andrew Gory, sales manager for an office-supply company and strongly supportive of her chosen career as self-employed bookkeeper. Her initial clients were small firms, such as painting contractors, that didn't have enough work for a full-time accountant. She also became a fifties working mother.

"You snuck around a lot," she grins. "Good mothers didn't work." She managed the two careers with aplomb, and some hired help, and ran a successful practice for more than thirty years.

Barbara Gory still works, helping small charities that can't afford to hire an accountant. She belongs to Associated Senior Executives (aside from her, all are men retired from big corporations), which donates advice to smaller businesses. She's a Fellow of the Institute of Chartered Accountants.

Is the working woman's battle for equality won? Not yet, she says. "I don't see too many women bank presidents. But on the other hand, you have to take responsibility for your own life. It's perhaps like any other discriminated-against group; you sometimes can do better by fighting against those barriers."

She remembers once standing at a long bank of elevators in the Toronto-Dominion Centre. At the other end was a man she'd known in university. Her mind flashed back to their graduation year. He won the most prestigious job in accounting and became a senior partner with a big firm – when no firm would hire her.

"Then I thought, 'But would I really want that job? No.' I've had a lot more fun having my own practice, dealing with entrepreneurs, doing my own thing. Maybe it was fortunate that I was never given that chance. But still, I would like to have had the choice."

Choices

Today's women have one enormous edge over their mothers and grandmothers in the fifties, concludes Mary Greey. "We never had the choice, or it felt like we didn't. We were refused that choice by our husbands or by society or by the lack of jobs or all those things. Now a woman can be in the workforce if she chooses. To me that's what women's lib is all about."

How did some of our fifties women cope with, compensate for, or overcome that lack of choice?

In London, Gene Tingley was once reminiscing with two close friends, "Maybe mumbling a bit about our husbands and their egos. Saying things like, 'Oh, what I did for my husband when we were younger!'"

She told the others, "When I think how many times in our early marriages when we wanted to walk away from it all, because our husbands were so intent on their careers, on their futures . . ."

Her friend Peggy said, "Aren't you glad you stayed?"

They all agreed. And Peggy said, "You know what that did for us? It made us strong women."

Gene muses that if she and cartoonist husband Ting had started out today with trial marriage or trial living-together as is the mode, "we would not be married. Yet it's been a wonderful life. Interesting. Frustrating." Along with raising two sons, she thinks she helped her husband's career in subtle ways. When Ting was foraging for ideas, as every creative person inevitably does, they would brainstorm together. "I would throw out subjects, enough to get that fertile and creative mind going, and he was off. And that was nice."

And where contemporary couples might throw in the towel or wage marital war, the Tingleys, with many other fifties couples, learned the art of accommodation.

"Ting sometimes calls me Pet," Gene says. "The first time our daughter-in-law Laurel heard it, she said to me, 'Are you going to take that from him?' I said, 'Oh, Laurel, don't be upset. It's his generation speaking. It's a term of endearment, and I'm not upset.'

"'But if I was your age,' I said, 'I'd smash him!'"

Beverly Watson – who as teenaged Beverly Holmes deplored and condemned World War Two – lives alone, deep in Ontario cottage country. Her chalet-style home of varnished logs smelling deliciously of pine looks down upon Pigeon Lake, near Buckhorn.

As we talked over sandwiches, her story unfurled. Beverly, after playing the standard role of wife and mother, grappled her way to a treasured independence.

After an arts degree and teachers' college, she taught for two years. Then she married and, heeding fifties protocol, quit work to raise a family. For a while the newness of marriage and children kept her occupied. "Then things weren't so new any more."

Her husband was television journalist Patrick Watson. "He was always doing exciting things, meeting exciting people, having incredible experiences. I was at home washing diapers, for heaven's sake, and he was meeting the Queen or something equivalent."

She discovered she didn't like being at home alone with children all the time. "They were my constant company. There was never time for anything but children. I found myself thinking, There's gotta be something better than this. The world was just passing me by."

With the children in public school, she took up volunteerism and for a long time worked for a women's shelter in the Ottawa area. After the divorce, she decided to go back to work full-time ("I was fifty and scared to death") and got a job at Algonquin community college as a community worker. It was fulfilling work and gave her an entrée to everything happening in the region.

Now in her late sixties, she works in the local library and revels in her autonomy. "It's taken me most of my life to learn what freedom to be yourself means, and what a valuable thing it is. I continue to be surrounded by people who have no idea what that really means. And I think, Just hurry up and find out, because there's a whole new life waiting for you!"

"I was so very happy with life," Suzanne Hamel says, thinking back to 1953. She and Louis, two years married, had a year-old daughter. Louis had a good job in the *Reader's Digest* art department, which pleased Suzanne's parents; although married to an artist, their daughter was not living in a garret.

Then she was struck down with poliomyelitis, at that time the scourge of our generation. Suddenly her choices in life – and life itself – seemed at a dead end. Within forty-eight hours she was unconscious, totally paralysed, in an iron lung. "My life held on to an electrical cord. That's how bad it was." She lay that way for ten days. Louis was constantly at her bedside.

After a month, she could move one hand slightly. She'd had a tracheotomy, and when they removed the tube she could hoarsely utter a few sounds. "Louis's being next to me most of the time I think helped me want to live."

Suzanne was in rehabilitation for five years. She started to paint, the one thing her damaged body could still manage, and took painting lessons. That, too, gave her courage to get on with life. They adopted a son. When he began school, it would have been easier – and it seemed the only option – to stay home on canes. No one would have faulted her for it. But Suzanne vowed to prove to the world and to herself that she could function and be useful.

She became co-librarian at a bilingual high school near their home, sharing the job and salary with a friend who didn't have a university degree. "The school director had a deal he could not refuse. He was getting two for the price of one."

The library was on a second floor, with no elevator. The students eagerly took turns carrying up the beautiful young librarian with the infectious smile. "They would be fighting at the bottom of the stairs at eight o'clock to see who would take her up," Louis says.

"But after three years, I had proved to myself that I could do it," Suzanne adds. She registered for more painting lessons, this time at the museum, and for five years was also a volunteer guide there (thus earning herself some additional art courses).

"There she was, guiding the people with her crutches around the entire museum," Louis says proudly.

"And then," Suzanne continues, "I wanted to do something more serious." She went back to university and got a degree in psychology. By then she and Louis were involved with the Vanier family's worldwide homes for the handicapped, each called L'Arche ("the Ark"). They visited Madame Pauline Vanier in France and came home to Montreal afire with commitment. Over four years they gave up most weekends and holidays to L'Arche near Quebec City. Suzanne helped the handicapped to communicate through drawings. Louis mended houses with hammer and saw.

Inspired by L'Arche, Suzanne studied art therapy. Getting her Master's degree "at the ripe age of fifty-odd" was the culmination of her life's dreams. Today, her kitchen wall is papered with the art of mentally ill patients who have studied and flourished under her. She began in a hospital studio, extended the work to patients in group homes, and, when the double duty became onerous (much of her time she's in a wheelchair), concentrated on her outside studio.

"Let your hand dance on the paper"

At sixty-seven, an age when some retirees while away their hours with bridge or golf, Suzanne Hamel — a blithe spirit who for forty-four years has refused to be defeated by the disability resulting from polio — offers art therapy for the mentally ill in Montreal.

I encourage them to make choices. First, the medium. "Today do you want to use watercolour, gouache, or crayons?" Then the paper. "Do you want to take paper, cardboard, coloured paper, white paper?" Imagine the choices they have. For some at the beginning it was too much; I could feel it was building up their anxiety. So I helped them slowly. After that they can decide. And you see the smile after. Wow!

And then the subject. I don't give painting lessons. I don't tell them, "Today you're going to draw this." I make them draw from their imagination. "What do you feel like drawing today?" Once it's on paper, I propose that they give it a title. A title helps to acknowledge what is on the paper.

After, I will tell them, "Do you want to talk about it? Or is this enough of a statement?" And they will tell me, "Okay, that's fine." Or else, "If you have a minute, I would like to go to your office. I need to talk."

It's good for me and it's good for them. That's what I like about this job. I'm not the expert. They are. That's what I keep telling them. "You are the expert. Trust yourself."

Some, when they come, will say, "I'm no good at drawing." I tell them, "Well, what I propose to you is to close your eyes and pick up any crayon and just let your hand dance on the paper. And after you open your eyes you will see something interesting there."

After divorce, Elsie Towson discovered that she – like thousands of other women of her generation – knew nothing about finances. Money was a husband's preserve; he held the purse strings, paid the bills, did the banking.

Elsie found herself bored, lonely, and needing money. She answered an advertisement: "Mature Women Wanted." It was for packing household effects. Corporations were sending their executives all over the map. If a man wanted promotion he went, and his wife followed as a matter of course.

Elsie liked the job. "You got picked up in the morning by a small van filled with packing material and boxes, and off you went to all sorts of beautiful homes, often with very unhappy women who did not like being moved around every two years. I've seen some real tragedies. I knew quite often that I'd end up two years down the line unpacking the same stuff. It had never been out of its boxes, because these unfortunate families knew they really couldn't put down roots."

Next Elsie led a book discussion group for seniors. It was so popular that a library invited her to work part-time, then full-time. She managed the book-mobile, a job she held until retirement, because it carried a small pension. It was important to set aside something for her old age. "Those were the glory days, when we were making something like 19 per cent on Canada Savings Bonds. I remember practically hocking the family silver so I could get some bonds and build up my RRSP. Yeah, from being a typical old country wife who'd never paid a bill and didn't know anything about finances whatsoever, I very soon sharpened up. Very liberating."

Irene Grant had a good marriage. The worst thing her husband Ted ever did, in his early years as a photographer, was turn their tiny apartment into a darkroom, putting their blankets over windows, ruining her baking pans with corrosive chemicals, and drying prints against the porcelain sides of the kitchen stove.

As a professional in great demand, Ted subsequently travelled all over Canada and beyond, often on short notice. Irene held the family together.

"If she had not been a strong woman," Ted says in Victoria, "who knows where our four kids would have gone?"

In 1946, thousands of British war brides followed their servicemen husbands to a new life in Canada, full of hope and apprehension. Canadian women grumbled that the Brits "stole" the flower of our nation's manhood. (Public Archives of Nova Scotia, H.B. Jefferson Collection)

She has, perhaps, just thrown something on to dash out to this Edmonton market in 1948 and cash in on the wonders of a Kraft products sale. "Serve yourself" was a new fascinating concept. (Provincial Archives of Alberta, GS-256)

Behind these impassive faces lurks high excitement. They've found a new place to buy consumer goods. It's the opening of a new Eaton's store in Kitchener, 1949. (The Eaton Collection at the Archives of Ontario, F229-308-0-317-1)

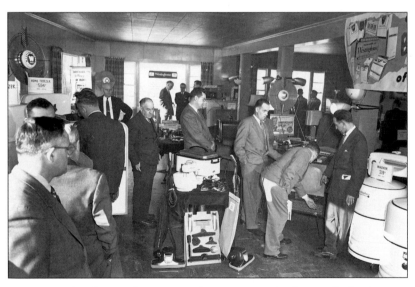

Many wonders but no bargains at this 1954 Westinghouse display in Ottawa. A washer with clothes wringer (dryers weren't yet common) at $219 and freezer at $594 represented from four- to twelve-weeks' pay for the average worker. (City of Ottawa Archives, CA-30411)

Don Mills in suburban Toronto was post-war Canada's first – and much-imitated – "planned community," with shops, schools, parks, industry, and affordable housing embraced by curving streets. (York University/Toronto Telegram Collection)

Top left: Courtly Louis St. Laurent (right), here in London with Britain's Lord Home, became our prime minister in 1948 – a refreshing, albeit unexciting, end to the interminable reign of William Lyon Mackenzie King. (Canapress Photo Service)

Top right: After chairing a Royal Commission that set the tone for post-war Canada's cultural life, Vincent Massey became Governor General. Here in Quebec City, he accepts a recording from André Payette of the Little Singers of Granby. (Canapress Photo Service

Bottom left: An ecstatic John Diefenbaker leads a minority Tory government to Ottawa in 1957 after a twenty-two-year hiatus. A year later, electors, captivated by the prairie lawyer's charisma, gave him an unprecedented majority. (Canapress Photo Service)

Bottom right: Nobel Peace Prize winner and mid-sixties prime minister, Lester "Mike" Pearson (right) meets Newfoundland premier Joey Smallwood in Ottawa. Their common ground: the Liberal party and bow-ties. (Canapress Photo Service)

By 1956 more than two million Canadians – like the Schiefner family of Milestone, Sask. – were glued to television. We enthusiastically watched everything, including what here appears to be a big rock or a giant loaf of bread. (Harrington, National Archives of Canada, PA-111390

TV gave us home-grown stars and programs, including three of Canada's most durable: Front Page Challenge (including regulars Pierre Berton, far right, and Gordon Sinclair, far left); Country Hoedown with Tommy Hunter, centre (succeeded by the Tommy Hunter Show); and comedians Wayne and Shuster. (Photos this page courtesy of the CBC)

A section of the St. Lawrence Seaway under construction in 1967. The great waterway, begun in 1954 and linking Atlantic shipping to the Great Lakes, had enormous economic impact on post-war Canada. (Canapress Photo Service)

Our wildly successful centennial-year fair, Expo 67, was for Canada a time of pride, joy, and coming-of-age. Among its dazzling exhibits and futuristic architecture: this U.S. pavilion, an immense geodesic dome. (Canapress Photo Service)

This 1967 view of Toronto's Yorkville area smacks of family. But Yorkville in the Flower Power years was also Mecca for dropouts, druggies, and runaways seeking the swinging life their square Generation M parents couldn't give them. (Globe and Mail)

"Grey Power" in action: a 1985 senior citizens' demonstration on Parliament Hill, protesting a proposed de-indexing of pensions. The government backed down – proving that seniors have teeth, and not just in a bedside water glass. (Canapress Photo Service)

With the children grown, Irene took a new run at life, study-ing nursing at age forty-four. Her fellow students called her Mom. She graduated second in the class and won the title Miss Congeniality ("Boy, somebody got *that* wrong," her husband grins). She worked twenty years until retirement.

"I give her credit," Ted says proudly.

"And I take it," says Irene.

In the thirties Kathleen Young of Souris, Manitoba – having presence, good looks, and a B.A., which in those days meant something – landed a job that would normally have gone to a man. She became advance person for Chautauqua, the then-famous road show that toured the West, Ontario, and the United States. Each night, Chautauqua, performing in tents or town halls, presented a play, a lecture, a comedy, and music at modest prices to rural and small-town people starved for entertainment.

Young earned an astonishing $32.50 a week but had to pay her own meal and hotel bills, and for a while existed on graham wafers, honey, and apples. She arranged billets for travelling players, found props for plays, signed up lecturers for the next season, and, sometimes, introduced the artists on stage.

She swept on to other jobs – booking lecture tours in the United States, working in a cocktail lounge, as a restaurant hostess, and as a beautician. The last led her to a job in England running a salon. There she married her university sweetheart from Manitoba, and they returned to Canada before World War Two broke out.

As Kathleen Foy, she was happily working in Birks in Toronto when she became pregnant. She resented having to quit work, but successfully raised four children. Then, when the marriage "got a little sticky because of alcohol," she went back to work to help support the family. She enrolled in teachers' college. "I hadn't written an exam for twenty-seven years. It was awful. I passed, but had a hard time getting a teaching job, because my B.A. commanded a higher salary than they paid the average elementary teacher."

As a teacher she was "a disaster. They gave me Grade Eight, and I was so scared and intimidated by those big kids. And they took advantage of me, knowing it was my first school." She quit teaching and studied library science. Over many years as a public librarian, her salary soared from $3,300 to $23,000 a year. After she reached sixty-five, and mandatory retirement, she worked another nine years in a private library.

Now, widowed and living alone in Montreal, Kathleen Foy still has the spunk of that long-ago Chautauqua girl. "We're all survivors," she says of our generation.

She's living proof.

Patricia Ritz Andrews's husband went into hospital with multiple sclerosis in 1960 (and later into a facility for the handicapped until his death ten years later). She was faced with a choice. She could sign over their house and go on welfare, or she could keep the house, continue working (she was a dietary clerk at Burnaby General Hospital in British Columbia), and her husband's hospital care would be covered.

For a woman with Andrews's Depression pride and work ethic it wasn't hard to decide. She opted to keep job and house and raise her son and two daughters on her own. It was not easy for the children. They were not allowed to hang out on street corners. They had chores. "I'd say, 'Gary, make a pudding for supper,' or 'Gary, peel the potatoes.' He and Judith had paper routes." All three turned out well (one writes a syndicated column, another has an M.A. in public health, another is a nutritionist).

Patricia paid off her mortgage in thirteen years. Along the way she took courses in deportment, in sewing, and in hospital-kitchen management. She had spare time because "I was neither single nor married. That was another tragedy in my life.

"I wonder how I did it. I don't look back too often. If I think about it when I wake up in the night, that's the rest of the night gone."

Helen Stauffer Collum and husband Howard lost their youngest son in a tragic highway crash in 1981. A few years later they divorced. It would be easy to say that the boy's death caused it; more likely, it laid bare and exacerbated their differences.

Howard remarried. For Helen, "The divorce liberated me. That means I wasn't my natural self in the years leading up to his departure. And that's a general indictment of marriage. I wasn't an abused wife or anything like that, but I did subject myself to many compromises against my natural feelings."

A powerhouse by nature, she has worked at up to ten jobs at a time. She teaches English as a second language, boards students in her Thornhill, Ontario, townhouse, is running hard continually.

"I've been wondering why I feel so happy," says Stauffer, who has reverted to her maiden name. "I have so many problems. My car is wearing out, I need money to pay bills. But I realize that I'm free now to be whatever it is I am. And that is a great relief."

"Something Terribly Wrong"

Moments after meeting Gwyn Griffith you are smiling. She radiates good cheer, looks years younger than sixty-five (whatever sixty-five is supposed to look like), and talks with ease and poise. No hint of the considerable obstacles or setbacks she has overcome.

Her mother died when Gwyn was ten. She had a stutter so severe that, when she said she wanted to teach some day, her Grade Ten teacher exclaimed, "You can't teach. You can't *talk*!"

Worse yet, Gwyn says, she was fat, wore glasses, and was a United Church minister's daughter. Then, in her mid-twenties, she realized she was a lesbian, the biggest handicap of all in the homophobic 1950s.

As a stutterer, she suffered the routine cruelty of other children who mimicked her or simply avoided her. She pushed on, and consistently got the best marks in class. Beginning at fourteen, she took speech therapy. It was slow and excruciatingly painful but she persisted.

Living in the manse beside the church, she and her sister felt the eyes of the congregation forever on them. The Griffith girls had to be preternaturally sweet and well-behaved. "We couldn't swear, of course. And one time a parishioner knitted me a coat with big white buttons. I hated it, but I had to wear it or she would have been upset." When she began university she stopped attending church to see how it felt. It felt bad, and she quickly went back. "The church was my family, my home."

In the early years, Gwyn Griffith expected to follow the conventional marital path. She even targeted thirty-five as the age she would marry and start a family. Her mother had married at that age, a little late for the times, but she had been a double gold-medal winner at Mount Allison University and, before marriage, national secretary of the Canadian Girls in Training for the United Church. Gwyn revered her mother's memory. She, too, wanted a career, but in social work, not the church.

Like most Canadians of her time, she thought homosexuality was "something terribly wrong." The fifties milieu was intolerant in the extreme. Males were "queers." Lurid pocket novels portrayed female "dykes" or "butches" preying on susceptible maidens.

Even now, many of our generation are, at very least, uncomfortable with the subject. According to sociologist Dr. Reginald Bibby of Lethbridge, author of *The Bibby Report: Social Trends Canadian Style*, only 27 per cent of Canadians over fifty-five approved of homosexuality in 1995. But that's a change from 1975, when only 12 per cent of that age group approved. It was rare, and refreshing, during my research to meet a few who remarked matter-of-factly that they had a gay son or daughter.

Gwyn's first lesbian relationship at twenty-five was brief and upsetting. "I knew it was an aberration of some kind, the worst kind." For years she was torn between her natural feelings and what society said was valid. Her church upbringing heightened her sense of guilt.

She compensated for all her perceived handicaps by striving harder at everything, and excelling: the top athletic award at University of Toronto's Victoria College one year, and secretary of the college athletic association; a B.A. with a psychology major and a master's in social work; director of individual services casework in the central Toronto YWCA; a fellowship to spend a year at Union Theological Seminary in New York.

Even during the sixties sexual revolution, homosexuality was barely discussed. Griffith kept her lifestyle and her inner conflicts under wraps as she rose in the YWCA hierarchy. In 1971 she become executive director of the Metro Toronto YW. Under her leadership, the Metro Y took a pro-choice stand on abortion. Although Gwyn still thought of feminists as "bra-burners," she was fully committed to the women's movement.

By now she had accepted her sexuality with a certain equanimity, yet when she left the YW in 1977, the organization – like Canadian society at large – was a long way from accepting homosexuals.

"Three or four of us on our management staff were lesbian. We only talked about it among ourselves." The YW recognized the need for sex education but was mainly concerned that women be taken seriously as sexual beings and "that marriage maybe wasn't the be-all and end-all for all women."

Gwyn earned a doctorate in education and became principal of the Centre for Christian Studies, a theological school related to both Anglican and United churches. "I was increasing in self-confidence. Yet in spite of all my accomplishments over all those years, I still didn't think I was worth very much."

After retiring from the centre in 1991 "and wondering what I would be when I grew up," she began freelancing in and around the United Church: occasional sermons, running leadership development programs, helping an occasional board of directors with its problems. Her stutter had virtually disappeared. "It just gradually got better, partly because I refused to withdraw and not talk."

And she is coming out as a lesbian. She is happily and openly in a relationship of many years' standing. For a woman of our generation, it has been difficult to admit "that this is as valid a lifestyle as any other. We've certainly got all the social analysis we need to attest to it. But it's damned hard when an eighty-two-year-old in church who thinks I'm absolutely wonderful says, 'You know, we can't have any of those kind of people in our church!'"

In her little living room in central Toronto, surrounded by plants, Griffith reads me her favourite poem, "Warning," by Jenny Joseph. It begins:

When I am an old woman I shall wear purple
With a red hat which doesn't go, and doesn't suit me.
And I shall spend my pension on brandy and summer gloves
And satin sandals, and say we've no money for butter . . .

"Well, I've started to wear purple," says the woman who once was fat and wore glasses and stuttered and dared not declare her sexuality. "I probably won't dare to do all that stuff. But I'm learning to not worry so much about what other people think."

The Politician's Wife

"I could write a book on the pleasures and pains of politics," Pemrose Whelan says. The pleasures evidently outweighed the pain. She was immersed in CCF/NDP politics long before 1946, when an Ontario socialist, Ed Whelan, came to Regina and a job with the Co-Operative Union of Saskatchewan.

Pemrose Henry, as she was then, was office secretary. Brimming with energy and efficiency, she came from a family of achievers in the southern Saskatchewan village of Shamrock. Ed arrived on her birthday. It was the nicest possible gift; they married two years later.

When Ed first ran for office in 1960, Pemrose, like every good political wife of the time, was "caught up in the pattern. Candidates' wives did thus and thus. One wasn't really consulted. It was all taken for granted – teas, meetings, accompanying one's husband. The older women steered us younger ones around."

For most of Ed's nineteen years in office, their Regina home was the constituency office and Pemrose was the volunteer unpaid staff. A born organizer and communicator, she did all his paperwork, helped him write speeches, and for many years wrote a column for the CCF newspaper, *The Commonwealth*. As the Whelan children grew older, they helped field the household's incessant phone calls.

Pemrose was Ed's campaign manager for two of his six winning campaigns. She was also party provincial vice-president for five years, chair of the federal women's committee, and appeared before the 1968 Royal Commission on the Status of Women in both provincial and federal capacities. Then she quit politics and got a degree in history.

"I doubt if I could have worked as hard as I did had I been objective about it all," Pemrose says. "But I was involved in something I believed in, associated with many fine people, and busy. Being busy is a good feeling."

Stylish Wanda Jones from Yellow Grass, Saskatchewan, was working in a Regina federal-government office when widower and war hero Frank Hamilton happened by. She liked his looks and down-to-earth ways but didn't give him a second thought – until he invited her to dinner. She rushed out and bought a "fire-engine-red pantsuit," then had last-minute qualms. Was it too flamboyant for a first date?

It was not. In due course Hamilton – then head of the Grain Commission – proposed. Just before the wedding he won the Tory nomination in southern Saskatchewan's Wood Mountain riding that would lead him into Parliament. The prospect didn't thrill Wanda, but she looked at her engagement ring and considered the options: "Political wife or old maid?"

Frank insisted on sharing the job with her, as much as the system allowed. But on life in Ottawa, Wanda Hamilton is eloquent and damning.

"To sum up the twelve years of political life, I would say I was like a trained dog. You sit, stand, and walk six paces behind. To this day I doubt that the bureaucrats have a file folder or any sort of document on what to do with a wife. When we went to Ottawa the very first time, we'd done everything together from the minute we were married. Then one word came up – caucus – and I was standing on my own."

She feels sorry for Margaret Trudeau, the flower child who shook Ottawa to its foundations. "People like Mrs. Diefenbaker and Mrs. Pearson were clones of each other. Then comes Margaret Trudeau. Nobody knew what to do with a young girl. Youth had never ever been involved in politics at that level. Then Maureen McTeer, that really did it!"

Wanda made friends with some political wives, but felt an enormous gulf between women from outlying provinces and from Ontario. "It was as though you were on a different planet. There was no communication whatsoever."

Like Frank, she enjoyed constituency work. "Yet after we first went out together with his campaign manager, and returned the next day, the manager turned around from the front seat and said 'Oh *you're* coming again?' That was women's lib in 1972. Your wife did not go with you. It was strictly a man's club."

The Hamiltons prevailed. They shared the long-distance driving around their sprawling constituency. One night, getting home at three a.m., Wanda said, "Wouldn't it be something if I had stayed home all day, you'd come home tired at this hour, and there'd be a wife saying, 'Now, what did you do all day, dear?'"

For twelve years they lived with a suitcase always packed. "So when Frank said he was going to retire, I thought, Gee, is this divorce? Is there life after politics?"

There certainly was. Most of all, she savoured her "divorce" from Fat City.

"When the TV program 'This Week in Parliament' used to come on, I couldn't handle it. I could smell the corridors. I could hear the footsteps. The doors shutting and opening. We haven't been back to Ontario since. If I never see Ottawa again, it will be way too soon."

V

"WE DO NOT LIVE IN THE OLD-FASHIONED WORLD"

Mixed Blessings

As the fifties wound down, we were getting ahead right on target. By the standards of the day, the money was rolling in. Almost 50 per cent of taxpayers in 1951 had annual incomes over three thousand dollars, versus 11 per cent in 1946. By 1953 more than 10 per cent of us were reporting incomes over five thousand dollars a year – nearly thirty times my father's annual disability pension from World War One, which in some Depression years was our sole income. By 1959 the average weekly wage was $73.47, about two-thirds more than nine years earlier.

We were whittling away our 5- and 6-per-cent mortgages, and beginning to trade in the original dollhouse bungalow for a two-storey job to fit our growing families and expectations. Our children were healthier than any generation in human history. Thanks to Dr. Jonas Salk's miraculous vaccine, the terrifying poliomyelitis was under control, after a 1952–1953 epidemic that killed more than six hundred people in Canada (and crippled thousands more, such as Suzanne Hamel). By 1965 not one child in Canada would die from polio.

Our diets were still loaded with red meat and fat. Not surprisingly, heart disease had become a major cause of death. Fortunately, the New Canadians – Czechs, Poles, Hungarians, Dutch, Italians, Yugoslavians, Ukrainians, nearly all of whom we called DPs (as in Displaced Persons) – were spicing our lives with lilting accents and exotic foods. Now we could feast on pastas, a multitude of cheeses, and delicious grainy breads that didn't bounce to the ceiling when you dropped the loaf. In rural greasy spoons, the *plat du jour* was still a hot beef sandwich drowned in yesterday's gravy, but in the city we were timidly experimenting with schnitzels, goulashes, fettuccine, spaghetti with meatballs. We carried home straw-encased Chianti bottles for candle-holders, which, once heavily encrusted with multicoloured drippings, adorned our coffee tables, the ultimate in fifties' chic.

Everywhere, visions of new expressways danced in the heads of urban planners. Canada had come out of the war with about 18,000 miles of paved rural highways and 6,200 miles of paved urban roads and streets. By 1966 we would have a grand total of 92,500 miles, of which two-thirds would be rural highways.

Inner-city parking was becoming a problem, and a measure of a car-proud society. About a hundred thousand commuters drove into downtown Vancouver each day, jostling for ten thousand parking spaces. In 1958 Toronto opened a three-million-dollar underground parking garage in City Hall square, a sensation of its time. It would eventually park 6,500 vehicles, at twenty cents an hour. This would leave a $1.60 daily dent in a working stiff's wallet, but, hey, that was the price of progress.

More wondrous still, the experts (faceless creatures whose numbers were burgeoning) said that a thousand computers – think of it! – would be at work in Canada over the next decade. Some even said that men would fly to the moon. Hard to believe, yet a clue was already at hand. One October morning in 1957, driving through some godforsaken corner of northwestern Ontario in yet another fruitless story-search to appease editor Ralph Allen of *Maclean's*, I heard on my radio the eerie *beep-beep* of Russia's Sputnik. Mankind had reached into outer space. With millions of others, I felt awed and small.

All this was a forward-march of achievement that had not existed in the thirties, and in the forties had been dedicated solely to war. But there was sour with the sweet, which, given our thirties' upbringing and our faith in Murphy's Law, surprised us not one bit.

For instance, television was less benign than we expected. No, we were not wallowing in TV gore and fornication as in the nineties. And yes, Desi Arnaz still loved Lucy; Ed Sullivan still dished up a weekly chowder of acrobats, comics, crooners, and performing animals. Everything was copacetic in Beaver Cleaver's house, as long as the family left everything to Beaver. But in our own homes – so the ubiquitous experts said – sinister forces were sneaking subliminal messages into our TV commercials. Subliminal? It meant messages flashed on screen in one three-thousandth of a second, or some such preposterous speed, supposedly making us do things we hadn't planned to do, such as buy a certain brand of perfume or booze because the hidden message equated it with power or sex.

The Americans, not content to work this insidious trick on humans, were allegedly playing mind games with dogs. A message was said to be built into a certain dog-food commercial, causing Spot to bark wildly, causing his master in turn to rush out and buy that brand. It was all a cruel hoax. Dogs were *not* mad for the doggie chunks as advertised; the come-hither yelp of *another dog* was embedded in the soundtrack, at a pitch audible only to Spot. Nobody asked why Spot was watching TV in the first place, instead of being out chasing cars.

Our economy was flourishing, but, as the 1957 Gordon Royal Commission warned, control of Canada was slipping out of our hands. Within less than a decade, the total foreign investment in our country would almost double to thirty-four billion dollars. Nearly three-quarters of it would be American. By the mid-sixties the United States would own 90 per cent of our auto manufacturing, 70 per cent of our oil and gas, 50 per cent of our mining and smelting.

Later, economic nationalists would castigate the Americans and offshore investors, but the foreigners were simply seizing opportunities that we let go by default. We needed British pounds and Yankee dollars to develop our resources, and we were too cautious, too immersed in our personal lives, to invest in our country.

Our little corner stores, once the essence of neighbourhood community life, were under siege. The *Financial Post* recorded the inexorable march of the chains. They comprised a mere 4 per cent of actual store numbers, yet already they accounted for more than one-third of the volume of sales. By 1958 the chains were supplying 44 per cent of our national food bill (about three billion dollars' worth). Soon, the *Post* predicted, supermarkets would sell clothing as well as food. At the time it seemed like more progress, which everyone said was good.

Awful things were happening to music. For those of us weaned on the silky melodies of Glenn Miller, Tommy Dorsey, Benny Goodman, Bing, and Old Blue Eyes, the new music and musicians were sacrilege. Early in the decade, guy groups such as the Crew Cuts, the Four Lads, and the Diamonds had elbowed aside our dreamy old tunes with their *wah-a-wah, woo-a-woo*. But at least they were clean-cut youths with ties, fresh shirts, and normal haircuts.

By 1956 our teenyboppers were screaming for a sulky-looking ex-truck driver with long oily sideburns, he who, it was said, Ed Sullivan's cameras would reveal only from the waist up, because of lewd things he was doing with his hips. Elvis somebody. What kind of name was Elvis? Nevertheless, old Ed, right there on national television – shoulders hunched, face contorted, arms flailing in his patented convulsive style – pronounced Presley one of the finest young men in the land. Elvis looked suitably humble, but he knew it was merely a sop for middle-aged America. The kids, who bought his records and loved his pelvic thrust, already idolized him.

Presley and a geeky-looking Bill Haley and His Comets were harbingers of rock and roll. Soon its cacophony would boom from the new stereophonic records, each costing about a dollar more than the old mono but worth every penny to our deafened young. Aficionados of noise were also buying up hi-fidelity equipment. Hi-fi was a form of sickness, *Financial Post* contributor Brian Cahill suggested, tongue-in-cheek and fingers-in-ears. Hi-fi enthusiasts, he wrote, were "victims of dark compulsions. . . . They are, in short, sick people who need sympathy, understanding, psychiatric care. . . . Some have even torn down whole walls of the home in order to accommodate ten foot horns. . . . The final stages of hi-fi addiction come when the victim becomes preoccupied with and dependent upon strange recorded sounds rather than upon music itself . . . rains, thunderstorms, running water . . ."

The family as we had known it was under assault. For our parents, and for most of us in early marriage, divorce was unthinkable. "It wasn't talked about, or no more than whispered about, like cancer," says Elizabeth Tucci.

In 1944 there were only 3,827 divorces in Canada. Now it was becoming a fact of life, given some imprudent wartime and postwar marriages: a record-setting 8,213 divorces in 1947, another 6,978 in 1948. We discovered that Canadian divorce laws were archaic and heartless. Yet, as *Maclean's* Ottawa correspondent Blair Fraser reported, reform was too hot a potato for mid-fifties politicians.

Quebec and Newfoundland had no divorce courts; people there had to petition the Senate. Elsewhere, adultery was the main grounds for divorce, sometimes with odd additions: in New Brunswick and Prince Edward Island, frigidity and impotence; in British Columbia, Ontario, the Prairies and Territories, rape, sodomy, and bestiality; in Nova Scotia, impotence, consanguinity (blood relationship), and cruelty. One lawyer estimated there were at least fifty thousand deserted spouses in Canada in 1956, yet nowhere was desertion grounds for divorce.

The mechanics of it were demeaning. A couple desperate enough often had to feign adultery. Usually the husband arranged to be "caught" by witnesses and cameras in a hotel room with a half-clad woman (a prostitute or anyone else willing to play out the charade). Civilized divorce was still a decade away.

Whether families were torn by marital strife or not, they were growing smaller and less authoritarian. Was that a bad trend? Dr. Robert Brockway, a Unitarian minister, pondered the question and came up with comfortable platitudes.

"In the end I suspect we shall have a much better kind of family than the old-fashioned authoritarian one," he wrote in *Maclean's*. "We shall find, I suspect, more ways of having the best of both worlds given time and maturity of experience. . . . It is not surprising therefore that we have not achieved Utopia."

In any case, Brockway concluded, "We can't go back to the old-fashioned family because we do not live in the old-fashioned kind of world."

The reverend certainly had *that* right.

AN OLD-FASHIONED TEACHER

In her Chatham, Ontario, home on an autumn afternoon, Marie Antaya — tiny, ninety-two, but full of fire — tells how she taught school for thirty years until the early sixties. Even then, her kind of teaching was becoming an anachronism.

My first school was about ten miles west of Chatham, one room, red brick. I was paid $1,025 a year. Four years later I got into a two-room school. I walked three-quarters of a mile through mud. I hitched up my long skirt and pinned it at the back under my coat and carried a clean pair of stockings.

There were no lamps or hydro in school, just windows on both sides. If the outdoor light was poor, it was hard to see writing on the blackboard. In the later years I had forty to forty-five students, eight to ten grades, and worked every night until midnight. I wish we had some teachers nowadays that would teach the kids something; they can't read, can't spell, no good at number work. Then, of course, about the time I quit, they started this nonsense that you weren't to touch a child.

They used to say, "She's so crabby." I don't think I was crabby, I was just strict. I insisted on things being done the way I wanted. I'd make them do their work in rough, then I took the books home every night and checked them. Next morning I told them how to correct it, then copy the finished work in their "good" binder. The inspector complimented me on the state of the workbooks.

There'd be one smart-alec in every school. I generally put him at the back, because if you sat him at the front he'd put on a show. I didn't use the strap too much, but sometimes some of the smart-alecs needed a good trouncing. That's all you needed to do. You could hear a mouse after that.

I think it's awful that a teacher can't lay a hand on a child today. The teacher doesn't have a chance.

Farewell to the Small Farm

The "most pathetic and puzzling figure" in Canada, I wrote in *Maclean's* in 1956, was the small farmer. Once the builder and backbone of Canada, our country personified, he was now on the social and economic fringe, his numbers declining, his influence and income waning. Nowhere was this more evident than in Saskatchewan, the heartland of Canadian agriculture.

Small farms were simply becoming obsolete. Mechanized agriculture was hitting its stride. A small farmer with the then-common half-section of land (320 acres), or even twice that amount, couldn't produce enough to pay for expensive machinery, particularly when fluctuating wheat prices and a restrictive marketing system governed his sales.

Between 1939 and 1951, Saskatchewan's rural population decreased by nearly two hundred thousand. Thousands moved to urban centres in search of nine-to-five jobs, electricity, indoor plumbing, and a wider choice of pastimes. Many were farmers' children who had watched their parents toil for a lifetime before and during the Depression – and for what? Of the 120,000 remaining farmers, 20 per cent lived away from the farm all or part of the time, usually commuting from neighbouring villages or towns that offered more creature comforts, a broader social life, and handier schooling. The rural landscape, always empty to the untutored eye, grew emptier.

But for those farmers who stayed to ride the tidal wave of change and survive, average income rose from $2,118 in 1946 to $3,869 in 1953. By 1951 more than half of the remaining farms Canada-wide were electrified. A Nova Scotia man gave his chickens electric light and electrically heated water; the hens rewarded him with 50 per cent more eggs. Farm women began to get refrigerators, deep freezes, electric stoves, vacuum cleaners, toasters, washers, water heaters – luxuries undreamed of by my mother and her neighbours a generation before. A good life, for those who could adapt.

Ted Turner grew up on a family farm, witnessed the revolution of the fifties and sixties, moved from the land to other jobs, and looks back now with a measure of detachment and affection.

During World War Two he was a teenager doing a man's work on his father's farm near Maymont, northwest of Saskatoon. Most able-bodied men were at war, and Turner's father had 960 acres (a large holding then), twenty beef cattle, a few dairy cows, and three hundred hogs.

Ted wanted to be a veterinarian, but there was no money to send him to college in Guelph, Ontario. Instead he took a two-year diploma course in agriculture at nearby University of Saskatchewan, graduating in 1948. That year he wanted to buy some land that would double their acreage, but his father advised against it. "Best to look after what we have," he said. In retrospect it was poor advice, but Turner accepted and made the best of it.

His father retired in 1950. Ted married Patricia Melville Bright (Mel for short), whom he'd known since Grade Three.

They took a ten-day camping honeymoon, then immersed themselves in farming. Mel had been working as a bank teller.

"I rescued her and turned her nine-to-four job into six-thirty a.m. to ten p.m.," Turner says. "Very nice of me!"

She kept her bank job, briefly, but when the first Saskatchewan blizzard closed the roads, she became a full-time farm wife. That meant housework, helping with yard chores, sometimes hauling grain or driving a combine, with long spells of isolation.

Already the neighbourhood population was dwindling. In 1940 there had been nineteen other farm sites within two miles of the Turner place; by 1950, there were ten. In the early fifties, the Turners and their neighbours still lived much as Ted, I, and thousands of others had lived on the farms of our childhood. No electricity, no plumbing, no passable roads in winter. The Turners used gasoline lamps and an outdoor privy.

Then life began to change, partly because Turner became an agent of change. As the community's youngest farmer, he persuaded his neighbours to help build an all-weather road into town. They chopped (by hand) five miles of brush lining the route that for years had created a snow trap. The municipality agreed to grade it. As a decent road emerged, twelve farmers led by Turner bought a snowplough. He drove it, when needed.

Electrical power was reaching into the rural West. Turner organized his neighbours again and worked out arrangements with SaskPower. "On July 31, 1952, we pulled a chain in the house and light came on!" Forty-four years later in his handsome Regina home, he still savours that moment. "To me that was one of the highlights of my life. Just like that, our whole lifestyle flipped over."

Right away they installed an electric motor on the washing machine and cream separator. Soon they had a milking machine. Small things, you might say, unless you have ever hand-cranked a washing machine or separator, or milked six or a dozen cows by the squeeze-pull method.

The Turners became highly self-sufficient. Ted doubled the beef herd, cut back on hog production, and added many more dairy cows. Half their income came from livestock; half from wheat. The chickens laid eggs for the table and for sale. The cows supplied cream for sale – it bought groceries and put gasoline in the car – and skim milk to feed the pigs. The pigs provided meat and more income. In 1958, sales from the beef cattle built a septic tank and put plumbing throughout the house.

"We were lucky, because so many of our wants were available within a span of years," Turner reflects. They couldn't afford a TV until 1957, and, typical of our generation, wouldn't buy it on credit.

Their lives changed again that year, when Ted became a local delegate to the Saskatchewan Wheat Pool. It was a natural evolution; his father had been a staunch Pool supporter. Three years later, Ted was elected a director, a job so involving that one year he was away from home for 115 evenings (Mel kept count). It stole time from family and farm. He reduced his livestock.

It would soon have to be a choice between farm and Pool. Turner loved farming and enjoyed his community and friends. Rural life was good for their three daughters.

"It wasn't an easy decision. But I was kind of a weird individual. When I hired seasonal help, I would sooner put that person on the tractor and let him do the summer fallowing while I fixed fences. I've always said my back was stronger than my head."

Truth was, he enjoyed physical labour, and the chance to work side by side with his children. "What is pleasure to us?" he asks, referring to our generation. "*Work* is pleasure. My greatest fear is not having something to do."

As well, Turner was gregarious, and the neighbourhood population was subtly dwindling. Not only was the number of farms decreasing, but rural families were averaging about three children instead of the five or six of a generation earlier. "I never got over the sense of isolation that you have on a farm. For some people, that's the biggest attraction. To me it wasn't." The Wheat Pool fulfilled his need for people.

In July 1966, he phoned Mel from the city: "I've been elected as the first vice-president of the Pool!" Mel understood, and was pleased for him. But no one at home could eat lunch that day, and their hired man was in tears. They rented the farm, moved to Regina, and the Pool became their life for the next two decades.

In three years Turner moved up to president. He thinks the organization enhanced rural pride. "When I started travelling for the Pool, you saw a lot of ramshackle buildings and messy farmyards. By the time I was through, the housing level had improved dramatically. A lot of beautiful farmsteads. People were obviously taking a great deal of pride in their operation. I like to think that because the Pool was there, farmers were better able to do those things."

After that he became chancellor of the University of Saskatchewan. But through all the years away, his heart stayed close to the land.

Has the disappearance of the old ways left a void in rural life? Turner thinks so.

"The family farm, where you had a little of everything, was about as good a training ground as you could get. Everybody had their jobs. There was a variety of things to do. You learned something about animal husbandry, plant husbandry, mechanics, economics. You had a full university course right there on the farm. Anyone fortunate enough to be raised in that circumstance had a good grounding."

Turner says it also fostered co-operation between neighbours. "I had a neighbour half a mile down the road. He was older than me, closer to my father's age, yet we ended up owning all our haying equipment together. We learned to work together. At the end of the year we never ever stopped to say, 'Well you owe me this or I owe you that.' We did the work that was required on the two farms and helped each other. It was fantastic."

It was one aspect of the so-called good old days that really was good.

Changing Politics

During World War Two, 66 per cent of us told Gallup that we approved of that supreme pragmatist and crystal-ball gazer, Prime Minister William Lyon Mackenzie King. In the immediate postwar years, we remained extraordinarily tolerant of our elected leaders. Even non-Liberals had kind words for dignified Louis St. Laurent and Lester "Mike" Pearson, with his superior intelligence disguised behind a self-deprecating manner and dorky bow-tie.

Were politicians better then? Stanley Westall, a reporter for Canadian Press and the Toronto *Globe and Mail* in the fifties and early sixties, says no: "I ran across a spectrum of politicians, from men of great integrity to rascals."

Edmonton's Ted Byfield, editor of the news magazine *Western Report*, agrees. But David MacDonald of Kingston, also a journalist, is one of several who flatly disagree.

"I think the overall calibre of people we now have in our cabinets is much lower than it was," he says.

In earlier years we were less aware of politicians' peccadillos. Journalists were more restrained (witness the non-reporting of John F. Kennedy's sexual escapades). Today, the media, although not necessarily better, are far more confrontational. "A press that had been extremely servile and unresourceful became not a lot more resourceful but critical and nasty and insulting," MacDonald says.

Sociologist Reginald Bibby notes that since the sixties we've steadily become more demanding of such institutions as government: "We don't hold them in awe; we have come to expect performance and accountability." His *Bibby Report* found that by 1985 less than one-third of Canadians had high confidence in federal or provincial governments, and, by 1990, that proportion was down to 22 to 25 per cent.

Was our generation politically naive? Not true, Byfield wrote in 1997. He remembers as a child hearing family conversations about King and R. B. Bennett, among others. "The tone was never one of adulation . . . and the expectations for virtuous conduct as doubtful for the politicians as for assorted members of the family." Yet they could still revere their politicians, he maintains. Today, "we elect our leaders, swoon over them briefly until the flaws begin to appear, then denounce them as frauds and consign them to villainy." By today's measure, if a politician is not entirely good then he must be entirely bad, Byfield says.

More likely, I think, it has to do with an unquestioning respect for authority figures of all kinds. We had it; young people today do not. We might not have liked politicians, but we accorded their office a grudging esteem.

"Mackenzie King, who was loved by nobody, was entitled to respect because he was the prime minister," agrees MacDonald. "The whole nation stuck out its chest when Mike Pearson won the Nobel Prize. And then we started making fun of the way he talked."

It's a rich or foolish country that twice rejected a Robert Stanfield for its leader, MacDonald adds. Stanfield's honesty and intelligence meant nothing to a Canada increasingly enamoured of TV sound bites, opinion polls, and big hair. He wasn't glib; he lacked charisma; and then he was gone, leaving our political scene poorer.

As the way of doing politics changed (if you accept, as I do, that it *has* subtly changed), Frank Hamilton, by his own account, went from high hopes to political dinosaur. Maybe it was partly a matter of charisma, although he certainly appealed to the Canada of 1944 when he returned from overseas with his bride, Mary Barlow of Manchester.

"The very best of manhood personified in his six feet, with a shock of hair the colour of a field of waving wheat and eyes as blue as any prairie skies," an Ottawa newspaper burbled.

Hamilton dutifully went out on War Bond drives, as was the lot of many servicemen with impressive records. A twice-decorated war hero who could speak coherently was political gold. In 1945, still in uniform, Hamilton ran as a federal Tory in the Saskatchewan riding of Wood Mountain. He lost once, lost again, and finally won in 1972. Then he discovered the frustration of the Ottawa backbencher.

"You go down there full of high hopes," he says in his home in Mazenod, Saskatchewan. "What a laugh! It doesn't work out that way, or it didn't for me. I was going to change the world, but found myself more and more just doing the little bits and pieces."

He served his riding diligently through twelve years and four elections. He and second wife Wanda (Mary died of cancer in 1968) put fifty thousand miles a year on their car. They were constituency people by choice and inclination. Week after week, year after year, they'd fly from Ottawa into Regina at night, find their car in the airport outdoor parking lot, and, in sub-zero weather, pray that it would start. Then the long lonesome drive through rolling prairie to Swift Current, arriving after midnight. And there was always someone to see early the next morning.

"I did a lot for the people, I think," Hamilton says. "We presented politics in a different light. We were always available. Box social, picnic, bonspiel, you name it, we were there. It gave people an opportunity to come forward with what might seem to you and me a very piddling little problem, but to them was serious."

Being an MP made him a better person, he says. "You think you have problems of your own until you meet people who just don't know where to turn for help."

He quit in 1984. He and two MP pals from the West didn't support Brian Mulroney's rise to the leadership. It worked against them. "We were up against young professional politicians. Young guys who had a university degree, never-met-a-payroll, never-missed-a-paycheque kind of thing. They could put a hell of a case in caucus, and they seemed to catch Mulroney's ear. We were sort of considered dinosaurs. So we all left, with no regrets."

DON'T FENCE ME IN

In his twelve years in parliament Frank Hamilton discovered that government largesse does not always win the local MP a standing ovation. Consider the old guys in the Gull Lake retirement home.

The senior citizens' retirement homes were really marvellous achievements. I had a hand in that. When the homes started going up at places like Shaunavon, Maple Creek, Gull Lake, it was tough getting some of the old birds in. They would set one up, there'd be a young matron running it, but you couldn't get the old guys to go in. Finally one or two would move in, but it'd be six months or a year before the thing would be accepted.

I'll never forget the Gull Lake home when it first opened. I went in, met the matron. There were three or four old guys in sort of a lobby. It had been done with two-by-twelve planks set at an angle. It was pretty dramatic. Sort of a room divider.

These old guys were sitting with their hats on, and they didn't know what to say. Finally I said, "I really like the architecture. I like the way this thing's done. It's very pleasing."

Nothing. Finally one old guy said, "It looks more like a corral to me."

What could you say? Nothing. Now those places are all full and have waiting lists.

A Compassionate Society

Whether we were conscious of it or not, the Depression left us with an abiding sympathy for people in need. Out of this came the social-services umbrella that shelters millions of Canadians today. In 1950, Canada's governments spent roughly a billion dollars on health and social welfare; by 1971 it was about nine billion. Although often abused, the social safety net is, many of us think, one of the two great achievements of our generation (the war effort being the other).

Going into the fifties, there was no medicare and no Canada Pension Plan (the CPP came in 1966). The old-age pension, later Old Age Security, was instituted in 1926, paying thirty dollars a month to all people seventy and over, and to persons sixty-five to sixty-nine if they passed a means test. In the fifties the pension for everyone sixty-five and over went up to forty dollars a month, then forty-six. According to the Gallup poll, 81 per cent of us endorsed the change, although a *Saturday Night* editorial demurred: "There seems to be no particular point in handing out an old-age allowance to a great many people who are already quite comfortable without it."

The family allowance, instituted in 1945, was improved in 1957: parents were paid six dollars a month for each child up to age nine, eight dollars a month for ages ten to sixteen. It cost the taxpayers forty-two million dollars a year, but 90 per cent of us, when polled, approved.

The University of Toronto that same year sponsored the first Ontario conference on aging – evidence that we, although never expecting to become geezers ourselves (for were we not immortal?), recognized that the elderly deserved more than a pension cheque and a ticket to an old folks' home. The conference discussed exempting the aged from school taxes and offering them educational courses, counselling, and low-cost housing and transportation.

Voices were rising against the death penalty. In April 1958, Minister of Justice Davie Fulton commuted to life the death sentence imposed on a forty-year-old who had confessed to beating a taxi driver to death for fifteen dollars. Executions seemed to be on the wane – thirty-two in 1946, seventeen in 1952, ten in 1953 – but opponents of capital punishment pointed to some thirty-five other countries that got along entirely without the gallows or electric chair.

All of this suggested an increasingly compassionate society. But the greatest achievement of our time was probably medicare. It came after bitter resistance, and was introduced first in the cradle of Canadian socialism: Saskatchewan. From its inception in 1932, the Co-operative Commonwealth Federation (CCF) was dedicated to social change. In January 1947, CCF premier Tommy Douglas, the charismatic Baptist minister, enacted the Hospital Insurance Act in Saskatchewan, introducing compulsory medical insurance with a uniform rate of contributions.

Medical-services insurance – to be known as medicare – was another CCF progeny, and the 1960 Saskatchewan election was fought on the issue. The CCF won but made mortal enemies of the province's doctors. The government passed its bill in

autumn 1961 and medical-services insurance took effect on
July 1, 1962.

Behind those bare-bones facts is the story of a province torn
by strife over a humanitarian idea, and Ed Whelan's personal date
with history.

Ed Whelan, a burly fellow of seventy-seven, hobbles about his
Regina bungalow, no longer the tireless MLA who pounded up
and down the hustings day and night for nineteen years and
never lost an election. But the timbre of his voice rises as he
relates that "unbelievable time in the history of the province."

Whelan was born and raised in a log house in southwestern
Ontario's Essex County, near Windsor, second oldest of seven
boys and two girls. Politics and public service were in his genes.
His maternal grandfather had been municipal secretary. His
uncle Herb Kelly, a Ford worker for forty years, was a shop
steward and strong CCFer. Ed's father, a farmer by occupation,
had been township reeve and county warden, knew all the local
politicos, and impressed upon his kids their obligation to serve
in public life.

Ed's father died of cancer at fifty-seven, when Ed was
eleven. "He would have lived if there'd been medicare,"
Whelan says bitterly.

Earlier, his father had sold their dairy herd to pay his medical
bills and support the family. The buyers gave him promissory
notes, not cash, and after her husband's death, Ed's mother had
virtually no money.

Ed wanted to be a lawyer but forsook higher education to
help support his mother and younger siblings. His job experience strengthened his political convictions. He worked for forty
cents an hour in nearby Amherstburg in a plant that made baking
soda. He tried for a job at Ford, stood for hours in a lineup of
three hundred men seeking work outside the gates, and got to
sixth from the front when they cut the hiring off.

Eventually he got jobs at Ford and Chrysler, joined the United Automobile Workers, and enrolled in the Ontario CCF before he was old enough to vote. In those days, all CCF roads led to Saskatchewan. Whelan went to a job with the Co-operative Union of Saskatchewan, and married Pemrose Henry.

"Now if you want to study law, you can," Pem said briskly. But most forties men didn't like the idea of being supported by their wives. Instead, Whelan began thirty years of public service, in and around government. He went to the Provincial Mediation Board (as inspector, then board member, then chairman), helping administer legislation designed to renegotiate debts and protect debtors. For ten years he travelled Saskatchewan from end to end, held hundreds of hearings, and helped negotiate mortgages that saved hundreds of family farms. Later, in the legislature, when an opponent challenged his knowledge of farming, Whelan said he'd walked over more Saskatchewan farms than all the other MLAs put together.

Throughout those years, he watched, admired, and learned from Tommy Douglas. The charming, feisty little premier was one of the ablest public speakers and shrewdest tacticians in Canadian politics, and Ed wanted to be with him. In 1960 he ran for election and won. (Two years later, brother Eugene was elected a Liberal MP. He became Minister of Agriculture under Trudeau and is now in the Senate. Some of the family, particularly uncle Herb Kelly, were shocked and appalled. *Eugene a Liberal! Where did we go wrong?*)

Ed fell into the thick of the medicare fight. Medical-services insurance – requiring doctors to collect fees solely from the proposed government plan – stirred fierce emotions on both sides. Saskatchewan's doctors and their supporters, the well-organized Keep Our Doctors (KOD) committee, were adamantly opposed. More than a hundred reporters from across the continent descended on Regina; their sympathies seemed to lean toward the doctors.

People whose family members went without medical treatment for lack of money cheered the government on. In seniors' homes, Whelan heard harrowing Depression stories of sick relatives being carted to the nearest hospital via boxcar, only to be sent away because they had no cash. He heard Herb Schienbein's story of his mother's botched operation. He studied dates on headstones in Prairie cemeteries and concluded that too many children and adults were dying too young.

The anti-government tactics intensified. Night after night, Whelan staggered out of bed to answer the phone at one or two in the morning. A man would snarl, "I'm gonna shoot you, you Red bastard!" and hang up. Finally Whelan got a quiet call from a restaurant cleaning woman. "Mr. Whelan, I'm quitting. What he's doing is a dirty trick." The nocturnal caller was her boss. Whelan told his tormentor the line was tapped. The calls stopped.

Other harassment went on. The Whelans, fearing vandalism, took out extra house insurance. One day Ed was accosted by a trio of pregnant women from his own neighbourhood. He was, they claimed, endangering their unborn babies. At school, children spat on the Whelans' daughter Sheila. (Unscarred by the experience, she became an accomplished trial lawyer and is now a provincial court judge.)

Many CCF MLAs received nuisance calls. Eventually they discovered a nest of what Whelan says were hired professional agitators, issuing bogus messages of distress ("My child is dying because of you") from a bank of phones in a downtown hotel.

Ed, Pemrose, and their children finally left Regina for a trailer trip into northern Saskatchewan. When they got back, it was over. The new act took effect on July 1, 1962. Ninety per cent of the province's protesting doctors closed their offices to take holidays or "educational leave." Later, they signed an agreement, winning the right to extra-bill patients if they chose.

But resentment lingered, and a few doctors left Saskatchewan for good. Others were brought in from Britain. Meanwhile, the Diefenbaker government appointed a royal commission on health services under Justice Emmett Hall. In a voluminous report in the mid-sixties, Hall recommended medicare for all of Canada. In 1966 Lester Pearson, by then prime minister, passed a federal medicare program.

Tommy Douglas had resigned his premiership in 1961 to head the new federal National Democratic Party (NDP), risen from the CCF. In autumn 1962 he ran for his first federal seat and lost, largely because of the medicare backlash. Vandals (Ed Whelan, who was Douglas's campaign manager, thinks they were instigated by the American Medical Association) painted the hammer and sickle on the NDP committee-room door.

"What they did to Tommy Douglas was an absolute outrage," Ed says, his voice thick with passion even thirty-five years later. "But in the end we won. We got the things that people really needed and wanted. We brought medicare to this country. It's the best thing that ever happened."

A Silent, Blinding Flash

All through the fifties, fear of annihilation lurked at the edge of our consciousness. We were living with the Bomb.

We now understood the awful reality of nuclear war. Many of us had read John Hersey's magnificent book *Hiroshima*, or the version of it that filled the entire August 31, 1946, issue of *The New Yorker*. It began:

At exactly fifteen minutes past eight in the morning, on August 6, 1945, Japanese time, at the moment when the atomic bomb flashed above Hiroshima, Miss Toshiko Sasaki, a clerk in the personnel department of the East Asia Tin Works, had just sat down at her place in the plant office . . .

and went on to tell the story of the bombing through six survivors. It was a masterpiece of reporting and eloquent restraint.

Those who hadn't heard of Hersey were nevertheless scared witless by daily newspaper reports. The Cold War was on. The United States and Soviet Union had the A-bomb (as in atomic) and later the H-bomb (as in hydrogen). They were far more powerful than the bombs that fell on Japan. Another war would be unlike anything in human history.

No longer could Canadians sit safe and snug beyond the oceans. With the new intercontinental ballistic missiles (ICBMs), there would be only a few minutes' warning at most. A silent, blinding, colossal flash and a city would be gone. A full-out war and the world as we knew it would be gone.

What, asked the Gallup poll in March 1951, would be the first question you'd put to the prime minister, given a chance? Top choice: "Will there be another war?"

Should we drop an A-bomb on the Russians first? Gallup wondered. Sixty-six per cent of us said yes. Which people of other nations do you like best? Gallup inquired in November 1951. We chose the Americans first, the British a close second, and the Russians a distant last, which wasn't surprising, considering we were ready to nuke them first.

In yet another poll (Gallup had turned the threat of global destruction into a cottage industry), 83 per cent of us wanted to ban communists from any public office, 57 per cent approved of banning them from voting in any election, and a similar proportion would have made it a criminal offence to belong to a communist organization. When Joe McCarthy, the Red-baiting U.S. senator, had his fifteen minutes of infamy, we watched his histrionics on television with mingled approval and disapproval. No God- and war-fearing North American liked commies, but McCarthy's smear tactics were more than many of us could stomach. Yet if Gallup were to be believed, a McCarthy might have flourished in Canada.

Newspapers described in gruesome detail how no one would survive within a three-mile radius of Ground Zero; how for dozens of miles beyond, radiation fallout would invade our bodies; how raging fire, flying shards of glass, and avalanches of rubble would kill and maim thousands more.

The *Financial Post* in 1950 delved into the state of Canada's home defence. (A sidebar warned against young closet-commies accosting us on street corners with peace petitions: "How Reds Would Trick You on 'Peace'") The consensus was that our cities' emergency services were pathetic. Toronto and Vancouver had civil-defence plans; Winnipeg, Hamilton, Windsor, Niagara Falls, Victoria, and Sault Ste. Marie were thinking about it; Montreal, Quebec City, Halifax, and Edmonton had none.

Whether any plan would have worked is another matter. As Western staff writer for *Maclean's* in the fifties, I attended a one-day civil-defence exercise in Calgary. One portion of the city tried to evacuate into the country. It was chaotic, and convinced me that if war *did* come, our last view of life on earth would be a gridlock of honking, cursing motorists.

Most of us pushed the fear into the backs of our minds, but it wouldn't go away. A few stocked their basements with canned goods and other non-perishables. In some schools, children were drilled on how to hunch under a desk and cover their heads if the sirens sounded. By 1957 our civil-defence gurus had evolved a warning strategy: first a "take cover" siren (a rising-falling wail), then the evacuation signal (a steady three-minute blast). Given that there was no place to hide, one might have been better off not knowing.

A YOUNG WOMAN'S TERROR

Antoinette MacDonald of Kingston, co-owner of a firm that sells specialty TV programming (educational, documentary, children's), is one of the most rational and intelligent people I know. And in 1962, when the Cuban missile crisis gripped North America, a young Antoinette Edwards, living and working in New York City, was overwhelmed by fear of nuclear annihilation.

I hadn't been concerned about nuclear war to that point. I read the newspaper and watched television, but I was young and didn't really pay much attention to those things. Then one day at work they said President Kennedy was going to talk to us that night. It sounded pretty serious.

We didn't have a television, so we went downstairs to watch with some friends. I remember Kennedy saying they would shoot over the bow of the boat [the Soviet vessel that was transporting armaments to Cuba]. All of a sudden, sitting on that couch, I realized that maybe we could be at war the next day. And it would be nuclear war, and I was in one of the target areas.

It had a paralysing effect on me. It just took over. And I thought, Where have I been? It's been leading up to this and it really could happen.

I went to work, but I was prepared to die. I found out where the shelters were – I worked right beside Grand Central Station – and it gave me a little sense of hope. But I thought, Probably I won't make it to the shelter.

We made it through the crisis, but I didn't make it through in terms of worry for several years. Every single day I thought,

It's probably gonna happen now. And the leaders, they'll do something behind our backs. And probably it's the end of the world.

I couldn't read a newspaper. I would read the headlines upside down, bits of a headline. And of course just the bits would bring the terror up inside me. For three years I lived in Spain that way. Then, for the first couple of years in Toronto, we used to get the *Globe and Mail* delivered, and I'd just bring it into the house and put it down. Then I'd ask if everything was okay. In trying to steel myself against it, I'd try to tune out. But part of me was tuned in. I'd get snippets of news in a radio broadcast, on the street, or in a store when the radio was on. And of course the little piece of information was far more dangerous than if I had had the whole story, and then dealt with it.

It was very difficult for Billy [her then husband]. He had great faith that things would iron themselves out. He always made me feel that it certainly was not going to happen. But I was convinced it was. Eventually I got over it, but it took at least five years before I would read a newspaper.

Although it may now seem like mass hysteria, nuclear war was a genuine possibility, and Canada was in an unenviable position smack between the two great powers. Ours seemed likely to become a no-man's-land; Soviet missiles aimed at the United States might drop on us by mistake, and Soviet missiles knocked down by U.S. defences might also fall on us. One official suggested that the American ICBMs, strung out close to the Canadian border, be moved into the far North.

"The Eskimos may not like it," the official said, "but it will be a good thing for the rest of the population." What the Eskimos thought (the politically correct "Inuit" hadn't entered our lexicon) didn't matter. They didn't have enough votes.

Washington correspondent Knowlton Nash wondered in print if Canada should start building bomb shelters on a large scale, or would this simply make the chronically angry Soviets even more irate? Shelters *were* going up for certain Very Important People, including our prime minister, whose hideaway was, naturally, dubbed a Diefenbunker. In 1958 the federal department of health and welfare issued a booklet, "Your Evacuation Pack," telling us what emergency food supplies to hoard. A year later a home builder in the Aurora subdivision north of Toronto offered a $1,500 bomb shelter as an optional extra on his $15,500 homes. With its reinforced concrete walls, steel door, and air-filtering system, you could stick it out for days and eventually rise up to a world laid waste.

"I remember being always afraid, particularly with our first two children," says Mary Parfitt of Mallorytown, Ontario. "I worried that they would never live to see adulthood. I wondered whether I should be joining anti-nuclear organizations and going out on marches and things, when really I had so much to do at home."

Madeleine Cranston of Victoria recalls waiting for a bus one day and thinking, "Why on earth would anybody want to have children? We're all going to blow up." But the Cranstons, like most of us, hoped and prayed and raised a family.

The fear haunted us beyond the fifties. In 1962 millions of us huddled in front of our TVs, watching Kennedy and Khruschchev play chicken with the human race in the Cuban missile crisis – the confrontation that tortured Antoinette MacDonald for years after. Norma West Linder, expecting a child at the time, asked herself, Is this a gift of life – or a liability?

As late as 1985, while writing a major magazine article on nuclear disarmament, I discovered that my oldest daughter,

Lesley, had been haunted by end-of-the-world scenarios, and holding her fright within, for nearly twenty-five years. Hers was not an isolated case; it was one of several things that alienated our boomer children from our generation.

We didn't dream that the nuclear threat would eventually abate, that the communist threat would dwindle and, much sooner, our children would create a revolution that would shake the very foundations of our comfortable lives.

VI

How we invented
the boomers

The World According to Spock

B y the early fifties we were awash in babies. Gurgling,
squalling, beaming, mewling, burping babies. Cherubic
infants with tranquil brows, nestling at their mothers' breasts.
Wrinkled red-faced morsels angrily demanding a cuddle, a
bottle, or a fresh diaper. Babies with chubby faces smeared in
canned goop, rewarding their anxious parents with beatific
smiles that turned out to be gas.

More babies than Canada had ever seen: 343,504 in 1946,
372,000 in 1947, more than 400,000 by 1952. In all, between
1946 and 1961, 6.7 million babies, give or take a pram-full.

A baby boom.

We came home from the munitions plants and the war, flung
off our uniforms and coveralls, and jumped straight into bed. Part
of it was our itch for licit sex, but we had nobler aspirations:
home, spouse, children, the warm and loving families that most
of us had, or thought we had, in the thirties.

If anyone *didn't* feel maternal or paternal, too bad. Having babies was expected, almost a duty. Not having babies was anti-social or, at least, to be pitied. Childless couples in the fifties drew suspicious glances and whispers. *They've been married* two *years and no kids! Is she frigid? Is he firing blanks?*

So babies came, hot on the heels of marriage (contraception was not yet an advanced art), and like most parents before us, we knew little of child care.

"We make people pass tests before they can drive a car, but we expect nothing of them if they're going to raise children," reflects Doug Gardner, social worker and member of our generation. "And yet this is the most important job you will have at that stage in life."

We made mistakes. The biggest one, in the view of Wolfville's Glen Hancock was that, "we were the first generation to depart from the authority of the family. We were too indulgent with our children. But we thought we were doing them a service."

It's true. As Douglas Owram, author of the definitive boomer history, *Born at the Right Time*, puts it, "This was a child-obsessed age." We wanted *so* much to make everything wonderful for them, for them to have all the things that we as children did not, to be spared the pain of poverty and war.

But how to do it? On matters of child-rearing we had, mainly, meddlesome mothers and mothers-in-law as our guides. Then the first of many would-be saviours rode among us. His name was Spock. Not the Vulcan with the pointy ears (he and "Star Trek" were barely a twinkle in Gene Roddenberry's eye) but Benjamin Spock, an M.D. with benevolent visage peering out from the jacket of *Baby and Child Care*. His book became our bible. It sold three-quarters of a million copies in its first year. The paperback edition, dog-eared and stained with tears and Pablum, was a staple in almost every home.

"I grew up with a child in one hand and Spock in the other," Elsie Towson says.

"Dr. Spock has been maligned for encouraging permissiveness," adds Elizabeth Tucci. "I don't agree. He gave a first time-mother a lot of confidence."

The doctor, biographers later revealed, had a difficult childhood himself. His mother was "very moralistic and excessively controlling," while his father, a lawyer, kept his head below the parapet. Spock overcame these beginnings to write a wonderfully sensible handbook. He talked to us as friends, not in the patronizing manner of many family doctors. From the opening words he soothed and encouraged us:

Trust yourself. You know more than you think you do. . . . Don't take too seriously all that the neighbours say. Don't be overawed by what the experts say. Don't be afraid to trust your own common sense.

Even Spock made mistakes, in the view of mothers on the firing line. "I thought he was a disaster," says Shirley Walbridge of Pointe Claire. "I'd let poor Jim lie there in his crib and yell for half an hour because the clock and Dr. Spock said it wasn't time to feed him. There's no way I'd do such a thing now. I didn't know anything about little kids. I relied on this Spock character and he led me astray. We did much better with Jamie when we decided that maybe Dr. Spock wasn't an authority after all."

Spock also recommended unpolished brown rice for pudding, but he neglected to tell us that you can lead a child to rice pudding but you cannot make her eat. Catherine, our second daughter, small of stature but indomitable of spirit, abhorred the very sight and texture of the stuff. She would sit at the table long after the dinner hour, an untouched bowl of loathsome pudding before her, her small face set stonily. In a battle of wills, her mother hovered nearby, equally stony, while I, rather like Spock's father, hid out behind the evening edition of the *Toronto Star*. Eventually Cathy might force down a spoonful and win a reprieve. She grew up normal and happy but has not touched rice pudding since.

But we didn't fault the doc for not knowing about pudding. "A lot of his ideas were excellent," concludes Mary Greey, mother and psychotherapist. "It's too bad that he was a man and the only expert around."

What's wrong with being a man? I ask, my dukes up.

"I don't think a man can really appreciate a woman's position. Mothers should talk about being mothers."

Which is probably why many young mothers, in the end, found that an ounce of Spock mixed with a gram of intuition was the best formula for child care.

"I had an absolute dream about what I was going to do with my child," Odile Winfield remembers in Vancouver. "He would have the very best of everything; I would have everything well organized and under control. I had absolutely no idea that this little human being came with a whole slate of his own.

"And I don't remember Spock ever saying, 'You have an individual in your hands. Watch, listen, observe. Be very respectful of this human being that you've brought into the world.' I had to raise my consciousness."

Other experts were soon swarming in the wake of Dr. Spock, contributing mightily to our bewilderment. As *Maclean's* reported in 1955, Spock's theory of scheduled feeding for babies was now replaced by "demand feeding"; that is, produce bottle, breast, or Pablum whenever Baby howled. Toilet training, once recommended at around three months, was now a no-no. Forcing rigid toilet rules on a child might turn him into a malcontent or an axe murderer.

"It's time parents stopped letting themselves be scared by the experts," *Maclean's* concluded. But we couldn't *not* listen to them; we wanted to do right by our kids.

Sometimes the experts were sound. Dr. Sam Laycock, dean of education at the University of Saskatchewan and a director of the Canadian National Committee for Mental Hygiene, told us how to teach sex (which no one had taught us). Don't feed kids that guff about the birds, bees, and flowers, he said. Don't delay instruction until the child reaches puberty. Try to be completely unembarrassed in the telling. (*That* was difficult, given our upbringing.) And be sure your child understands that personal family sexual matters are not to be shared with the kids next door.

We were receiving mixed signals about education, particularly the teaching of reading. The experts, in whom we were placing far too much faith, were weaning youngsters from phonics to the whole-word technique. This upset many of us who had learned to read perfectly well under the old method. It particularly disturbed the guru Rudolf Flesch (author of *Why Johnny Can't Read*). In a 1955 issue of *Maclean's* he spurned the new method, offering as Exhibit A the Robert Louis Stevenson poem "The Swing," from a 1929 Grade-Two reader:

How do you like to go up in a swing,
Up in the air so blue?
Oh, I do think it the pleasantest thing
Ever a child can do!

Flesch contrasted that with Exhibit B, a piece from the 1954 Grade-Two reader, in which, he said, words were "brutally hammered into a child's brain; no resemblance to the English language." It was titled "Over I Go":

"Hurry, Jim," called Jack. "Faster! Here I come! Here I come behind you."
Jump, jump, jump went Jim.
He jumped over Billy, over Patty, over Dick.

"Over I go," called Jack. Then he began to jump.

He jumped over Peter . . .

This was "whole-word recognition," and many of us thought it was pap. Two or three decades later, as young people submitted botched job applications, or reached university unable to spell, some experts wondered if, at the very least, a combination of the two methods might produce a more literate population. And in early 1997, a study conducted in Texas found that children taught the phonics method were miles ahead of their whole-word counterparts.

Whole-word recognition was only one disturbing trend in the schools. "The educational system was designed to affirm self-esteem," writes Douglas Owram. "Every pupil was to be given the opportunity to show that his or her personal experience was worth while." He quotes a 1959 teacher's manual for grade three: "See that each child has a chance to taste success in some area . . ."

On the face of it, what could be more fair? Except that it would one day reach an extreme wherein excellence would take second place to feeling good. The real message of fifties education, Owram concludes, was "child-centredness to an unparalleled degree." This, along with everything else in their tiny lives, persuaded the boomers that, "This society is designed for you."

The greatest outpouring of advice and confusion in our child-rearing years centred on discipline. To spank or not to spank? Chastise, or soothe recalcitrant moppets with sweet reason? Most of us had grown up with strict discipline, or the threat of it, at home and in school. In my grade school, the thick leather strap reposing in the teacher's desk was rarely used, but its mere existence was, like the fifties H-bomb, a massive deterrent.

"If you got into trouble at school, you sure got in trouble at home," says Marion Pratt of Tillsonburg. "Nobody ever asked whether you were right or wrong. They assumed that the teacher was right." Although the teacher wasn't always right, and although those ancient practices appal modern educators, they kept order in the schools, unlike today's child anarchy.

We found it difficult to accept the emerging philosophy of "let them do their own thing." It seemed, and still seems to us, as harmful an extreme as our forefathers' primitive "spare the rod and spoil the child."

"My wife and I found that children would test us to see how far they could go, how much they could get away with, how ornery they could be, until they were disciplined," says Reverend Ken Campbell of Burlington. "Then they loved you and were your best friend."

Helen Margison was a "very strong disciplinarian. Consequently my youngsters were welcome everywhere. Somebody once said to my daughter, 'You're not free to do anything, are you?' And she said, 'Oh, yes, we're all free to behave ourselves.'"

Norman Currell of White Rock, British Columbia, feels he benefited in the fifties from being Saskatchewan vice-president of the Canadian Mental Health Association. A visiting psychologist offered four "I's" for administering discipline: It must be immediate, inevitable, invariable (same sort of punishment for same sort of misdemeanour), and impersonal (punish a child not because he made you angry but because he knowingly broke a rule).

Currell applied these principles, banishing a son to some neutral place (not his bedroom, where he'd probably enjoy himself) until he was ready to come back. "I only had to do it once or twice, but it worked like a charm," Currell reports. "I never had a moment's trouble with my boys."

Neither Margison nor Currell admits to spanking. Others do. Tony Parfitt, educated by Jesuits, remembers getting "a lot of whacks" from a piece of whalebone covered with leather. As a parent, he also dealt out whacks – fewer and more humanely, but whacks nevertheless.

Once only did I attempt to spank a daughter, whereupon her little sister began pummelling my back with her tiny fists. The whole thing dissolved in laughter. The discipline in some of our own childhood homes had been unnaturally harsh, but by the fifties, our experts would have none of it (they now speak of outlawing it), filling us with guilt and remorse.

"I spanked Jim, and I shouldn't have," Shirley Walbridge says. "You're supposed to love them, not chastise them. But our doctor in Sarnia, when I told him about some of Jim's escapades, said, 'Spank him.' I said, 'I do.' He said, 'Spank him harder.'"

Persuaded that corporal punishment was bad, some parents of our generation tilted to the other extreme. In the worst-case scenarios (a phrase we wouldn't have used then) nothing was denied the children. Their whims and temper tantrums were indulged.

The result, according to Toronto psychiatrist Dr. Joseph Berger, could be disastrous.

"If you try to raise a child by satisfying his each and every wish, you don't end up with a well-adjusted child," says Berger, who has taught psychiatry at university, has been an examiner for the American Board of Psychiatry for nearly twenty years, and currently teaches psychotherapy to family doctors. "You end up with a totally self-centred, self-indulgent and demanding narcissistic personality who can't live within his reasonable natural limits. Narcissism is the problem of our age."

On top of this, most boomers grew up in the new homogeneous suburbs, surrounded by homes and creatures exactly like themselves. Unless there were grandparents – and in the fifties and sixties young families were scattered across the land far from their roots – they rarely saw an old person.

It gave little boomers an exaggerated sense of their importance and produced, declares Douglas How of St. Andrews, New Brunswick, "the most permissive generation in human history."

Just the kind of carping you'd expect from a geezer, right? Then let's hear from Peter Menzies, self-proclaimed boomer, writing in a July 1996 edition of the *Calgary Herald*:

> History, one suspects, will not be kind to my generation, which may be recognized not so much as Boomers but as a wave of self-righteous, self-satisfied, and self-serving Babies.
>
> We are, after all, the demographic segment that successive governments catered to as they ran up national and provincial debts. We are the ones who abused unemployment insurance. . . . And we are the self-obsessed generation who, fully aware of how the system could be scammed, pulled the plug on it when it was no longer of value to us.
>
> When we were young, university tuitions were kept low, bursaries were abundant and student loans were, if not forgivable, at least offered at modest rates. But today, having fed at that trough as youths, those in mid-life show little or no inclination to help those who follow.

Wish I'd said that. But if I had, a boomer would have run me down with his Beemer.

"I Guess He Was Trying To Get Away From Us"

Our children were rebelling against everything: the suburbia that had sheltered them; the parents who had cosseted them; the war that had saved them from being drafted into the Hitler Youth; and, of course, Vietnam. The veil of ignorance had been lifted from their eyes. They saw a venal, hypocritical society, and they would save us, or at least themselves, from it.

They were becoming alien creatures. Our sons, with hair to the shoulders, were carrying *purses*, for God's sake! Our daughters, with hair to their waists, were burning their bras, donning long, flowing, psychedelic gowns, or miniskirts, then micro-skirts, then hot pants, pasted to every crease and contour.

They mated casually and said they were making love, not war. They wore beads and vibrant colours, smoked funny cigarettes, and danced all night in the surreal blink of strobe lights to the mindless deafening throb of rock bands. They hitchhiked across the land, guitars and packs slung on their backs, converging on the inner-city equivalents of Toronto's Yorkville or Vancouver's Gastown.

A CASE OF MISTAKEN "YORKS"

In which two aspiring hippies end up among pots and pans instead of pot. Douglas Gardner, head of the Toronto Children's Aid Society in the troubled sixties, explains.

One day the supervisor of a special unit I had just set up said, "Doug, I've got two kids from your old home town. You should have a look at them. They just blew in last night, and they're as mad as hops."

They'd decided to leave home in Sudbury and hit Toronto's Yorkville, which was, of course, Mecca for kids all across Canada. Didn't tell the parents. It was raining, it was cold, took them three days to get here. The last ride they hitched was from Barrie [forty miles north of Toronto]. The driver said, "Where do you want to go, kids?"

They said, "Oh, we're going to Yorkville."

He thought they said "Yorkdale" [a shopping centre in the

northern reaches of Metro]. So he let them off at the Yorkdale shopping complex late at night. I guess they thought, This doesn't look quite right, all these department stores.

Driver said, "You're *sure* this is where you want?"

But they were out in the world, trying to be sophisticated, so they said, "Oh, yeah, this is it."

And of course the police picked them up, hauled them in overnight, and brought them to us in the morning. My supervisor, knowing I came from up there, was pulling my leg: "Those kids from Sudbury aren't very bright, are they, Doug?"

They didn't want to divulge their names, but eventually they did. We notified their parents and they were sent home.

Maybe Sudbury looked good to them after that.

We of the Ozzie and Harriet generation were amazed, shocked, apprehensive at the blossoming of these flower children. Yet part of us secretly envied them, doing so openly and freely what we had done furtively or not at all. Mothers dutifully went on making grocery lists and pushing shopping carts around gleaming supermarket palaces, hoping the kids would come home on Sunday for a good dinner. Fathers plodded diligently to office jobs so proudly won – three-weeks' holidays with pay! – in Warren K. Cook suits and skinny neckties, earning money to bail the children out of a jam if necessary.

We tried to understand our half-grown babies, and sometimes tried to emulate them. I recall an early-sixties evening with my then in-laws, all lubricated with the ubiquitous rye-'n'-ginger, enthusiastically doing the Twist led by a limber twelve-year-old niece. Our headaches in the morning were as nothing compared to the lower-back pain.

Middle-aged women let their hair and their skirts flow long and free. Middle-aged men wore sideburns down to their jawlines and bum-hugging trousers with flared cuffs. I succumbed quickly to sideburns but resisted the mod clothing until 1970. Then, heavy with hubris and a new job as editor of the magazine *Toronto Life*, I yielded to the pleas of stylish friends who felt my looks were a discredit to my high station. I presented my body, in venerable tweed jacket and flannel pants, to the clerks at Harry Rosen's high temple of haberdashery. They blanched, and hastily clad me in a chocolate-brown blazer with brass buttons and bell-bottom slacks of green-blue plaid, the sort that latter-day geezers sometimes wear for golfing or a morning of vacant gazing in the mall.

Rosen's lads followed up with a double-breasted suit of shimmering blue with chalk stripes and acres of lapel. Getting the hang of it, I added a shirt of midnight blue, another of orange, and a very wide blue necktie with a chicken-wire pattern in red. When I walked, pulsating, onto the street, mothers shielded their children's eyes and salesmen gave me standing ovations.

Then I went right off the rails and bought a white sport shirt with a deep, deep collar and an appliquéd pattern of red dots and writhing circles. My daughters said the pattern looked like paramecium, so they called it the Bacteria Shirt. They named my chalk-stripe the Nathan Detroit Suit, after the two-bit mobster in the musical *Guys and Dolls*. And they waited for me to butt out of their generation. In due time I did, returning to the drab protective colouring of my generation and my profession. Writers should be heard, not seen.

Many of the parents I interviewed remember their children as paragons. What about all those dropouts, hippies, and pot-heads? Must have been someone else's kids. But a few, on reflection, admitted, "Yes, our youngest was a druggie. She caused her mother and me unimaginable grief" or "Oh, yeah, he had a ponytail, smoked marijuana, the whole bit. Actually, we had a lot of problems with him. He ran away from home for four days . . ."

And a few, even after thirty years, still remember those years with puzzlement and pain. Here are four stories exactly as the parents recounted them. Because the children of that era, now middle-aged adults, have put those times behind them (or are trying to), I have omitted the names.

"We're Still Not Sure Why"

She is a Toronto widow in her late sixties. Subject in question: her oldest daughter.

"She was born in 1949, so she'd be in her forties now. We were too strict with her. We believed in spanking, and I didn't believe in just a little tap. My husband used to spank her too, realizing later that we were spanking her for the wrong things.

"Maybe that's why she always tried to please us. Maybe it was fear. I remember my sister saying to me, 'Why should a great big adult hit a little child?' And I thought, *It's terrible*. Later, I went to work for the Catholic Children's Aid, and I realized that it is child abuse. So our first one got the brunt of it. The second one got some. The last three didn't ever get spanked.

"I'm not in touch with my oldest daughter any more. We got alienated from her, and we're still not sure why. She was almost a beatnik. She started playing the guitar and singing 'The Times They Are A-Changin''. I was shocked at the words of that.

"She didn't exactly get into the drugs and everything, but she'd go down to Yorkville and all the coffee houses and everything. She was really a product of the sixties.

"She was going to become a nun at one point. We had a priest over at the church who was almost a sixties person himself. He was quite young, and he introduced the folk mass, which wasn't heard of in those days. And my daughter and her two cousins sang in the folk mass.

"Anyway, when she wanted to become a nun, I said, 'Talk to the priest about it. You're only nineteen. I think you should work for a while and see what life is like.' Then she came home from school and said, 'I'm gonna be a beatnik. I can do more good in the world that way than being a nun.' This is what the priest told her. That she could do more good by going around and talking to young people and singing. He was a little bit way out.

"That was it. I mean, I was glad she was going to be a nun, but I didn't like the idea of a beatnik. She didn't really become a beatnik, but she never did enter the convent.

"She went kind of overboard on religion. Actually, the Catholic religion, but a charismatic group that was almost like a cult. And she got so you couldn't even talk to her. You'd say, 'What a beautiful day.' 'Yes, the Lord has given us a beautiful day.' That sort of thing. You couldn't talk for ten minutes. She had to go to a psychiatrist.

"She didn't get married till she was thirty-six. We went to her wedding. But I don't know if she ever had any children, because I haven't seen her for ten years.

"Maybe she should have entered the convent. It might have been better."

"You're Up and Down Like a Yo-Yo"

The father, a Westerner and war veteran, still looks a trifle shell-shocked as he tells his story.

"In the sixties, our two oldest . . . how do I describe it? They became very mouthy. That wasn't normal with them. They'd be yelling at us, and, of course, I'd react in no uncertain terms. I used to spank them. They don't resent that now. I guess they did at the time.

"So the oldest took off. I had tried desperately to get my kids to go to university. I didn't care what they took, but I wanted them to have some foundation when they got to be working age. But I couldn't interest them. They'd say, 'We don't want to end up like you.' I said, 'What do you mean?' 'Well, you're working all the time.' This was the thing that I got. And as a result, none of the four went to university. They regretted it later. They said, 'You should have made us.' I said, 'How do you make people learn?'

"The oldest took off with one of the rock groups, flying all over North America. She ended up in Hollywood and made a movie. Something about cheerleaders, it was tame compared to what you see now on the screen. I went to see it, thinking, My little baby! But anyway she came around.

"The next in line, she followed this kid to Kansas City. And phones us and tells us that she wasn't with him but she married this lawyer who was writing a book on Kansas City jazz. They came up to visit and asked me to invest in the editing of a film. I said, 'Uh-uh. I haven't got that kind of money, and anyway, I'm not a risk-taker.' So she stayed away for a number of years. She used to phone in the middle of the night that she was being beaten up. I finally sent her a ticket to come home, which she did.

"That lasted for a while, and then she took off to live in a seedy part of Toronto. God, I went down on a convention once and visited her – my kid, in squalor, living like a real hippie!

"Anyway, she came out of it. She married, and they're happy and have a big property and a lovely house. I don't know. As a parent you're up and down like a yo-yo!"

"What Happened in the Sixties? Marijuana."

Before his death, this Quebecer's husband had a drinking problem. She handled many parenting problems on her own, including this one.

"My son couldn't live under the same roof as his father, because my husband picked on him for some reason. So I said, 'I want you to go elsewhere. You're university material.' He was accepted in a college out West. I sent him the hundred dollars I got for playing the church organ every month. He worked at Eaton's Thursday night, Friday night, and Saturday. He was a workaholic, and a perfectionist.

"He only lasted two years at college, partly because of finances, partly because a young professor got him into marijuana. I heard this long afterward, through the grapevine.

"He drove back East for Expo '67 with six others in an old hearse. They all got jobs at Expo. But he got deeply into drugs, although I didn't know at the time. He was twenty-one. All of a sudden, he and a friend bought a boat and sailed to the Caribbean. He spent years there, dealing marijuana. I thought he was chartering his boat. He made so much money he went to Europe, got a bigger boat and lived over there with his second wife.

"Then he got pinched. I was in Paris, visiting my daughter, when we got a phone call saying he was in jail. I was widowed, nearing retirement. I said to myself, 'This is the worst year of my life. I don't know whether I can survive this.'

"We went to the jail. Outside the gate, I said to myself before going in, I'd better pray. It was a horrible old place. He was in solitary, because they thought he was Mafia. They let him wear good clothes for the visit: a camel-hair jacket and grey flannels. My daughter, who was with me, said, 'What do you do all day?' Big laughs. He said, 'Don't cry or I'll cry.' We got through by making jokes, mostly.

"They spent months trying to decide what to do with him. About eight months later, he was sent to the States for trial. I spent four months down there in a motel, little kitchen, sixteen dollars a night. And I went looking for a church. A woman at the hairdresser's took me to her Baptist Bible-study group. She introduced me: 'Her son is in prison.' Nobody groaned or moaned or looked surprised. I thought, Here's my church. They had marvellous music, and I'm into church music.

"After four months, my son went to trial. We had two very expensive American lawyers. They said he'd get a minimum of fifteen years, maybe twenty-five. Anyway, he got four years and we were elated. He served two – they took off the time he'd been waiting for trial – in a correctional centre in a rural area. I went to see him a lot.

"He went back to the Caribbean to operate a charter, legally, but the Americans caught up with him, told the local people about his past and he was thrown out. He came back to Canada. He's fifty now, trying to start over.

"So you ask what happened in the sixties? Marijuana. That was a very, very, very hard part of my life.

"I Just Don't Know What He Was Trying To Prove"

The speaker, a father in his late seventies, lives in the Maritimes.

"Our son went through a period in which he was ashamed of all the stuff his mother and I had. Well, Jesus, we didn't have a hell of a lot by most standards, but all the kids were kind of ashamed of their elders. When he came near the end of his courses at Dalhousie, he suddenly takes off without getting his degree, heading for Australia.

"He got to India, and as far as I can make out, he was living in the depths, sleeping on the streets. I had bought him a lovely sleeping bag for Christmas. He sold it to keep alive. Came back with hepatitis and possibly some parasites. I just don't know what he was trying to prove. I guess, to be blunt about it, he was trying to get away from us.

"He came home and said, 'Dad, would you mind if I became a carpenter?' He's been a carpenter ever since. I don't mind. You do whatever you want to do with your life."

WHY JOLINE DIDN'T RUN AWAY

Chick Childerhose, now of Sooke, British Columbia, tried an intellectual approach on his children. "Actually, you are adults in a little body," he said. "You were born because you wanted to be born, and you chose me and your mother to be your parents. I know it's a tough choice but you did it, so you're stuck with us."

He was surprised at how quickly they took to the idea. "I came to the conclusion that kids basically want to grow up."
Then . . .

When Joline was thirteen she said, "I'm leaving home." So I said, "Well, if that's what you want, okay." I asked her what she had in mind. We kicked it back and forth. So I said, "Okay, I'll write you a letter." I sat down at the typewriter:

To Whom It May Concern: The bearer of this letter, Joline Childerhose, is in all respects trustworthy, of good character and a hard worker. Any help that you can give this person will be appreciated. Here is my phone number if she needs any assistance that I can provide.

I wrote it so broadly that I thought for sure she'd see it was all a big spoof. Just a paragon! And she read the letter, and I could see her thinking, That's me, that's me. You've got me to a T.

So she folds up the letter, and I said, "How do you plan to travel?"

"I'm going to hitchhike, I think."

She was heading for Toronto. We lived in North Bay. I said, "Well, along the 401 there's a lot of cases of girls hitchhiking and guys in vans getting them and raping them." So we talked about rape a little bit.

And I could see, the more she talked, she just sort of needed reassurance, which I hadn't thought about. She didn't run away. She's a hard worker and has three kids.

Them and Us

In due course the boomers shed their beads and sandals and took straight jobs. But we are still light years apart; many of them don't ever want to look or be like us. They are better educated and trim from rigorous exercise, surgical tucks, and low-cal, high-fibre diets. They are postponing marriage deep into their thirties or beyond and earning more and casually spending more on things we considered luxuries.

"They'll always be a little bit of a mystery to us, and we'll be a little bit of a mystery to them," Mary Parfitt says. "Always."

Although the oldest of them are now in their early fifties, mortality snapping at their heels, they continue to command an inordinate amount of space and time in magazines, books, newspapers, and on TV, confirming their belief that they are Chosen People. They even have their own association, Canadian Baby

Boomers Inc., for group discounts and to help preserve retirement plans.

What *is* a boomer? The admirable Douglas Owram maintains that the baby boom ran from 1946 until 1962 and that 6.7 million were born in that period. University of Toronto's David Foot, high priest of demographics, says the boom ran 1947 to 1966 and that there are 9.8 million boomers in the land. This wildly inflated figure includes boomer-age immigrants. Owram's numbers make more sense.

So, if we were to draw a generational tree, it would consist of:

1. Generation M (for Mature): all of us wonderful folks who came through depression and war and invented the boomers. I have included in this group everyone who is now sixty-five or older.

2. The *half*-generation behind us, born from, say, 1933 to 1945. Some call them the Silents. I say they were born with diamonds in the soles of their shoes; they suffered little or none of the privations of depression or war, and cashed in on all the postwar prosperity.

3. The boomers, beginning 1946 or 1947 and ending 1962 or 1966, depending on whether you prefer Owram's or Foot's definitions. Foot, with categories for every occasion, divides his boomers into "front-end" (oldest) and "back-end" (youngest).

4. The baby busters (Foot's definition): the half-generation following the boomers. This would include what author Douglas Coupland erroneously (but profitably) dubbed Generation X. The Xers are not a generation. Coupland himself describes them as born between the late 1950s and the 1960s. By that definition they are, as the ubiquitous Foot points out, really late boomers with a few spotty busters thrown in for ballast.

5. The third distinct generation, our boomers' children: what Foot calls the echo.

Again and again, my respondents asked rhetorically, Why are baby boomers the way they are? The question plagues us still, you see. They are mostly good people, they are our children, but their outlook toward marriage, family, religion, work, and possessions is totally unlike ours.

"What in their parents' day would have appeared a sumptuous standard of living became for the first wave of boomers a normal way of life to which they were entitled. It was as simple as that," writes McGill University professor François Ricard in his *The Lyric Generation: The Life and Times of the Baby Boomers.* "Any object, any idea, any *person* is there to be acquired and then rejected as soon as something better or newer – a more modern idea, a more attractive mate – comes along to replace it and plunge it into obsolescence."

Here's another perspective from Catherine Collins, the not entirely typical boomer who still hates rice pudding. She has always held a job and is responsible with money, although nowhere near as parsimonious as her father. She saves and invests but, like most children of middle- and upper-class families, she knows if she really needs more money she can turn to her parents, as our generation could not.

As for jobs, she says, "The boomer attitude was, jobs should not bore us. Work, for a lot of us in our generation, is as important as – or more important than – many other things, such as starting a family. Work for some of us *is* family. It's such a big part of life, we *expect* it to be creative and fulfilling. Going into a dead-end job just isn't acceptable unless we're in desperate straits."

Aha! cries Doug Harvey of Victoria. That is the boomers' (and their successors') Achilles heel!

"Immigrants are succeeding in this country 'cause they're ambitious," Harvey says. "They'll live in the back of a store. They will work very hard to accomplish something. They're smart. No smarter than our kids, but our kids can't stand up to that competition. They've been spoiled somehow, and they say, 'Hey, I don't have to do that. I ain't gonna wash dishes, and I ain't gonna do this, and I ain't gonna do the other thing.'

"But our generation would have, 'cause we were hungry too, and had drive and really knew what work was."

Boomers grew up, writes Douglas Owram, "amid a cult of family and childhood, and they would themselves shift the emphasis towards a cult of youth as they reached adolescence. . . . Indeed, adult 'judgement' was mistrusted in a world that looked ever more to the spontaneity of youth." A rallying cry of the sixties and seventies was, Never trust anybody over thirty. Right away, a barrier between us.

The boomer craving for instant gratification was another. Gene Tingley once asked a young couple what they wanted from life. "I was reminiscing about how, when we were newly married, if anybody needed a new roof, the gang got together and the women got food and we put the roof on.

"They said, 'That sounds wonderful. But we want it all now.' I said, 'Why? Getting it is half the fun. Why do you want it all now?'

"He said, 'Well, all our friends want everything now, so we do too. We want what our parents had, and more.'

"It's dreadful. I don't understand that."

It baffles Sheila Hanson of Mallorytown, Ontario, too. "We grew up with parents who were frugal, careful. And so did our children. So where has this materialistic, hedonistic society come from?"

The answer: from us. We made them what they are. Not intentionally. But the boomers, as Owram points out, never had to struggle for survival and had few worries about economic security. They were "the best-fed, best-educated and healthiest generation in Canadian history. . . . Thus, the generation could turn its attention to its own sensibilities. The boomers' sense of self was due, in no small part, to the fact they had the luxury of being free to think about such things."

Edmonton's Ted Byfield, editor of *Western Report*, thinks we're to blame for more than that. "Besides our commitment to materialism, we were also completely enthralled by what we· thought of as modern research and technology," he wrote in 1995. The educational psychologist and the sociologist spoke with the same authority as the chemist and the physicist, Byfield contends, "but they had not earned that authority. And we didn't realize it. We eventually were to discover that what many of these pseudo-scientists talked and taught was pure poppycock but by then it was too late. We had entrusted our children to them and, in effect, they used our kids to produce the Sixties Revolution."

But they *are* our kids. No matter how much angst they may have caused or are still causing, nearly all my interviewees regarded the raising of them as one of the greatest, if not *the* greatest, personal achievements of our lives.

Despite everything I have said about profligate boomers, they are not all wastrels and lay-abouts. Meet Riitta Louhimo. During cuts in Ontario government spending in 1995, social services minister David Tsubouchi produced a sample shopping list for those on a limited income. It proposed that one person could eat for $90.21 a month. It brought down an avalanche of ridicule and outrage from journalists and social activists.

Even us Depression refugees, knowing *we* could live on such a budget but wanting to be fair, wondered if the Harris government had flipped its lid. Then came a letter to the *Globe and Mail* from a Riitta Louhimo, describing the forgotten art of thrifty shopping.

She *had* to be from Generation M, hadn't she? Surprise! Ms Louhimo was a boomer, but not the product of North American wretched excess.

Her family came to Canada from Sweden in 1959 "for the opportunity to better our situation," she told me. "And that's the key; it was an opportunity, not a right. We lived in a basement apartment during those early years, while my parents worked, learned English, and began to save up for a better life. I left home at a fairly early age and put myself through college one semester at a time. I didn't expect to live in a large apartment when rooming houses were in my budget."

As students, she and her husband lived over an empty store in three rooms with an unheated kitchen. They discovered that "good cooking is less expensive than prepared food" (no news to Generation M but a revelation to most younger Canadians). They learned to make hearty stews with oil, garlic, beans and potatoes; graduated from salt and pepper to curry and basil; shopped from the priced-to-clear racks.

They used public transit. It took most of a day to travel to the stores, shop every aisle for listed bargains, line up to pay and trek home with frequent rest breaks for tired arms. They never shopped at convenience stores unless they were too sick to travel.

"Life is more fulfilling, in my viewpoint, if one never reaches that perfect moment when everything hoped for is here," Louhimo told me. That's our generation's philosophy exactly.

Just for the hell of it, Louhimo tried living within the dollar guidelines of Tsubouchi's much-maligned shopping list. She discovered it could be done, and done well for around seventy-five dollars – *less* than the guideline. "Although we can afford to live higher on the hog now, it still gives me pleasure to know that if the world collapses around me, I will survive."

Her detailed shopping list (different from Tsubouchi's) and techniques are fascinating but too long to recount here. But "this is not a starvation diet. I didn't lose any weight while eating this way. I missed things like chicken wings, but that's a taste issue. I got plenty of bulk to fill the stomach and plenty of calories and nutrients."

The biggest secret, Ms. Louhimo says, is to buy what's on sale and cook in bulk right away. It requires budgeting and such logical tactics as avoiding prepared foods and junk foods, skills that many boomers and Xers never acquired.

"Perhaps Harris should institute some classes for welfare recipients," she concludes, "although I'm afraid that may be considered somewhat fascist." She's probably right on both counts.

Our generation tends to lump boomers together with the later arrivals as variously defined on page 239. It's a mistake. They are not much alike, nor particularly fond of one another.

The very late boomers and the busters, including what Coupland called Xers, came of age during the early-eighties recession to discover that all the good jobs and houses were gone. About 25 per cent of them, according to the research firm Canadian Facts, think that only fools pay income tax. According to a scathing 1995 article in *Next City*, a Toronto-based periodical, among the busters and younger there is "a frightening kind of morality, the idea that honour doesn't count, that individuals bear no responsibility for their behaviour. It is an extension of the old 'anything is OK as long as you don't get caught' brand of morality. And it is endemic among today's youth, a growing malaise nourished by the welfare state."

Busters certainly aren't all on welfare, but they are otherwise identifiable. They complain a lot (my contemporary, David MacDonald of Kingston, calls them "a bunch of unmitigated whiners"). Their guts churn with what Douglas Coupland called "boomer envy." In a 1995 article in *Canadian Living*, writer Laura Pratt quoted one of the malcontents: "The reason we are like this, so sullen and unresponsive, private, confusing, and completely non-user-friendly, is largely tied up in the generation that's just before us. We are like this because of the baby boomers."

An American twentysomething once sneered that the main boomer wave "gleefully shifted from sixties hedonism to eight- ies materialism." The boomers didn't take *that* lying down in their Jacuzzis; one of them shot back that the Xers/twentysome- things (busters, to David Foot) are a "faceless, colourless, odour- less transition group."

When Generation M gripes about the lack of common courtesy in young people, we're referring at least as often to the busters and echo generations as to boomers. There's some sta- tistical basis for our plaint. Sociologist Reginald Bibby finds that the number of Canadians under thirty-five (particularly male) who value honesty, kindness, politeness, and forgiveness is consistently lower – by as much as eleven percentage points – than it is for those over fifty-five. "In short," concludes Bibby, "a value shift is taking place." Anyone who has been shouldered off a sidewalk by a gaggle of teenagers or young adults – perhaps not intentionally rude but totally self-absorbed – will attest to that.

Jack Brown of Waterloo points to the boorishness of athletes – from kids to young adults. Child hockey players *and* their boomer parents heap gutter language on referees. Baseball's petulant millionaire Roberto Alomar spits on an umpire. Such behaviour was not tolerated in our time; ours was an age of civility.

Not to deny there are mean-mouthed nasty old seniors among us, but, Glen Hancock maintains, good manners were a hallmark of our growing-up. "If someone on the street was ill, every mother said to the children, 'Now, you be quiet when you're passing their house,'" Hancock says. "Can you imagine that today?"

Elizabeth Tucci can't stand children, encouraged by their boomer parents, using an adult's first name. "And I don't see the necessity of teaching four-year-olds all the medical names for all parts of the body. When a four-year-old does this, calling me 'Liz' in the process, it's a bit too much."

"In some ways we weren't as indulgent as they are today," Jim Lamb agrees. "Ruby and I certainly wouldn't take our children to a restaurant until they learned to behave. Behaviour was a much bigger factor in our day. The house was oriented to the adult. When guests came, there was never any question as to who was in charge. Any disturbance would be squashed. Whereas today grandchildren raise hell regardless of who's there."

That kind of conduct sends Hancock into orbit. He tells of conversations with young parents being routinely interrupted by their children: "The parents don't look upon it as being undisciplined. They regard it as the rightful freedom of young people. For the present that might be fine, but I really fear for the conflicts those children will have when they get away from home, have to start sharing, and have to start seeing another person's point of view. Rather than simply always being right themselves."

All that aside, Generation M – being famed for its moderation and fair play, along with wisdom, humour, and good looks – is not without sympathy for the busters, even if they do want to send us to bed without supper.

"My heart goes out to this generation, especially where the woman has to go out to work," Bernice Holmes says. "We can say 'Does she really have to? Does she need the three-bedroom house or the second car?' With all the diversity in raising children nowadays, the answer in most cases is, 'Yes, she does.'"

Perhaps the greatest discrepancy between us and them (boomers in particular) – and certainly right up there beside outlooks towards money – is the attitude towards love, marriage, and familial ties.

Among younger generations it is fashionable, if not *de rigueur*, to blame one's parents for every failure, disappointment, or sin. The most appalling crimes, if not forgiven outright, elicit understanding and sympathy from younger generations if, say, the serial killer's mother failed him at toilet training.

Conversely, members of Generation M, almost without exception, speak of their parents fondly, sometimes with reverence. Is it the rose-coloured-glasses syndrome? Maybe. Some parents of my contemporaries were drunks. Sometimes one parent abandoned the family. Child abuse no doubt existed, but it was never discussed.

Generation M seems unwilling to condemn its parents' errors and omissions. Perhaps it is because respect for elders was implanted in us at earliest childhood. We would never dream of dissecting parental rights and wrongs as the young do freely now. They analyse everything; we at their age did not. Neither extreme is right.

To marry or not to marry? That's another question. "Speaking as a Catholic, the boomers kind of crossed lines that we would never have crossed," observes Tony Parfitt. "Things like living together and all that."

The boomers were the first generation to postpone marriage past the magic age of twenty to twenty-nine. One reason: career (especially for young women) came first. They were the first to live, and even bear children, as couples out of wedlock. Their intent, in part, was to find the appropriate mate, to avoid getting locked into the boring or loveless marriages (so perceived) of their parents.

Initially this shocked Generation M; some still can't handle it. But many of us realized that the new mores, although flouting traditional doctrine, had potential merit. Many of us plunged headlong into matrimony long before we were emotionally ready for it.

Are the boomers better off? Hard to say. Many of their "relationships" (buzzword for today) break down regardless. As one boomer told me, "Talking about failed relationships is one of our favourite topics." In 1975, reports Reginald Bibby, only 7 per cent of Canadians were divorced over a lifetime; in 1995 it was 14 per cent.

Divorce has taken its toll on Generation M, too, but many of our "dearly beloved" of earlier chapters are still together, fifty-odd years later, by luck or good management.

Dearly Beloved – III

And others of us, late bloomers and second-time-arounders, were – during the chaotic sixties – quietly falling in love and marrying in the sweet old-fashioned way, but with the wisdom of middle years . . .

It is the early sixties. Clifford Bell has worked painfully hard all his life, from the time he and I left our one-room grade school together in southwestern Saskatchewan. He's had little time and few opportunities for romance. Now, partner with his father on the family farm, Clifford is coming up to age forty and a cross-roads in his solitary life. It's about time I do something – either go on the booze or get married, he tells himself, somewhat in jest. Getting married is better. Probably.

He is a faithful member of the neighbourhood Anglican church, a wee, white wooden building served by a minister in summer when the roads are open. In the winter during childhood, Clifford and others took "Sunday School by Post."

In the sixties, his name is still on its mailing list, and he still enjoys its occasional letters and booklets. Particularly the seasonal messages from the secretary in Regina, a certain Olive

Farnden. She, too, has a farm background, is in her forties, came out of three and a half wartime years in the Canadian Women's Army Corps as a lieutenant in personnel, and has teaching credentials earned with her DVA credits.

One December he sends her a personal letter along with the Christmas donation. Just a friendly note, but it seems to call for a personal reply. To her surprise, more letters come thick and fast. It's obvious this stranger is looking for a marriage partner.

They arrange to meet in the spring on neutral ground, in front of a Moose Jaw funeral home (nothing morbid; just a handy landmark). She sees a tall, raw-boned, quietly humorous fellow. He sees a short woman with a merry smile and eyes warm with wisdom and compassion. Circumspectly, as you'd expect of our generation, their first "date" is in the home of Clifford's sister Edith, a Moose Jaw teacher. They marry a year later, in 1966.

Thirty years later, Cliff recalls it as "the divine push in my life. Closer to divine than anything else that's ever happened to me."

New Year's Eve, also in 1966. The slim, dapper ex-sailor Larry Holmes is general manager of the Ontario Brewers' Institute. His first wife died young. His second marriage has broken up. He is just back from a lonely Christmas in Hawaii on his own.

During his holiday, he has periodically phoned his secretary, the dark-eyed ebullient Bernice Quinto, to see if the office can live without him. But this is Saturday, which seems an odd time to phone.

"I just wondered," he begins. "It's New Year's Eve . . ." (as if she didn't know.) "What are you doing?"

Bernice thinks, I'm old enough not to lie about stuff like this. "Not a damn thing," she says.

"Would you like to go out?"

They do, and they marry the next September.

Years after, when they have a family, Bernice's friends, remembering the naive teenager who thought babies came off a hospital assembly line, say, "Hey, did you find it hard delivering your babies with your underwear on?"

Bernice is ready for them.

"No," she says, "but I found it really hard *conceiving* with my underwear on."

VII

THE WAY WE ARE

Money and Us

In 1995 Roy Bonisteel, former host of TV's "Man Alive," wrote in the United Church *Observer* of "the increasingly negative attitude I seem to sense toward the old. It's called ageism. We tend to discard the elderly whenever we can. . . . Stereotypes and common misconceptions about the aged are held as truth in our society."

He's right. When certain of the younger generations discovered that the good times were gone, they vented their wrath on an easy target: us. A July 1995 study, "The Generational Accounts of Canada," produced for Vancouver's Fraser Institute by a youthful Ph.D. candidate, is a commendable examination of how governments are spending Canadians into the poorhouse. But it also characterizes our age group as "the most fortunate" generation, receiving a lush assortment of government benefits and, during our retirement, paying only about 40 per cent of those benefits' total cost. All right, but what about *before* retirement?

Barbara McNeill, who spent most of her working life as a corporate financial officer, calculates that the Canada Pension Plan premiums she and her employers contributed during her working years were capable, at an actuarial rate of interest, of paying her current CPP *and* OAS – $10,800 a year – indefinitely. Whether federal governments put those premiums to work properly to *achieve* that result was out of our hands.

The sniping goes on. A *Saturday Night* article, cheekily titled "Grandma! Grandpa! Back to Work!" opened with: "Retirement isn't a birthright. Those who enjoy it haven't earned it. . . ." Did they mean us Generation-M layabouts who worked our buns to the bone all our lives?

In 1996 Toronto *Globe and Mail* columnist Michael Valpy discovered in Regina a casino packed with old folks (locally dubbed the "Greedy Geezers") happily feeding the slots. Valpy fell back in alarm. "This is what our wise elders are doing?" he intoned from his editorial pulpit. Banning gambling, or alcohol for that matter, both of which cause untold human misery, would be another issue. But why pick on the elderly? They were having fun, and, according to Valpy, all profits went to the Saskatchewan government, local charities, and the Federation of Saskatchewan Indians. You could almost call it charitable giving.

In Vancouver that same year, a thirty-one-year-old theology student, at a hearing on the plight of the beleaguered CPP, wailed that his generation would be "paying through the nose," and that "wealthy" seniors should be denied benefits from the CPP entirely. But as Dick Martin, secretary treasurer of the Canadian Labour Congress, pointed out in a 1996 *Globe and Mail* article, "nearly half of the income received by the elderly comes from OAS and the CPP," and "large numbers of older Canadians today live barely above the low income (*i.e.*, poverty) line as defined by Statistics Canada."

An item on TV's "Canada AM" called us the "Blessed Generation." To the youthful commentator, we were blessed with "low taxes, low housing prices, forty years of booming economy." No mention of the low wages we earned during much of our working lives.

We are not without pity for young Canadians in the current merciless job market. Over and over, my age group has expressed genuine sympathy for today's young job-hunters. But all their mewling and snivelling gets under our skin. A generation that struggled through depression and war is hardly "blessed" or "fortunate."

"So I've taken all this money?" demands Doug Harvey from Victoria. "Did *you* ever have a cup of hot water, that's all, for breakfast? Did you? Did *you* go to school with the sole off your shoe as I did? Oh, no!"

"Our generation worked for those pensions," snaps Gene Tingley. "Our generation got this country going. We'd work till two o'clock in the morning with no overtime and think nothing of it."

Rae MacLeod, a retired actuary living in Thornhill, Ontario, once told a young acquaintance, "I'm going to leave you the museums and airports. Might even leave you the subway. No rent required. So maybe you can consider what we seniors get as advance payment."

MacLeod was in the pension business most of his working life. He watched and studied the OAS and CPP from their inception. In 1951, he says, the revised OAS was predicated on a 2 per cent sales tax, a 2 per cent personal-income-tax levy, and a 2 per cent tax on corporate profits.

"Would there have been such widespread approval in 1951 if there were any suspicions that the federal government, without consultation or even a background paper, would retroactively change the universal OAS into a means-tested program through the income tax act?" MacLeod asks, referring to the OAS clawback.

MacLeod was involved with a 1983 parliamentary task force on pension reform, which included a fresh look at the CPP, established in 1966 when seniors' poverty was one of Canada's urgent problems. For many years, the premium was 3.8 per cent, then was gradually increased by 0.2 per cent a year. By 1996,when McLeod provided these comments, it was 5.6 per cent, split equally between employer and employee or paid in full by the self-employed.

"From the outset, it was well known that the premium rate would rise to over 10 per cent as the program matured," MacLeod says. So, the need for higher premiums (according to reports in early 1997, they will eventually reach 9.9 per cent) should come as no surprise and need not be blamed on fat-cat seniors.

Nevertheless, the people I polled were surprisingly fair-minded over the OAS clawback whereby the government takes back part or all of one's old age pension depending on level of income. By a ratio of two to one, they claimed not to resent it. Those who object do so more on principle than over income lost. One respondent calls it a breach of faith. Another replied, "I provided that money, dammit!"

"If such a clawback were the answer to Canada's economic problems, then I wouldn't resent it," says Hal Sisson of Victoria. He's sure the government will fritter away any savings, and most of us agree. We've had our fill of wastrel governments and are tired of taking the rap for society's contemporary ills.

So it was a treat to read in the *Globe and Mail* a letter from a right-thinking boomer in response to yet another Gen-X bleat.

"I am a baby boomer whose parents are senior citizens," wrote the admirable Anne Marie Doyle of Ottawa. "They and their friends are people who paid their dues every step of the way, provided for their own retirement income and rarely if ever complained about some of the tougher hands they were dealt."

The excellent Ms Doyle concluded, "It seems that while Generation X differs in many important respects from my generation, they have acquired the boomers' knack for whining."

Obviously some of the younger generation turned out just fine. We are nominating Ms Doyle for the Order of Canada.

What about our wealth, the trillion dollars that we allegedly squirrelled away, a good portion of which is expected to fall into the laps of our children and grandchildren? The "trillion-dollar fairy tale," as Canadian Association of Retired Persons (CARP) president Lillian Morgenthau dubs it, arose from a late-1980s study. It found, in a sample of Canadians over age fifty, $350,000 in assets per average household. Roughly 30 per cent of that estimated stash was in real estate, mostly homes we bought for peanuts, on our peanut incomes, that appreciated over the years.

But by 1997, rock-bottom interest rates were leaching away seniors' savings and causing us to dip deeper into the nest egg. That, coupled with predictions that more of us will live into our nineties – sorry, Generation X! – means we may spend the whole damn trillion before we drop dead.

True, a minority of affluent snowbirds flies south every winter to frolic in Florida. But most seniors stay home and shiver. Sixty-nine per cent have incomes in the ten- to twenty-thousand-dollar range, according to CARP. More specifically, Statistics Canada finds that average income for senior men is $24,500 and for senior women, $15,000. Maud Barlow, national chair of the Council of Canadians, reports that four out of ten seniors are classified as "very poor."

Scott, the young "runner," climbs to the second floor of the shabby building, packaged dinner in hand. He knocks. "Meals on Wheels!"

The door opens slowly. A shaggy grey head peers through the crack – rightly cautious about admitting strangers in this part of town – before letting us in. His single room (no bath-room), about twelve feet by twelve, is chaos. The unmade bed is a tangle of grubby sheets and blanket. Beside it is a cluttered table and an overflowing ashtray. A few clothes are bundled on top of a wardrobe and in stray corners. It's the disarray of a man who has given up caring. He is one of our generation's elderly poor.

Scott sets out a hot meal: bean soup in a styrofoam cup, roast beef with corn niblets and mashed potato in a tinfoil container.

"How's it going?"

Instead of a knee-jerk "Okay" to my knee-jerk question, the man says matter-of-factly, with no apparent bid for sympathy, "It's lonely living on your own." And I think ashamedly, But for the grace of God . . .

Scott and I may be the only other people he will see until the next meal delivery. Back at the Mid-Toronto Community Services office, Jacqueline Arrindell, in charge of volunteer pro-grams, says that for 95 per cent of Meals on Wheels clients this visit is their only contact with the outer world.

Meals on Wheels is the centrepiece of Mid-Toronto Community Services' impressive array of programs for elderly or disabled persons living on their own, all aimed at helping them retain a modicum of independence and dignity. It serves a large swath of the inner city. Seven days a week, if clients choose, a hot noontime meal is brought to their door; four dollars a day for those who can afford it, less or nothing for those who can't.

The district houses people of all ages, in rooms, mediocre apartments, or public housing developments. The seniors, here, are people who never cashed in on postwar prosperity – or did but got lost along the way.

Today, volunteer driver Ernie smoothly weaves through the neighbourhood maze of one-way streets. Volunteer runners Scott and Michael unload the meals from a trunk full of thermal bags and trot them to nineteen doors.

Last door. Her white hair is tousled, but her smile is huge and radiant. As with most of the others, TV is her only companion, but there's a bright, defiant touch amidst the dreary clutter of her single room: two clusters of dried flowers in browns, oranges, and reds. *She* hasn't given up.

"God bless you!" she says as we leave.

And I hope God blesses *you*.

A *Maclean's* headline, probably composed by a querulous boomer, perpetuates the myth: "More Seniors Are Living It Up. But Will Baby Boomers Retire in the Same Style?" A lot of boomers will, and then some. A couple of years ago, the Farrell Research Group of Vancouver reported that roughly half of all the personal wealth in Canada is concentrated in the 12 per cent of Canadians who will retire in the next few years. These will be the early boomers – who lately have broken out in a frenzy of RRSP savings – and the Silents.

The Toronto pundit Robert Fulford once wrote in the *Globe and Mail* that "the Depression generation . . . ran the country deep into debt." More recently, another *Globe* deep thinker, Jeffrey Simpson (born in 1949), said essentially the same: "Never before in Canadian history . . . has one generation bequeathed such a fiscal mess to the next." Lillian Morgenthau, CARP's doughty president, begs to differ.

"The reality is that the vast majority of Canada's seniors had little to do with the government's fiscal mismanagement over the last twenty years, and there is no reason they should now pay a disproportionate share of the cost," she says. "Nor did most of today's seniors ask for or benefit from most of the government's foolish fiscal excesses."

But we did – along with Fulford's age group and older boomers such as Simpson – elect the politicians who ran us into the ground. We must carry that on our consciences. And we did enjoy times of high employment, healthy real-estate markets, and a vibrant stock market – as did the Silents and the early boomers.

Many of Generation M have adequate RRSPs and paid-up homes because we were and are extremely careful with money. We started worrying and saving when we were young. Consider Steve Walbridge of Pointe Claire, Quebec. When he was seven, his father gave him a little notebook, a freebie from a life-insurance company. Steve, who grew up to be an accountant, began a lifetime habit of record-keeping. His weekly entries included: "allowance, 7¢; Sunday School, 2¢; candy, 1¢ . . ." The biggest salary he ever had was $31,000 in 1979, his final year of work, yet he always managed to buy a savings bond.

"We're comfortable, now," Walbridge says, then adds defiantly: "*Why* are we comfortable? Because we were careful with every darn penny from day one!"

Barbara Gory, another retired accountant, is also penny-conscious, although she doesn't have to be. "It's not that we spare ourselves. It's just that it would seem absolutely wrong to waste money. It's a fear that it could run out, something could happen."

Gladys Byrnes, widowed and renting a fine old red-brick house with gingerbread trim in Creemore, Ontario, has enough pension money to travel, including winters in Florida. Yet she won't splurge on a special treat, such as the fresh asparagus that she loves, "unless it's a good buy." Irrational? So it might seem to a boomer. To us it's called getting a bang for your buck.

One of our canons is, Don't let credit charges drag you down. We are genuinely perplexed when younger generations seem unable to grasp the wisdom of this, or simply ignore it.

"I pay for everything, totally," says Douglas Gardner, a typical case. "I use credit cards, but I pay the full amount each month. I've never paid those guys one cent of interest, and I have no intention of it." At one time, when he saw signs in banks urging customers to borrow today and have a car tomorrow, he turned them face down. "False advertising," he told the startled tellers, who thought he was a nutcase.

When he was a child, Gardner recalls, his mother sent him to pay the telephone bill on the way to school, long before it was due. "It had nothing to do with the fine. It was just you paid your bills on time. It was your responsibility."

Same with Joe Ghiglione in Moose Jaw: he walks downtown to pay the phone bill the same day he receives it. A boomer, with her fiscal head screwed on straight, reminds me that this is not financially smart, that Joe could hold the bill until a day or two before the due date and earn interest on his money in the interim. Of course. But the way we see it, what if, by putting off, we somehow missed the due date and ended up paying interest to those suckers? Anyway, the current monthly interest on, say, thirty dollars from your phone bill wouldn't even buy a fortune cookie.

Dr. Mary Wright, retired professor in London, Ontario, says she now has more money and property (through bequests and financial caution) than ever before. Yet she retains the instincts of the young assistant professor who earned two hundred dollars a month. When I visited her, she had just bought a second TV – small, and, if memory serves, a black-and-white – and was wondering if she'd been extravagant.

"When I was working, I asked a well-to-do farmer his advice for success," recalls Leonard Shiels of Craven, Saskatchewan. " 'I'll tell you, boy,' he said. 'You pay for what you get, and see that you get what you pay for, and you will turn out all right.' " Leonard did, and so do we all.

Well, almost all. I met two or three of our age group – mutants, perhaps – who admit to reckless spending. Elizabeth Tucci was married to one. "I guess he was a reincarnated member of the Light Brigade," she says, clearly relishing the line, "because his motto was 'CHARGE!' "

Akin to our fiscal conservatism – and just as baffling to our children and grandchildren – is our compulsion to save things; precious clutter that they call junk. We are a generation of packrats.

Recently, at a Sunday brunch, a well-dressed stranger, upon hearing of my book-in-progress, asked, "Do you layer the soap?" I understood instantly. He meant, do I keep the slivers from nearly used soap bars, the kind my kids chuck in the garbage, and squish two or more together to get a little more mileage from them. Yes, I do. So does this fellow. Neither of us is destitute (he, as I recall, is a former realtor or insurance man – either of which I regard as a licence to print money). We just have to do it.

In Paradise Valley, Alberta, Cyril Flint stockpiles bits of wire, old rags, even old shoes in his garage. His wife, Lillian, hoards old towels, sheets, cardboard boxes: "They *might* come in handy some time." Around Foxwarren, Manitoba, Lillian Falloon still scrapes the wrapping papers from pounds of butter as liners for baking pans. Mary Arnold of Mississauga saves "elastics and silver paper. I have a drawer full of string. When I taught kindergarten, I saved empty toilet rolls and wax paper rolls for school projects."

Marianne Harvey still picks up stray pennies from the street, although "my kids would pass by a dime or a quarter." Merle Tingley of London has "saved every little scrap of wood, every little piece of metal – 'cause you never know when you're going to need it – rather than go to the hardware and spend fifteen cents for a new one."

"If I use a piece of Saran Wrap twice – and I do – my children say, 'Mo-ther!' in that put-down tone of voice," says Patricia Andrews. "And tissue paper. When I unwrap a gift, my kids say, 'Oh, Mother, careful, careful, don't tear it!' They know I'm going to fold it and put it away to use again."

Clifford Bell owned only one suit until he was thirty. "I got it to go to church in. I still wear shirts with holes in the back.

Olive gets after me about it, but I take a fancy to one shirt and stay with it."

None of this has to do with lack of affluence. It is simply the way we are. Peter and Madeleine Cranston own a handsome home in Victoria. He topped off his flying career by piloting cabinet ministers and VIPs for the federal Department of Transport. Yet, he says wryly, "I still have to steel myself to take a taxi if I'm not paying for it out of expense money. But I've finally accepted that long-distance calls are a cost-effective way of communication."

Waste pains us. "Young people today throw away three times what our parents ever *had*," complains Ron Cason of Calgary. Glen Hancock surreptitiously turns off the lights that his boomer children leave blazing in empty rooms when they visit his home. So do I. Neither of us lets the young people know we do it, lest they think us eccentric, stingy, or both.

On any pleasant summer day, Bill Williamson of Don Mills reclines on excellent lawn chairs that he salvaged from a (younger) neighbour's garbage five years ago. Ben Robertson of Surrey told his wife one day, "Just tell me what kind of exercise machine you want. They're all out there on the curb with the garbage. It just breaks my heart!"

I understand, Ben. In the immortal words of President Bill Clinton, I feel your pain.

The Way We Are

Sometimes I pull on my old-person's disguise (wrinkles, grey hair, vanishing jawline, advancing waistline) over the lean, taut, dark-haired matinee idol that is really me, and take to the streets. I could be the Amazing Invisible Man. Younger people generally look through or around me. When you are old, you don't count in Canadian society (unless that society covets your pension cheque).

Several years ago, financial planner Barbara McNeill and I, collaborating on a book about money management, interviewed demographer David K. Foot. Baby boomer Foot, a nice-enough fellow, gladly shared his theories, then did two things that caused our gorge to rise. He absent-mindedly patted Barbara on the knee (not realizing how close he came to losing his arm), then remarked that we (geezers) probably didn't like to use banking machines.

I, a gadget freak, had been using the one-armed bank tellers since they were invented. McNeill – who has a B.S. in chemistry, an M.B.A. in finance and organizational behaviour, and whose last job before retirement was treasurer and vice-president of finance for Syntex Inc. – was doing her family's banking at age twelve. Only our Generation-M good manners kept us from depriving the world of the now-famous co-author of *Boom, Bust and Echo*.

Foot didn't mean to be patronizing. His offhand remark simply reflected the prevailing assumption that when you are old you are out of it. (The same condescending attitude is at work in a notorious TV commercial wherein two elderly twits, sitting with their minds in neutral, are galvanized into paroxysms of joy when their idiot son phones home to say he's just bought life insurance.)

If we are not all incompetent twits, what wisdom did we acquire in our three-score-and-something years? What are the virtues that we extol so often and so annoyingly to our children and grandchildren? What values and attitudes set us so proudly apart, like alien creatures from the distant planet Good-Old-Days?

And (perish the thought) do we have any imperfections?

The following observations are based on many months of archival research plus interviews with 181 Canadians of my generation from many walks of life. They were not, I stress, selected by scientific pollsters' methods. Some are school or university friends; others were met during my forty-five years of journalistic travels around Canada; still others responded to my advertisements in various news media across the country. All of them answered my questionnaires, or were personally interviewed, or (most often) both.

Several of the people I interviewed claimed that only history will be able to measure our worth, if any, fifty or a hundred years down the road. Sorry, I can't wait that long.

Most of my interviewees modestly, diffidently (tooting one's own horn was not encouraged in our childhoods) found some good in us. Former teacher Kay Belbas of Rossburn, Manitoba, gives us an A for effort: "We did the best we knew how."

Peter Cranston suggests that success may be measured in what *doesn't* happen. "They used to say, if you completed a flight and the next day the people didn't remember anything about it, you did a heck of a good job," the former pilot explains. "The same goes for what we did in our lives. We didn't succumb to any wild radical movements that persecuted people wholesale the way so many countries did. We were cautious, and we didn't run off in directions that were bad." Quintessentially Canadian, some would say.

So, what kind of people are we?

1. Survivors

Dr. Edward Pleva, retired geographer at the University of Western Ontario, considers survival our dominant trait. We will doggedly see something through to the end, no matter how long it takes. We learned never to quit, because keeping on was usually the only option. We fervently hope there will never be another depression or war, but if they came, we would prevail.

2. Smarter than you think

University of Manitoba researcher John McIntyre says seniors are enormous repositories of general knowledge, even allowing for what they may have forgotten. *U.S. News and World Report* notes that the brain doesn't necessarily decline with age: in tests, one-third of subjects over seventy showed no loss of mental acuity; one-quarter to one-third of those in their eighties performed as well as younger people. Older brains are not necessarily worse, just different. The *Canadian Journal on Ageing* reports that, while cognitive function often declines with age, it's not a given. In some studies, the elderly show no mental deterioration if they stay busy. (Generation X is *really* going to hate that.)

3. Decent

"Fairness," "honesty," "decency." Over and over, my respondents nominated these as our redeeming qualities. "Decency pervaded our generation, from the time we were growing up at home, through the war, and after," says Glen Hancock. "We still live by that code. It's one of the good things we inherited that is not extant in the rising generations. We think it's right. Whether it is or not, we're stuck with it. It's as much a part of us as our blood corpuscles."

"We tried so hard to be something and at the same time be fair," says Regina's Dr. John Archer. Jack Brown, who spent the last twenty years of his working life as secretary of the University of Waterloo, adds, "If we did one thing and one thing only, we gave an honest day's work for an honest dollar."

4. Charitable

When I think of the deeds I've
done to help my fellow man

And of the things I didn't do
for want of thought or plan
It occurs to me the balance
may still be changed a bit
If when I see a chance to help
I do get on with it.

Those lines are from Tim Seeley, the thoughtful Peace River, Alberta, farmer and occasional poet, who also offered me a quote from Cicero. Younger Canadians, hearing us gripe about society's freeloaders, may think we are a couple of pints short of the milk of human kindness. Yet taking care of each other was part of our growing up. "It was sort of a code," says Arnold Steppler of New Westminster.

"We didn't expect the government to take care of us," adds Olive Bell. "We helped each other."

We've always distrusted government promises and government aid. Toronto's Barbara McNeill, who after retirement set up shop as a financial planner, habitually asked her older clients, "What is your first priority?" Without exception they answered, "I want to be sure I'm not a burden on anyone."

Precisely *because* of that, we draw a sharp line between needy and needless. We have little patience with generations who think the world and government owe them a living.

"I was brought up to believe that one earns a 'right,'" says Bill Finnbogason. "There is no question that people in need are entitled to assistance if they qualify. Today, to the detriment of society, we have a situation where government assistance is, in a sense, in competition with industry in its attempt to fill lower-paid positions. In the minds of many, the difference in the wage being offered and assistance being received is not sufficient to warrant getting off the dole. The work ethic is, in many cases, a thing of the past."

That aside, when financial aid is needed in families, the

money often flows from the elders to the middle-aged or younger. Of the persons I surveyed, about 90 per cent had financially supported their children into higher education or beyond. They reported it with pride, not resentment.

As a group we are the biggest givers of money to charity. A Revenue Canada survey for a recent year showed that 38 per cent of seniors make charitable donations, compared to only 30 per cent among all Canadian taxpayers. An average senior's contribution was $890, compared to the overall Canadian adult average of $634. Sometimes the charity extends far beyond our shores; for instance, from their little farmhouse north of Selkirk, Manitoba, Ernest and Helen Beck regularly support Third World children.

We also freely donate our time. True, we *have* spare time (so do many younger people), but that alone is not reason for giving it. We do so because it's right, and because it makes us feel good. Louis Hamel voluntarily adapts houses for the elderly or disabled in the poorest area of Montreal. His helpers are young dropouts, all hard cases, some with drug problems. He tries to instil in them discipline, respect for authority, and craftsmanship. Once they are reasonably trained, Hamel's team fits houses with access ramps, accessible kitchen drawers, bathroom rails, tables screwed to the floor so a disabled person can lean against or hold onto them. Along the way he tries to create understanding between his clients and his unruly kids. Sometimes it works.

Why does he donate so many hours of his life? "I feel I owe this world," Hamel says.

A 1990 study by the Vanier Institute of the Family found that 55 per cent of Canadians over age sixty-five help provide volunteer transportation, financial support, child care, home maintenance, housework, and personal care. The value of that effort, if performed by full-time workers earning an annual salary of twenty-five thousand dollars, would add up to 1.7 billion dollars a year.

Ex-merchant seaman Eric Golby of Tottenham, Ontario, is a shining example; he's been a volunteer driver for cancer patients and crippled children since 1979, and in 1987 was awarded the Ontario Medal of Citizenship for his work. Norman Currell of White Rock, in his eighties, performs a similar service for the elderly. And around Canada, the "Seniors for Seniors" organization does just what its name implies.

The Vanier report concluded, "Many of those who worry about whether society can care for an increasingly older population often overlook the contributions that seniors themselves make to others."

5. *Sexy*

According to *The Bibby Report: Social Trends Canadian Style*, 30 per cent of men ages sixty to seventy lead "highly active" sex lives; they say they do it at least once a week. Even one in five men and one in fifteen women over age seventy claim they have sex once a week or more. And a *Reader's Digest* article cries, "Sex! It Gets Even Better!"

Could have fooled me.

6. *Naive*

Our tendency to trust, perhaps a legacy from our simpler beginnings, and once a noble attribute, proved near-fatal in the postwar years. Most of us think our blind faith in our politicians was one of the great errors of our time. "We became too docile and impotent in respect to political issues," says Gordon Smart of Victoria.

"We elected politicians who felt they had to keep sweetening the pot to get re-elected," add Joyce and Bob Brack of Saskatoon. And Jean Holt of Edmonton sums up bluntly, "We've elected and re-elected spendthrift nincompoops for decades."

7. *Cautious*

Excess caution, probably born of the Depression, has plagued most of us through our lifetimes. We can't shake it. We are bankers' nightmares, not because we default on loans but because we don't borrow.

"It *scares* me to borrow money," says Clifford Bell of Moose Jaw. Ben Robertson in Surrey understands completely: "One reason I never had my own business is I was scared stiff to borrow. How are you gonna pay it back?"

That attitude inhibited our entrepreneurism as a nation – we didn't invest in Canada when Americans and other foreigners did – and as individuals. Maurice Falloon remembers that "we were scared to take a chance. When I think of all the bargains I could have had in land! But it was always a lot of money, and I backed off."

Before his death, Fred Hamilton told me how he once had a chance to buy into the board game Trivial Pursuit, when its inventors were looking for backers. "The shares, I think, were fifty dollars. On the salary Canadian Press was paying me, fifty dollars was a lot. Of course, those guys became millionaires."

8. *Concerned*

Although society may have written us off, most of us care deeply about our society. By a ratio of about two to one (in my limited survey), we are more concerned about crime than ten or fifteen years ago. By comparison, sociologist Reginald Bibby found 46 per cent of the general population – and 56 per cent of those over fifty-five – view crime as "a very serious" concern.

That is partly because the elderly feel more vulnerable, partly because, as Bernice Holmes put it, we wish "our children could feel that free sense of well-being when away from their homes" that we enjoyed. We speak nostalgically of those gone-forever days when we never locked doors.

"I think it was about 1960 before I took the key out of the truck in the yard, or out of the tractor," says Ted Turner of Regina, recalling his farming years. "If you left it there, you always knew where it was. It never occurred to you that somebody would steal it. In fact, you left it there because your neighbour might need it."

Given our worries over crime, do we favour capital punishment? Forty per cent said no, 36 per cent said yes, and 24 per cent gave a qualified yes (depending on the crime). One woman said she had opposed capital punishment until the monstrous Paul Bernardo murders. Many of the no's were tempered with indictments of the justice system: "A judge's sentence should not be set aside," "Parole boards are staffed by weaklings," and "A life sentence should be for life." In this respect, my respondents were kinder and gentler than seniors overall. Or perhaps, aware that they might be quoted in a book, they were curbing vengeful tendencies. In Reginald Bibby's survey, 82 per cent of the general population favoured capital punishment, and 87 per cent felt the courts were not harsh enough. (For persons over fifty-five, those figures were 85 and 90 per cent respectively.)

Do we approve of the Draconian cost-cutting measures of the Ontario and Alberta governments? Forty-three per cent said yes, 38 per cent said no, and the remaining 19 per cent gave a qualified yes (agreeing in principle but feeling the methods were too harsh).

For about 75 per cent of my respondents, the most important issues facing Canada are deficit reduction and national unity (almost equal in importance). About 18 per cent rated unemployment and the need for jobs as a priority – interesting in that none of us is job-hunting. By comparison, Bibby found that 72 per cent of the general population deems the national debt to be its top concern, with unemployment a serious problem to 55 per cent and national unity a serious concern to only 25 per cent.

Interesting, too, were the miscellaneous comments that this thoughtful generation scribbled on the questionnaires I provided. Pemrose Whelan wishes that "values such as civility, courtesy, willingness to work could have been cultivated to a greater extent" among the generations that followed us. Douglas Gardner feels that, "in an effort to clarify individual rights, we did not stress efficiently the responsibilities that go with those rights."

Lawyer Hal Sisson, author of many funny songs and skits for amateur productions, has a somewhat pessimistic view of our future.

"Our expectations began to outrun the ability of a finite planet and the ecology thereof to meet the Western World's desire for immediate material prosperity and gratification," Sisson wrote, "while the majority of the grossly over-populated world starves. Demographics and stupidity will get the human race in the end."

A few of us even think Generation M will carry the can for society's latter-day ills (Generation X is going to love this). John Dodds of Vancouver says flatly, "Our generation will be remembered as greedy, mean, and narrow." He's no crank. Well-educated, well-groomed, silver hair coiffed, even in sweater and open-neck shirt he looks like the retired broker that he is. He lives alone, reads extensively, thinks Pierre Trudeau was "the only fun politician we ever had," and believes we have clung too long to our emotional ties to the British royalty. In some respects, then, he is not typical of our lot, but that makes his opinions all the more intriguing.

Nova Scotia's Jim Lamb, although less judgemental, also thinks our generation slipped up along the way.

"Up until about maybe the seventies, we did all that was expected of us," he says. "Then I think the affluence of the age corrupted us. Against our better judgement and our experience, we allowed our standards to fall in just about every field.

"The coarsening of society is one thing. Not just the language, the violence, the bad manners, the terrible dress. (Look at the wealthy people out there today, dressed like a bunch of bums.) All our standards slipped. Lawyers no longer observe their principles. Doctors don't. Journalists certainly don't. Where there's any kind of standard, all the standards are lowered."

O Canada

Partway through this project, I began asking people what Canada and being Canadian mean to them. A few were flummoxed. Others rose to the challenge.

"A Canadian identity?" replied Olive Thorne of Edmonton. "I see it every day in my neighbourhood when I look at very patient individuals, very giving individuals, very un-American individuals, very down-to-earth individuals, very hardworking individuals, somewhat naive individuals, and not very protest-minded individuals. I treasure what I observe in what I consider as 'Canadian.'"

To Ben Robertson, Canada means the freedom to vote, work, or speak out as we please. "Freedom is so wonderful, and we don't wave our flag or blow our horn nearly enough."

"Primarily it means the land, the lakes, the whole geography," Beverly Watson says. "It means fairness and caring. It means the democracy that still, for the most part, works here. I think it also means pride."

And to Bruce Lundy of Niagara Falls, Canada means "treating one and all in a decent manner." If only that were so. But Canada and its institutions haven't measured up for all of us.

Frank Moritsugu, the kid whom Canada didn't want, ended up in some of the top journalistic jobs of his time: *Maclean's* magazine, the CBC, *Canadian Homes & Gardens*, and the *Toronto Star*. He finished off his career with a long stint in the Ontario government.

"I've done all right," Moritsugu says diffidently from his Willowdale home. "I had a chance to overcome a lot of that shit [meaning his internment along with so many other Japanese Canadians], partly because I bust my ass to do it!" He "bust his ass," he admits, to prove he was as good as anyone else.

The wartime banishment left Frank and his fellow Nisei "blasted with psychological problems, and a lot of them won't accept it." In the 1980s, Moritsugu worked with others for redress. Initially he wanted only an apology on national television. He came to accept, however, that there had to be a decent financial settlement, otherwise "the rest of Canadians wouldn't realize this had been a bad thing." The settlement and apology came too late for his father and mother, who died in 1962 and 1984 respectively.

For Moritsugu, personal healing came long before that. In 1968, Douglas How – then editor of the Canadian edition of *Reader's Digest*, preparing a landmark two-volume history of Canadians in World War Two – asked him to write about his evacuation experience.

"You have to write it like you are the nineteen-year-old kid that it happened to," How told him.

Moritsugu, living at the time in a minuscule apartment in Montreal, begged a spare basement room from the janitor and sat alone typing day after day. When he reached page seven of his final draft, a strange thing happened.

"Suddenly tears started flowing down my face and even splashed on the typewriter keys. I had to stop, not only to wipe my eyes, but to think, 'What the hell is going on here! This is so weird!'"

He was not at that moment recording a particularly searing experience. "The only conclusion I could come to: I had finally peeled away all the scab that had covered over all those years. Now I *was* that nineteen-year-old guy, and it hurt like hell."

It was cathartic. He had broken the psychological block. Now, although he would never forget them, he could talk about those ignominious years when his country let him down.

"It frightens me, how little value Canadians place on citizenship, unless they've had to acquire it," Moritsugu says. "Japanese Canadians were the only ones who had to prove our citizenship after the fact."

One day long ago, on the Whitefish River Indian Reserve, little Lillian McGregor asked her father, "What's on the other side of those hills?"

"A couple of other reserves."

"What's a reserve?"

Augustine McGregor explained how treaty Indians were assigned to designated land.

"Are we in jail?" she asked.

"In a way," he said. "In a way, yes."

Sixty years later – although she built a successful career in the white man's world, primarily through her own drive and intelligence – Lillian feels her people are still imprisoned by the Indian Act.

"Aboriginal people are the only people in this country to live under an act like that. As soon as it's abolished – that won't be in your time or mine – then there'll be progress."

Aboriginals, she feels, are third-class citizens. They don't own their land as do, say, a white farmer or a city householder. They don't have MPs representing the reserves. The billions of federal dollars allotted to the native "problem" by successive governments don't seem to have accomplished much.

"I feel very frustrated. So I encourage the young people to

educate themselves. Learn their own backgrounds and learn the issues and speak up. We don't want to resort to violence, which is what they [officialdom] may drive us to."

The respondents in my informal poll rated the Quebec problem high among their concerns, but were divided about solutions. Some said we should get tough with Quebec. Others felt we should accommodate its demands "within reason." One thinks Quebec "should be treated like any province within Canada." Another says we should "call Quebec's bluff by telling them and the rest of Canada exactly what is to happen if Quebec separates." The iconoclastic John Dodds says if separation occurs, it is Generation M's fault. "We will be remembered," he says, "for one thing: that we let the country go."

To most Anglos in the prewar years, Quebec was an anomaly; thousands, maybe millions, had never seen the province nor met a French Canadian. The war changed that, but even in the fifties the invisible wall remained.

French Canada still meant Montreal – cosmopolitan, tantalizing, atypical Montreal, pragmatically accepting its unilingual visitors and ringing up its cash registers. We revelled in the city's civilized drinking, superb dining, and such exotica as Lili St. Cyr, the celebrated stripper. We didn't know a Quiet Revolution was brewing. Most of us bore no ill will. And most of us are still fumbling toward a realization of Quebecers' aspirations.

Louis Hamel – tall, with thick grey hair and dark, burning eyes – is passionate, voluble, and witty. He would never present himself as a "typical" Quebecer, but he is a wavering federalist: "Let's say I'm on the borderline."

He feels the English Canada he has known intimately for most of his adult life is turning against him and that no one outside Quebec understands what Quebecers want. A deal is a deal, Hamel says. Quebec's historic deal with Canada was autonomy in language, religion, and civil law. "We have the civil law. We have our religion. But our *language* is what makes us different."

LEAVING HIS CULTURE ON THE HANGER

Louis Hamel, artist, my friend for more than thirty years, is explaining how he feels about his language and Canada. Hamel is fluently bilingual; his mother told him when he was twelve that to earn a living he would have to learn English. I am unilingual, steeped in good intentions and many fruitless French language courses, including an agonizing month-long immersion in Tours.

You see, we're talking today in English. That may hurt you, but I'm gonna say it, because it says I'm a Canadian more than a hell of a lot of other Canadians, because I'm bilingual.

When I travel to Toronto, I have to leave my culture on the hanger as I arrive at the airport, because I cannot carry my culture into Toronto. If I go to the hotel lobby to get a magazine, I can't find a French magazine. It's all English. So when I arrive in Toronto, I just don't feel I'm in my country.

Now, when I go to New York, I have no expectation that I'm gonna talk French, and yet there's more French restaurants there than in Toronto. So I have no displeasing aspect when I'm in New York, because there's no expectation. I'm in a foreign country, so I change my language like if I go to Italy.

When I go to Toronto, I have to change my culture, but I'm told, "That's your country." So I'm always in conflict. I'm anxious to come back to *my* country, which is French Canada.

"I'm still a Canadian," Hamel stresses. "But Canada is really putting me into a position to say, The Hell with it. I'm going to become a French Canadian first."

As art director of *Reader's Digest* in Montreal, Hamel had to "bastardize my French language. I had to, because I was an artist. I could not show the emotions that artists should have." If he had, he maintains, he would have been written off as just another emotional French Canadian. "I had to be beautifully anglophone, with all the expressions and the dynamic and so on in English." French-speaking colleagues, who had to use English in joint staff meetings, often couldn't get their points across. They came away "looking like second-rate types. It's a bit like being black."

French Canada at the moment is like a teenager who loves his mother but wants to leave home, Louis concludes.

"It could be such a beautiful love story," adds his wife, Suzanne, of our two solitudes. "We could have the best of both worlds if we really respected each other. But there's an enormous amount of ignorance on both sides."

Many of us think Canada would work better if its Senate — rather than continuing as a rich haven for the halt, the weary, and the politically faithful — were an elected body representing the regions. As such, it might give Eastern and Western Canada a more meaningful voice in national affairs.

Will the Senate ever change? Who better to ask than one of Generation M: Gil Molgat, known to his old Winnipeg friends as Number Four.

It's an in-joke. In Canada's political pecking order, the governor general is No. 1; the prime minister, No. 2; the chief justice, No. 3; and the Speaker of the Senate, the Hon. Gildas Molgat as recently as mid-1997, is No. 4. Molgat rose through the ranks in Manitoba to become leader of the provincial Liberal Party. In 1970 he was named to the Senate. Now in his seventies, thick, grey hair fringing a bald pate, genial but politically as sharp as the proverbial tack, fluent in both official languages, Molgat is equally at home with the gaggles of schoolkids who flow constantly through his handsome offices in the Centre Block as he is with visiting heads of state.

And as co-chairman of the Joint Committee of the House of Commons on Senate Reform in the early 1980s, Molgat helped produce a report that in essence recommended instituting a Senate elected for one long term only, but not elected at the same time or in the same manner as the Commons.

Nothing happened. The recommendations were lost in the shuffle of a subsequent general election. Molgat doubts that Senate reform will ever come.

"The Canadian public wants change," he says, "but I don't really think the people in power in the provinces or in Ottawa want it."

In its present state, the Senate is non-threatening to the Commons and to provincial premiers, he explains. It questions Commons legislation, proposes amendments, occasionally blocks a bill. "But in the final analysis, the Senate will not usually completely obstruct the Commons. We try to get them to change their minds."

An elected Senate would become much more aggressive, Molgat says, "a real counter to the House of Commons. I predict that it would eventually supersede the House of Commons." Elected MPs, and maybe even their constituents, wouldn't like that.

Provincial premiers don't want a powerful Senate, either, Molgat thinks. Elected senators in their provinces could mean the premiers would no longer be the biggest frogs in their puddles. Molgat speculates that, in terms of public profile and prestige, the premiers would end up rather like governors of American states — definitely lower down the food chain than today.

If all this be so, Canada is stuck with the old-folks' home on Parliament Hill for the foreseeable future. But at least one of our generation tried to change the system.

Do Seniors Have a God?

Most of us are of that age when we can count our remaining years on our fingers and toes. (Five of my interviewees have died since this project began.) Are we therefore more spiritual? Or, have any events in our lives altered our faith?

"I KNEW FOR SURE"

Some eleven years ago, David MacDonald, now of Kingston, was in hospital with cardiac arrest. For two days, his condition was critical.

When I woke up, they said, "Well, you've had a little turn," and let it go at that. A couple of days later in the coronary care unit, I heard a doctor on rounds use the term "semi-miraculous" to some of his young residents, and realized he was talking about me. So I started asking questions.

Now, I was brought up to believe in God, but we don't know, do we? We don't know for sure. But suddenly, when I thought about it, I knew for sure. I just knew. I had been at least halfway there [to death] and came back.

And I not only knew there was a God, I knew that I didn't have to fear death. This doesn't mean that I think I'm ticketed for heaven, but I don't fear it. And I can't tell you why. It

doesn't prove anything. I can only tell you how I felt before and
how I feel now.

"When you get older," Peter Cranston believes, "you start
thinking about final exams." But as in so many other matters,
and in spite of our advancing years, we run the gamut from
churchgoer to atheist with many shades of belief, opinion, and
soul-searching in between. Joe and Mary Arnold, for example,
go to church every Sunday. Lillian and Cyril Flint attend services in the Paradise Valley Gospel Hall twice on Sunday and
again on Wednesday.

The Catholic religion is a strength and solace to the
Cranstons. "It's something we wouldn't do without," Peter says.
"I keep finding new insights and angles on it all the time. It's
much more interesting than it ever was before."

But, Madeleine adds, their attitude has relaxed. "We're far less
conservative than our parents were."

"Well," Peter says, "when your kids grow up and quit going
to church and live with each other without benefit of clergy,
you're either gonna cut them off or . . ." He shrugs.

"That doesn't change my view," Madeleine stresses. "But it
has forced me to be more receptive to their ideas and more
accepting."

As a child, Ben Robertson thought he might become a minister. He'd climb into the hayloft and preach to a bemused congregation of livestock. He soon abandoned his invisible clerical collar,
but grew up believing that "honesty was the thing. My uncle, he
didn't go to church at all, but he was a good-living man. He said
– whenever he got a dirty deal from somebody on the farm about
something, buying a cow or machinery or whatever – you always
had to watch out for the guy who went to church all the time."

When Ben's wife, Louise, was gravely ill with TB meningitis, friends and strangers across Canada and abroad prayed for her. Finally she came out of the coma and eventually recovered her speech and most of her memory. "And that," Ben says, "made me decide that there was a higher power, that's for sure."

At the other end of the spectrum, Hal Sisson has no respect for religion. Sociologist Reginald Bibby found that 85 per cent of Canadians over fifty-five believe in God, but Sisson isn't one of them. "I'm an atheist, and I don't care who knows it. I think religion has a lot to answer for. It's merely a power hierarchy and structure that, shortly after it was invented, tried to self-perpetuate itself with dogma."

Larry Holmes is a fatalist, not an atheist. "In the navy I found it very difficult sleeping in a hammock with my clothes and boots on. Finally, I thought, 'This is ridiculous. If we get hit by a torpedo, I'm not going to get out, anyway.'" He figured he could get into his clothes, boots, and lifebelt in about thirty seconds, so went through the war sleeping in some semblance of comfort. "And I had no real fear, because I was a fatalist, I believe in some greater force. But the dogma of religion leaves me absolutely neutral."

Glen Hancock has always considered himself a religious person. In the war, his encounter with the mystical A. E. Helliman and the subsequent terrible night over Duisburg strengthened his belief in a supreme being.

"I have a feeling, if there wasn't a God, we'd create one, because I think people need that kind of symbol," Hancock says. "Something that is stronger than themselves."

Going into the war, Fred Hamilton was "a not-very-interested Anglican." Being in battle changed him, but raised new misgivings.

"The padres we had were not all adequate for the work they were supposed to be doing. They were good men and brave men, but a lot of them had rather foolish ideas about your relationship with a god, if there is a god."

Whenever the men went on a large night patrol, a padre usually visited them. The Protestant padre spoke about dying and bravery: "What you owe your country and so forth. These guys didn't give a good goddamn about their country or anything else. All they were trying to do was stay alive."

Conversely, the Catholic padre seemed to have a soothing influence on the Catholic troops. "When he finished talking to them, they all seemed rather relaxed, not tense and nervous and anxious the way the rest of us were. They seemed to have something that helped them with the work they were going to do that night."

After the war, Fred met Kay Heaney, "and they told me, 'You either become a Catholic or you can't have her.'"

He was a practising Catholic for the rest of his life.

A PRACTICAL VIEW OF THE GOOD BOOK

At eighty-seven, Leonard Shiels of Craven, Saskatchewan, has been a farmer all his life, dealing with the realities of nature. Have his religious views changed? "I kept out of religion and politics. I think they are both for the same goal: to keep people divided." But he has an observation on the Bible.

I could never go for the story in the Bible. It starts out, There was morning and evening, and that was the first day. Then on the fourth day, He made the sun. How could there be morning and evening without the sun?

In the Flood it rained for forty days and forty nights. The air can't hold that much moisture. Four men with no knowledge of boat-building built an ocean-going vessel to carry all the animals and enough feed to keep them thirteen months? It's more than I can swallow.

For some, the force-fed religion of childhood created a back-lash in adulthood. Kay Macdonald, a minister's daughter steeped in church, now attends only "once in a while." Norman Currell, after a childhood diet of three church services on Sunday ("couldn't even bounce a ball that day"), became an agnostic. In Patricia Ritz Andrews's family, every day began with worship. The children knelt on their chairs to pray. Dancing was forbidden, "and that set us totally apart from other kids." The wrath of God forever hovered over them.

Patricia thinks her parents' rigid beliefs helped them through hard times, but as an adult she decided that religion "has a lot of baggage that has nothing to do with faith in God. I began to think for myself. I am free, unfettered, and have more faith than ever. Sometimes we serve a church or a denomination rather than the Lord."

Beatrice Quinto Holmes went to Catholic schools and was taught by nuns. One day in grade school, the teacher, presumably testing the depth of their faith, asked how they'd react if a murderous enemy charged among them.

"I remember all of us putting our hands up and saying, 'Oh, I'd be strong, I'd let him kill me!'" Bernice says. "I remember her talking about bayonets. By the time I got home, I was hysterical. 'Mom, I don't want to die! I don't want to be with a bayonet in me!'" Her mother walked her back to school and accosted the teacher: "Sister, I'm awfully sorry to say this, but you are an insult to your habit." Bernice remained Catholic, but with open eyes.

At age thirteen, Odile Bidan Winfield had doubts. "Some

things didn't make sense. We learned catechism, a whole series of questions and answers, by rote. What is God? There is no answer to that. After the war seemed a good time to question all of this. If there was such a wonderful creature up above, why did He allow all this to happen? I went to my priest and said, 'There are some things that I really don't understand. Could you help me?' He said that 'faith is a state of grace, and you do not question.'"

She quit the church in anger and remains not at all religious to this day. Her husband, Stan, went through several convolutions of the soul, hating his Jewish faith as a boy, returning to it as a man. When he married, he forced it upon himself and his family. "It was a disaster. It had a very adverse affect on our firstborn son." Today, Winfield doesn't like religion but strongly identifies with his heritage, a feeling strengthened by the profound wartime experience of Belsen.

In yet one more variation of faith, Gene Tingley says, "I think George Bernard Shaw put it better than I can: I have a cathedral within my heart. My joy and my religion is in planting a seed and seeing a flower grow. It's in listening to the birds sing. It's based on nature. I think I respect Mother Earth more than anything else in this world. That's my religion."

Staying Out of the Mall

Early one recent summer morning, the corner table in a suburban Hamilton Tim Hortons was packed with men, mostly my age, chugging back coffee, munching doughnuts and trading gossip. It had the air of a daily ritual, a stereotypical oldsters' diversion, like the bridge games, bingo games, golf games, mall-sitting, and Florida vacations that, most Canadians assume, is the retiree's way of life. And so it is, for many.

Still, I admire the eclectic pastimes of some of our cast of characters. They're staying out of the mall. Edna La Rocque of Sudbury attends university part-time to "keep my mind active and also to get some insight into today's generation." In Halifax, retired nurse Elizabeth Murray is indulging her lifelong love of music with vocal lessons and choral singing. Olive Thorne of Edmonton obtained her B.A. at age fifty-eight and is making up for lost time with "a keen interest in all of life's affairs."

Glen Hancock leads his travel club, the Nova Scotia Globe Trotters, on tours all over the world. Ben Robertson of Surrey, a confessed workaholic in his youth, is still at it, despite a battery of ills. Twice a week he delivers four hundred community newspapers to four hundred doorways on foot.

Fran Murray Peacock (who used to breakfast with her school chum atop a Fredericton hill) wanted to be an artist. But in adult life, she says, most of her creative energy went into making drapes. As an executive wife she moved thirty-two times, to temporary homes as far-flung as Bombay and Australia.

"Each time we moved, I spent two months organizing a house. I'd work day and night making drapes and turning the place into something homelike."

Her marriage ended in the early nineties. An elegant woman of slight build, she lives in a condominium in Ridgeville, Ontario, with time for art at last; her walls are tastefully decorated with her own and others' paintings. "I wake up every morning with a new idea, and that's pretty tiring!"

Her condo, incidentally, has handsome drapes. Made them herself.

In Vernon, British Columbia, lawyer Neil Davidson, with a long record of public service behind him (mayor of the city for three years, city solicitor for seventeen years), was, at age eighty, helping raise $2.3 million for a local hospice and service agencies. He was a championship skier deep into his seventies until his bones cried "Stop!"

Vancouver lawyer Stan Winfield taught courses at the University of British Columbia law school before and after retirement (a bench on campus bears a plaque in his honour). In 1995 he led Ted Aplin's sons back to Belsen, where their father had salvaged so many lives. A year later, at seventy-two, Stan was back in Europe as part of an observer team monitoring the elections in Bosnia.

Sheila Hanson of Mallorytown, Ontario, is an accomplished potter who refines her craft with constant study. Husband Malcolm is an artist in rock. Their home is perched on a lump of the Canadian Shield overlooking the St. Lawrence River. Malcolm has lugged and gut-wrestled hundreds of granite slabs onto the property, and coaxed and fitted their odd shapes, like pieces of a jigsaw puzzle, into walks and flowerbed edging.

Their neighbour Stanley Westall teaches English as a second language to Asian immigrants. So does Beatrice Shaw of St-Laurent. Ron Laidlaw, a computer whiz at seventy-seven, fills the air with e-mail and, in his spare time, makes wine. Larry Holmes, having studied the culinary arts, bakes bread and cooks gourmet meals. Erol Hill plays guitar in a country and western music group called Crystal River, for seniors' audiences around Murillo, Ontario.

Frank and Wanda Hamilton, after quitting politics, returned to the Mazenod, Saskatchewan, farm. On the several acres surrounding their home, Frank is giving something back to the prairie: a green and glorious habitat created with native plants and shrubs. Beverly Watson, active member of the Pigeon Lake Environment Association, is also paying back nature. She says she owes it to her grandchildren for having helped "leave the world in such a mess for them."

Douglas How, one of many full- or part-time authors among us, had two new books in print at age seventy-five, both short-listed for awards. Rae MacLeod, retired accountant, is into Scottish dancing. I'm into t'ai chi when not writing books. The

Cranstons of Victoria, the Hannahs of Frobisher, and Bernard Brouillet in Montreal, are among scores who devote volunteer hours to their churches.

In White Rock, Peter Marchant – tall, with pleasant square-cut features and a quick, shy smile – locks up the community club-house each night for a few dollars and has compiled a personal history for his grown son and daughter. But he feels frustrated. "I've got a million things I want to do, a million things, but I have no money at all. Yet I want to make some contribution."

Something of Value

Society farms us out at sixty-five. Many of us could be, and want to be, productive beyond that age, as Peter Marchant so earnestly desires. "We're the elders of our society," Beverly Watson points out. "We are the ones with the knowledge and experience. Other cultures seem able to recognize this, but Canadians tend to hide our older people away."

"We could have a tremendous input into the upcoming generation if they'd only listen and ask for this experience," adds Tony Parfitt, who, like Watson, has boomer children. "But they don't seem interested. We're old codgers in their view." He wanted to learn from his father. "The generations coming up, their idea of getting information is to seek it off the Internet."

Many of us *are* useful, in the giving of time as described above. Mid-Toronto Community Services, for example, uses hundreds of volunteers, about a quarter of them senior citizens. Ernie Edmondson, ninety-two, is one of their stars. Tall, lean as a whippet, with a bright, bespectacled gaze, Edmondson has been driving for Meals on Wheels since he retired from the income-tax department thirty years ago. He's out anywhere from once to four times a week, skilfully piloting his six-year-old Honda through the convoluted traffic of east-central Toronto.

"I'd miss it if I didn't have this," he says. Meals on Wheels would miss him, too.

Volunteers are the backbone of rural communities and small towns across the land. Ron Jeeves of Wolseley, Saskatchewan, has belonged to and often presided over every imaginable local organization all his adult life. The list includes a seniors' club, the Canadian Legion, church board, co-op board, and agricultural society (in 1996 he was named one of four honorary members of the Saskatchewan Agricultural Societies and Exhibitions).

"These things are important," Jeeves insists. "Today, you try to get young people to go on a board – council or school or whatever – they just won't do it. In our generation, it was part of life."

Volunteerism *is* important, but might we offer something else before we say goodbye? Dorothy Noyes, *Newsweek* columnist, eighty-nine when she wrote this in 1994, suggested that teenagers and seniors share a bond. Both groups are facing a profound biological change, the teens moving into adulthood, the seniors confronted with waning physical powers. Both, Noyes said, are distrusted or disliked by other generations:

One of our [teens' and seniors'] most difficult challenges comes from the outside world. It's another factor that makes our struggle to mature so alike: coping with those numerous unsympathetic, contemptuous and sometimes downright hostile others.

Like those folk who accuse teens of being too self absorbed, irresponsible, sex driven, booze drinking, "no good" and for those who look upon seniors with much disdain, not as national treasures.

That may astonish the kids ("Us the same as *old* people? Yecchh!") and the seniors ("Us bond with those foul-mouthed little creeps with their hats on backward?!") Yet maybe Noyes is on to something.

Maybe there is a potential link between us and our grandchildren (those under twenty) or great-grandchildren; a bridging of the triple- or quadruple-generation gap that will make their lives and what remains of ours more meaningful.

I doubt we could penetrate the teenagers' private domain of self-absorbtion, but pre-teens might be receptive. Already, they've been exposed to more information than our own parents ingested in a lifetime. Yet perhaps there is something they can learn from us about touch and caring, manners and civility, friendship and humanity.

"Although Bill and I had none of our own, we both love children and would like to pass on our values and moral standards," says Kay Belbas. "In this day and age, that is not easy. We can only set an example."

"It would be nice to pass on some sort of work ethic," says Lillian Flint. "On the farm, our grandchildren have learned you work or you don't eat."

"I wrote a booklet covering the first twenty years of my life," says octogenarian Neil Davidson. "I was surprised to find more interest in it from my grandchildren than from my children."

Maybe not so surprising, if Dorothy Noyes was on the right track. The Toronto Intergenerational Project (probably other cities have similar projects) has seniors telling stories to schoolchildren. Apparently, the kids are enchanted with the tales of "olden" days. Such stories could fill some of the void in history instruction for those young people still wondering who won World War Two, and who think Depression is something you have on Monday morning.

Generation M's streak of naiveté, the quality that sometimes got us into trouble, has a flip side: the childlike sense of wonder that some of us retain. We have seen so many marvels, yet many of us, happily, continue to marvel. I still find it remarkable that I can punch a few buttons and instantly talk to a friend in Vancouver or England; that pages of words fly in and out of my office by fax or modem; that I have boarded hundreds of huge metal people-containers that have no damn right to fly like birds, and been transported far abroad and safely home again.

"Even today I am fascinated by such advances as the Hubble telescope and joining the Mir station in outer space," Neil Davidson says. "To the present generation, that is pretty ho-hum stuff."

So it is. If, say, more daycare centres or grade schools could use us – help us impart to the young our fanciful thoughts, our rich memories, our splendid history – could we enhance that sense of wonder in younger kids before it becomes stunted by adulthood?

It would do them good to hear a Stan Hoffman, the Moose Jaw working man. Hoffman has never travelled outside of Canada nor much within it. Many youngsters have already seen more of the world than he. Yet in telling me of his dreams of seeing the Pyramids, the Nile, Africa, he burst out, "I'm gonna be cremated. When they scatter my ashes maybe my spirit will go to all those places!"

If the young should want it, the spirit of all our not-uneventful lives could be part of theirs, and help carry them, and us, to undreamed of places. And if that seems idealistic – well, that's another part of the way we are.

"We have lived through a remarkable century," Elsie Towson concludes. "When they look back at this century, they'll say we came through it with our colours pretty well flying."

We did. Meeting this sampling of Generation M, hearing a little of their hopes, dreams, and accomplishments (more stories by far than could fit into this book), weighing bad against good, I am proud to be one of them. Let Helen Margison, eighty, have the final word for all of us:

"We were in no way without fault. Our best may not have been good enough. But I have to believe that we got it gloriously right some of the time."

BIBLIOGRAPHY

Books

Bothwell, Robert, Drummond, Ian, and English, John. *Canada Since 1945: Power, Politics and Provincialism.* Toronto: University of Toronto Press, 1981.

Braithwaite, Max. *The Hungry Thirties, 1930/1940.* Toronto: Natural Science of Canada, 1977.

Creighton, Donald. *The Forked Road: Canada, 1939-57.* Toronto: McClelland & Stewart, 1979.

Foot, David K., and Stoffman, Daniel. *Boom, Bust and Echo: How To Profit from the Coming Demographic Shift.* Toronto: Macfarlane, Walter & Ross, 1996.

Ferguson, Carol, and Fraser, Margaret. *A Century of Canadian Home Cooking.* Toronto: Prentice Hall, 1992.

Franklin, Stephen. *A Time of Heroes, 1940/1950.* Toronto: Natural Science of Canada, 1977.

Gilbert, Martin. *The Day The War Ended: VE-Day 1945 in Europe and Around the World.* London: HarperCollins, 1995.

Granatstein, J. L., and Neary, Peter, eds. *The Good Fight: Canadians and World War II.* Mississauga, Ont.: Copp Clark, 1995.

Hersey, John. *Hiroshima.* New York: Alfred A. Knopf, 1946.

Himmelfarb, Gertrude. *The De-Moralization of Society: From Victorian Virtues to Modern Values*. New York: Alfred A. Knopf, 1995.

How, Douglas, ed. *The Canadians at War: 1939/45*, vols. 1 and 2. Montreal: Reader's Digest Association (Canada), 1969.

Johnson, Sara E. *To Spread Their Wings*. Spruce Grove, Alta.: Saraband Productions, 1990.

Lamb, James B. *On the Triangle Run*. Toronto: Macmillan of Canada, 1986.

————. *Press Gang: Post-war Life in the World of Canadian Newspapers*. Toronto: Macmillan of Canada, 1979.

Leacy, F. H., ed. *Historical Statistics of Canada*. Ottawa: Statistics Canada, 1983.

Lower, Arthur. *A Nation Developing: A Brief History of Canada*. Toronto: Ryerson Press, 1970.

Owram, Doug. *Born at the Right Time: A History of the Baby-boom Generation*. Toronto: University of Toronto Press, 1996.

Redman, Stanley R. *Open Gangway: The (Real) Story of the Halifax Navy Riot*. Hantsport, N.S.: Lancelot Press, 1981.

Ricard, François. *The Lyric Generation: The Life and Times of the Baby Boomers*. Toronto: Stoddart, 1994.

Ross, Alexander. *The Booming Fifties, 1950/1960*. Toronto: Natural Science of Canada, 1977.

Smart, Reginald G., and Ogborne, Alan C. *Northern Spirits: Drinking in Canada, Then and Now*. Toronto: Addiction Research Foundation, 1986 and 1996 eds.

Spock, Dr. Benjamin. *Baby and Child Care*. New York: Dutton Books, 1992 ed.

Whelan, Eugene. *The Man in the Green Stetson*. Toronto: Irwin, 1986.

Pamphlets and Reports

Good, Christopher. *The Generational Accounts of Canada.* Vancouver: The Fraser Institute, August 1995.

Divorce: Law and the Family in Canada. Ottawa: Statistics Canada, 1983.

Facts About Alcohol Policy in Ontario. Toronto: Addiction Research Foundation, 1996.

Suicide in Canada: Update of the Report of the Task Force on Suicide in Canada. Ottawa: Health Canada, 1994.

Newspapers and Periodicals

Calgary Herald, July 18, 1996.

Canadian Banker, Winter, 1955.

Canadian Business, December, 1949; December 1950; June 1951; February, April 1952; September 1953; February, June, November 1954; March, October 1955; March, April 1956; February 1957; February 1958; September 1959; August 1995.

Canadian Forum, March 1956.

Canadian Hobby-Craft, January/February 1949; March/April 1950.

Canadian Homes & Gardens, October, November 1948; March, May, September, October 1949; January, February, September 1950; January, November 1951; January, May, August, December 1952.

Canadian Living, March, September 1995.

Canadian Plastics, September 1956; November 1957.

Canadian Unionist, September 1952.

Canadian Welfare, June 15, 1955.

CARP News, February, October, 1995.

Chatelaine, April 1995.

Dalhousie Review, April 1949, Winter 1953.

Economic Annalist, August 1954; October 1955; August, October 1959.

Financial Post, February 12, July 30, September 17, December 3,
1949; April 22, August 12, August 19, September 16,
September 23, October 7, November 4, 1950; January 27,
May 26, July 7, August 25, October 27, October 31, 1951;
February 23, March 22, June 21, July 5, October 4, 11, 18,
December 20, 1952; February 21, March 7, April 18, July 25,
August 1, October 3, 10, 31, November 21, December 5,
1953; February 13, 20, April 3, 10, June 9, August 14, 21, 28,
September 18, 25, October 23, 1954; January 8, February 12,
May 14, June 9, 25, September 17, 24, October 8, 15, 22,
November 5, 1955; January 14, February 4, May 12, 19, June
16, 23, October 20, November 3, 10, 17, December 8, 29,
1956; January 12, March 23, 30, May 18, June 8, 22, July 6,
August 3, September 14, October 19, 26, November 23,
1957; January 4, 18, 25, May 3, 17, 31, July 12, 26, August 2,
September 13, 20, October 18, November 8, December 6,
20, 1958;   January 24, 31, February 7, April 18, May 30,
June 6, 27, July 4, 18, August 2, September 26, October 3,
November 7, 14, 21, 1959.

Food for Thought, December 1947; January 1949; February 1951;
November 1952; December 1953; November 1957; February
1958.

The Globe and Mail, December 1, 1994; July 24, October 20,
December 9, December 14, 1995; February 15, February 26,
February 27, March 7, June 5, July 1, August 12, August 13,
August 28, September 28, October 1, November 11, 1996;
February 15, February 18, February 19, 1997.

Health, November/December 1947; November/December
1948.

Home Building, April/May 1950; October/November 1955;
February/March 1959.

Homemakers, January/February 1994; January/February 1995.

The Idler, July/August, 1991.

Industrial Canada, February, 1959.

Labour Gazette, March 1954; July 1957; March 1959.

Maclean's, November 1, 1948; March 15, April 15, June 15, August 1, 15, November 15, 1950; May 15, June 15, 1951; January 15, April 1, June 15, August 15, December 1, 1954; January 1, October 1, 29, December 10, 1955; August 4, October 13, 1956; March 15, July 19, 1958; August 15, 1959.

Manitoba Business, July/August, 1995.

Marketing, October 31, 1994.

Monetary Times, February, December, 1953; July 1955; August 1956; March 1957.

New City, Fall 1995.

New Scientist, February 19, 1994.

The New Yorker, May 20, 1996.

Newsweek, February 22, 1993; September 5, 1994.

Report on Business Magazine, September 1994.

Saturday Night, March 20, August 28, September 4, November 13, 1948; July 19, October 11, November 1, 1949; January 31, May 23, June 20, October 24, 1950; June 5, June 26, September 11, November 17, 1951; February 2, March 29, October 25, November 8, December 20, 1952; January 10, August 15, 1953; March 6, September 25, 1954; April 27, 1957; January 3, 1959; June, 1995.

Scientific American, January 1995.

Toronto Star, February 1-18, 1935; May 5-19, 1939.

Trades and Labor Congress Journal, January 1953.

United Church Observer, August, September, 1995.

U.S. News and World Report, November 28, 1994.

Utne Reader, May/June, 1996.

Vancouver Sun, June 11, 1996.

Western Report, March 28, 1994; August 14, 1995; April 8, 1996; September 16, 1996; January 20, 1997.

World Affairs, December 1951; January 1952.

Cast of Characters

(The Interviewees)

Bob and Velma Adams, Scarborough, Ont.; Helen Allison, London, Ont.; Patricia Andrews, White Rock, B.C.; Marie Antaya, Chatham, Ont.; John Archer, Regina; Joe and Mary Arnold, Mississauga, Ont.

Murray and Marg Barnard, Halifax; Michael Bartolf, Oxbow, Sask.; Ernest and Helen Beck, Selkirk, Man.; Kay Belbas, Rossburn, Man.; Margaret Belcher, Regina; Clifford and Olive Bell, Moose Jaw; Dr. Joseph Berger, Toronto; Diane and Ian Bickle, Regina; Roy and Doris Bien, Regina; John Bigham, Burlington, Ont.; Arthur Bishop, Toronto; Michael Bliss, Toronto; Margaret Boyd, Kinistino, Sask.; Joyce and Bob Brack, Saskatoon; Bernard Brouillet, Saint Laurent, Que.; Jack Brown, Waterloo, Ont.; Gladys Byrnes, Creemore, Ont.

Ken Campbell, Burlington, Ont.; Lloyd and Marie Cartwright, Walkerton, Ont.; Ron and Cora Cason, Calgary; Robert "Chick" Childerhose, Sooke, B.C.; Ruth Collins, Toronto; Alan Cooper, Okanagan Falls, B.C.; E. M. Cooper, Calgary; Peter and Madeleine Cranston, Victoria; Norman Currell, White Rock, B.C.; Lily Currie, Regina; Jean Marie Danard, Thornhill, Ont.; Neil Davidson, Vernon, B.C.; Kay Davis, Kelowna, B.C.; Evelyn de Mille, Calgary; Phyllis Dixon, East York, Ont.; John Dodds, Vancouver; Rose Dyson, Toronto.

Ernie Edmondson, Toronto.

Maurice and Lillian Falloon, Foxwarren, Man.; Bill Finnbogason, Winnipeg; Lillian and Cyril Flint, Paradise Valley, Alta.; Kathleen Foy, Montreal; Roy Francis, Cambridge, Ont.

Herb and Arlene Gallifent, Hamilton, Ont.; Douglas Gardner, East York, Ont.; Irene and Joe Ghiglione, Moose Jaw; Elisabeth and Eric Golby, Tottenham, Ont.; Barbara Gory, Etobicoke, Ont.; Ted and Irene Grant, Victoria; Mary Greey, Toronto; Gwyn Griffith, Toronto.

Louis and Suzanne Hamel, Outremont, Que.; Fred and Kay Hamilton, Sydenham, Ont.; Frank and Wanda Hamilton, Mazenod, Sask.; Glen Hancock, Wolfville, N.S.; Jim and Olive Hannah, Frobisher, Sask.; Malcolm and Sheila Hanson, Mallorytown, Ont.; Marianne Harvey, Willowdale, Ont.; Doug and Helen Harvey, Victoria; Erol Hill, Murillo, Ont.; Stan Hoffman, Moose Jaw; Willard Holliday, Victoria; Larry and Bernice Holmes, Willowdale, Ont.; Jean Holt, Edmonton; Jean Hook, Flin Flon, Man.; Douglas How, St. Andrews, N.B.; Ted Howard, Mallorytown, Ont.

Patricia Ingraham, Hamilton, Ont.

Ruth and Ron Jeeves, Wolseley, Sask.; Sara E. Johnson, Spruce Grove, Alta.

Donald King, Toronto; Earl and Myrtle Kleeberger, Sylvan Lake, Alta.

Ron and Vibeke Laidlaw, London, Ont.; James and Ruby Lamb, Baddeck, N.S.; Mona and Eddie Laporte, Moose Jaw; Edna La Rocque, Sudbury, Ont.; Norma West Linder, Sarnia, Ont.; Stanley Logan, Hemet, California; Riitta Louhimo, Toronto; Bruce Lundy, Niagara Falls, Ont.

Max and Kay Macdonald, Regina; David and Antoinette MacDonald, Kingston, Ont.; Lachlan and Barbara MacLean, Blenheim, Ont.; Peter Marchant, Surrey, B.C.; Helen Margison, Toronto; Walt McConville, Brentwood Bay, B.C.; Elizabeth

McEachern, Scarborough, Ont.; Marilyn McFadden, London, Ont.; Lillian McGregor, Toronto; Patricia McLaughlin, Winnipeg; Duncan Rae MacLeod, Thornhill, Ont.; Barbara McNeill, Scarborough, Ont.; Gildas and Allison Molgat, Ottawa; Frank Moritsugu, Willowdale, Ont.; Hope Morritt, Point Edward, Ont.; Elizabeth Murray, Halifax; Gilbert and Madeline Murray, Burlington, Ont.; Alex and Beatrice Nickason, Peterborough, Ont.

Jean Orpwood, Toronto.

Tony and Mary Parfitt, Mallorytown, Ont.; Hazel and Keith Paton, Oxbow, Sask.; Fran Peacock, Ridgeville, Ont.; Alice Pearson, Govan, Sask.; Edward Pleva, London, Ont.; Bill and Marion Pratt, Tillsonburg, Ont.

James Redditt, Burlington, Ont.; Mary Louise Richmond, Willowdale, Ont.; Ben and Louise Robertson, Surrey, B.C.; Agnes Robinson, Ajax, Ont.

Herb Schienbein, Regina; Tim Seeley, Peace River, Alta.; Beatrice and Ed Shaw, Saint Laurent, Que.; Leonard Shiels, Craven, Sask.; Hal and Doreen Sisson, Victoria; Gordon Smart, Victoria; Charles and Hilde Smith, Vancouver; Helen Stauffer, Thornhill, Ont.; Arnold and Dorothy Steppler, New Westminster, B.C.

Olive Thorne, Edmonton; Merle and Gene Tingley, London, Ont.; Elsie Towson, Scarborough, Ont.; Elizabeth Tucci, East York, Ont.; Ted Turner, Regina.

Steve and Shirley Walbridge, Pointe Claire, Que.; Beverly Watson, Buckhorn, Ont.; Stanley Westall, Mallorytown, Ont.; Ed and Pemrose Whelan, Regina; Olive Williams, Etobicoke, Ont.; Bill and Norma Williamson, Don Mills, Ont.; Stanley and Odile Winfield, New Westminster, B.C.; Arthur Witt, Brantford, Ont.; Mary Wright, London, Ont.

INDEX